STUDIES IN HISTORICAL GEOGRAPHY

Southern Africa

for Anne

The first land grant on the Liesbeeck River, 1657

STUDIES IN HISTORICAL GEOGRAPHY

Southern Africa

WITHDRAWN

A. J. CHRISTOPHER

DAWSON · ARCHON BOOKS

First published in 1976

© A. J. Christopher 1976

Wm Dawson & Sons Ltd, Cannon House
Folkestone, Kent, England

Archon Books, The Shoe String Press, Inc
995 Sherman Avenue, Hamden, Connecticut 06514 USA

British Library Cataloguing in Publication Data

Christopher, Anthony John
    Southern Africa
    (Studies in historical geography)
    Bibl - Index
    ISBN 0 7129 0694 0
    ISSN 0308 6607
    1. Title
    911:68 DT753
    Africa, Southern - Historical geography

Archon ISBN 0 208 01620 1
LC 76-21207

Printed in Great Britain
by W & J Mackay Limited, Chatham
by photo-litho

Contents

Illustrations

9

Tables

Preface

HISTORICAL GEOGRAPHY in southern Africa has suffered serious neglect in the present century. A recent survey (1972) of studies in Africa failed to refer to any work produced south of the Zambezi River.[1] This is all the more surprising when it is recalled that southern Africa has been the subject of inordinate debate and investigation for the past fifteen years. The basis of the controversy revolves around the place in the subcontinent of the European settlers, who, over a period of more than 300 years, have transformed the landscape on lines similar to those to be seen in other mid-latitude colonizations. The result has been the creation of a landscape which owes much to Europe, through the introduction of new crops and animals, town foundations and industrial development, as well as to its African environment, which enforced modifications of the European cultural perceptions of the pioneers.

The emergence of a new and distinctive landscape in the south of Africa is a phenomenon worthy of study. The theme fits closely into the main stream of landscape evolution studies appearing in historical geographical literature, and as such differs markedly from the two previous studies by Lucas (1898) and Pollock and Agnew (1963), which were more traditional in approach.[2] The parallels between southern Africa and other eighteenth- and nineteenth-century European colonies of settlement are therefore useful guidelines in methodology.[3]

Southern Africa has been regarded through its recent history as related to North America and Australasia, rather than to the rest of Africa, and the influence of European immigration on the subcontinent has been profound.

The theme of European colonization solves one of the major

problems of many historical geographies — when to start. The year 1652, when the first permanent settlement at the Cape of Good Hope was founded, provides the 'new beginning in history' so often sought after. When to end presents greater problems. Traditional conclusions at major dates such as 1910 (the formation of the Union of South Africa) or 1914 (the outbreak of World War 1), appear remote, yet the recent past has been so bedevilled by political considerations as to make objective writing virtually impossible. So 1960 has been taken as the terminal date. The main outlines of southern Africa had then emerged, yet the latest rapid transformation, 'the wind of change' associated with the breaking of political ties with Europe in the 1960s had not yet had a great impact.

The areal extent of southern Africa presents several problems. Clearly South Africa, with its peculiar political boundaries, makes an unsatisfactory unit of study. European settlement from the hearth at the Cape of Good Hope spread over a wider field. The extension of the settlement frontier in the eighteenth and nineteenth centuries resulted in the emergence by 1914 of a distinct southern Africa settlement area, linked by a common historical experience (Fig 1). The Zambezi became, as it remains today, the boundary of substantial European settlement as, in Zambia, African interests remained paramount in the colonial era. South-West Africa, with its German imprint, and Mocambique, with its long Portuguese association, separated the southern African European settlement frontier from the Cape, and are therefore excluded.

Clearly other themes, time-spans and areas could have been selected. The African imprint upon the landscape, in particular, deserves attention. However, African geographical studies have been neglected and the emergence of African historians and geographers to investigate the other thread in southern African development is awaited.[4]

I wish to express my gratitude to the host of people who assisted me in the research for this book. The primary documents and other works were drawn from sources in southern Africa and England: in Cape Town, the Cape Archives, the Surveyor-General's and Deeds Offices; in Pietermaritzburg, the Natal Archives, the Surveyor-General's and Deeds Offices; in Bloemfontein, the Orange Free State Archives, the National Museum, the Surveyor-General's and Deeds Offices; in Pretoria, the Transvaal Archives, the Surveyor-General's and Deeds Offices; in Johannesburg, the Africana Museum; in Kimberley, the Deeds Office and the Alexander McGregor Memorial Museum; in Durban, the Local History

13

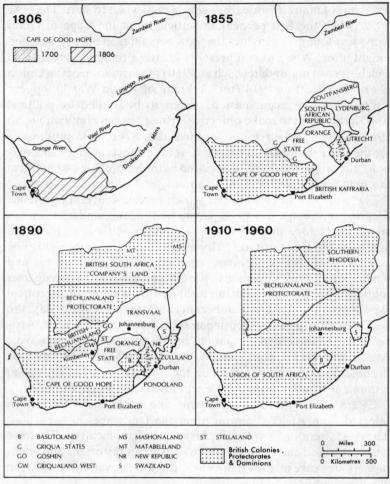

Fig 1   The political development of southern Africa

Museum and the Killie Campbell Museum; in Gaborone, the Botswana National Archives and the Department of Surveys and Lands; in Salisbury, the National Archives of Rhodesia, the Department of the Surveyor-General and the Deeds Office; in Bulawayo, the Department of the Surveyor-General; and in London, the Public Record Office and the British Museum. I am most grateful to all these institutions and their staffs for their permission to consult their records and libraries, and for their assistance with my enquiries.

Financial assistance of the Human Sciences Research Council towards the costs of the research is acknowledged. Opinions expressed or conclusions reached are, however, solely those of the author.

The work owes much to its diagrams, which were drawn with considerable skill by Mrs Catherine Lawrence. The arduous task of typing the manuscript was diligently undertaken by Mrs Dalene Vorster. Finally I wish to record my thanks to my wife, Anne, who accompanied me on much of the field work — for her encouragement and considerable assistance, and for helping to make the whole exercise so enjoyable.

A. J. Christopher
Port Elizabeth
July 1975

1

Assessments
of Southern Africa

IT IS THROUGH contemporary records that a picture may be built up
of the problems and possibilities which southern Africa offered to
prospective settlers. The varying assessments of the subcontinent as
a field for colonization are important in comprehending why, in
1960, after more than 300 years of European endeavour, the European population numbered little more than 3 million. The contrast
with other lands of settlement is glaring. In 1960 Canada possessed
18 million inhabitants, Australia 10 million, and even the smaller
and younger New Zealand 2.4 million. In the great age of European
migration (1815–1914), only 4 per cent of emigrants from the
United Kingdom went to southern Africa, compared with 11 per
cent to Australasia and 17 per cent to Canada.

Why should southern Africa have fared so poorly? There are two
major reasons. The first was the contemporary assessment of the
physical environment, and the second the presence of a substantial
indigenous population. These factors influenced the course of
European settlement, both in broad outline and in detail. The
physical environment was variously assessed, but generally considered to be unsuitable for large-scale European agricultural settlement, while the indigenous population was looked upon as a source
of cheap labour, and therefore working-class European labourers
and convicts were generally unwelcome. It was, however, the physical environment which was considered by contemporaries to be the
overriding factor.

The Physical Environment

In terms of physiography, southern Africa may be divided into two broad divisions, separated by the Great Escarpment. This can be traced from the Victoria Falls in north-western Rhodesia, through the eastern highlands of Rhodesia to the Limpopo, where it is not well marked, then southwards through the eastern Transvaal, the border between Natal and the Orange Free State and Lesotho, and finally through the southern Cape Province. Above the escarpment lies a series of tablelands, with the Kalahari Desert basin at their core. Below the escarpment, in the south-western Cape Province, lie folded mountain belts with ranges parallel to both southern and western coasts, and elsewhere a series of terraces or steps descends to the coastal plains, which in many places are not extensive.[1] Thus physical barriers impede movement inland from the coast, while the rivers are mostly unsuited to transportation owing to rapids, waterfalls and small volume of flow. Above the Great Escarpment there exist few barriers to movement, as the plains generally merge into one another with only minor mountain chains to separate them. The barriers encountered in the interior were, until the arrival of medicine and mechanical transport, largely those of disease, drought and isolation.

Thus southern Africa, even more than Australia, lacked internal water-transport possibilities, and the physiography was such that at the coast there were few suitable areas for large agricultural settlements. Nevertheless, the physiography, although highly significant, particularly in the early years of the settlement, was not so important as the climate, which presented severe drawbacks to agricultural settlement. Rainfall totals are in general low, and temperatures are high. Thus over all but the southern and eastern margins of the subcontinent, evaporation rates exceed rainfall. Apart from the south-western Cape with a winter rainfall maximum, rainfall is concentrated into the summer months. Over half the subcontinent receives, on average, less than twenty inches per annum, with increasing variability as totals decline. Once the initial settlement had been established and penetration of the interior began, it was the climate and the vegetative cover which attracted most attention as indicating agricultural or pastoral potential.

Assessments Prior to 1806

The initial impressions formed by explorers in the Age of Colonization and Exploration were that southern Africa had little to offer by way of trade or settlement bases. Portugal settled Angola and Mocambique, but made scant use of the coastline between them, and the Dutch were initially content with islands such as St Helena and Mauritius as ports of call for their vessels sailing between Europe and the East Indies. It was only with the virtual exhaustion of St Helena as a supply base that the Dutch East India Company was forced to consider southern Africa as a provisioning station.

Most reports up to the 1640s had little comfort for prospective settlers, as to either the potential productivity of the land or the character of the indigenous inhabitants. However, a report (1649) based on the experiences of a shipwrecked captain, Janssen, viewed the vicinity of Cape Town in a different light:[2]

> The soil of the said (Table) valley is very good and fruitful, and in the dry season all the water one could wish for could be led through the gardens with little toil. Everything will grow there as well as anywhere in the world . . . Since everything is to be had there in sufficient quantity, abundance of fish . . . further elands and steenboks are abundant . . . There are all sorts of birds there in thousands.

On the basis of this report, the European settlement of southern Africa began.

The initial years of settlement were concerned with the problems of supplying passing ships, rather than with providing a livelihood for settlers. However, curiosity about the nature of the land at the Cape soon led to exploration of the area beyond the vicinity of Cape Town, in search of minerals and livestock. These expeditions were confronted by mountains and drought.[3] Descriptions of dreary desolate wildernesses and deserts abound, and comments on periods of drought are common. In 1685 the Governor of the Cape, Simon van der Stel, led an expedition to Namaqualand. He found water reasonably plentiful, but the land was certainly no agriculturalist's paradise, and only the lure of minerals — in this case copper — could have attracted men to the area.[4] The minerals were, however, too remote to render exploitation worthwhile, and official interest in the interior lapsed.

The second half of the eighteenth century witnessed a number of major expeditions which attempted to produce a more comprehensive and scientific account of the colony.[5] These effectively showed the barren heart of the Karroo and, by contrast, the improvement eastward towards the lands occupied by the Xhosa, and northeastward to the upper Orange River. A number of patient observers such as Le Vaillant, Thunberg, Gordon and Barrow left substantial volumes of field sketches and drawings, from which it was possible to piece together some idea of the country, before European settlement on any scale took place.

The body of knowledge built up in the final years of Dutch rule
reveals a vast arid land. In the 1770s Thunberg described the
interior plains of the Karroo as 'very dry, sterile and bare of grass'.[6]
Barrow in 1797 noted at Graaff Reinet that 'water in fact is everything in southern Africa'.[7] In a topographical description of the
Cape Colony as it was then constituted, he stated that seven parts in
ten were 'for a great part of the year, and some of them at all times,
destitute of the least appearance of verdure'.[8] Referring to the
'lonely wastes' of South Africa, he said that 'Nature seems to have
withheld her bounteous hand, and doomed them to cheerless,
irremediable and consequently perpetual sterility.'[9] Such accounts
remained basic reading in the early nineteenth century and do much
to explain the lack of interest, both by the Imperial and Colonial
governments, in the interior of the colony.

Nineteenth and Twentieth Century Assessments

The nineteenth century witnessed a vast expansion of knowledge
about southern Africa. However, as perception and colonization
became bound up with one another, a new element was introduced,
which had been absent in the Dutch period.[10] Unlike the British, the
Dutch had never sought to attract agricultural settlers to southern
Africa, and official and later promotional literature vied with similar accounts from other parts of the world in the highly competitive
struggle for immigrants. Travellers visited southern Africa more
frequently. Settlers with ties in Europe wrote copiously. The result
was a confusing explosion of knowledge.

Official accounts were at first enthusiastic about the agricultural
potential of southern Africa. Lord Somerset, the Governor of the
Cape, wrote in 1817 that the Eastern Province of the colony was[11]

> The most beautiful and fertile part of this settlement. I know not how to
> give an idea of it unless by saying that it resembles a succession of parks
> from the Bushman's River to the Great Fish River, in which upon the
> most verdant carpet, Nature has planted in endless variety; the soil well
> adapted to cultivation is peculiarly fitted for cattle pasturage.

In reality, the scrub and bush of the Eastern Province proved to be
generally unattractive, while the need to promote it stemmed from
the depredations of the Xhosa of the Ciskei, rather than from its
inherent worth. Later (1848), Sir Harry Smith, High Commissioner
in South Africa, stated of Natal:[12]

> In this vast District there is Space for a Population of 2,000,000. This

> District embraces a most beautiful Country strongly undulating and intersected by many Streams, where Waters never fail. The land in many Parts is rich and fertile beyond Description.

Official accounts thereafter were largely pessimistic about the development of southern Africa, as a result of the difficulties encountered in the Eastern Cape and Natal settlements. Imperial officials tended to discourage settlement, emphasizing its dangers, and in the 1880s only 2.8 per cent of regional enquiries to the Emigrants' Information Offices were for details about southern Africa.[13] Thus the Colonial Emigration Commissioners in 1870 stated of the Cape Colony: 'The soil . . . produces an immense variety of indigenous plants, many of them very beautiful, but few that are directly useful either as food or medicine.'[14]

Promoters of colonization schemes were similarly divided. Some became highly poetical with little regard for reality, while others attempted to provide some factual basis. An almost idyllic picture of South Africa, particularly Natal in the 1840s, was built up:[15]

> What an immense extent of hill and dale is spread around; what myriads of gorgeous flowers, that glow like gems amidst the verdure of this grassy ocean; the vast primeval, where the huge straight trunks of trees are wound with gigantic vines and blossoming creepers, forming at an immense height, a canopy of the thickest foliage of the deepest green, whose tints never vary, but throughout the seasons are clothed with the same richness and verdure.

In the promotional accounts the land was said to be 'peculiarly suited' to this or that beneficial purpose; the climate was universally 'solubrious', and indeed the fertility of the soil, the lack of drought and so on produced a picture of Natal which could not fail to attract settlers. However, the promoters of Australasian settlement were equally emphatic that southern Africa was not the place to go to:[16]

> The general character of everything, animal or vegetable, earthly or atmospheric in these as well as other parts of the huge African continent, is extreme and contrasted. Either the earth is stone and dust, or rankly prolific in vegetation; there is parching dryness or deadly swamp, the animals are of the most gentle or the most ferocious character; the vegetation produces luscious fruit or deadly poison. Naturally, a place with such characteristics is one of risks and alterations in fortune. Whatever the settler pursues, especially far inland, he must prepare himself to meet great and often overwhelming risks.

Promotional accounts in the second half of the nineteenth century were more realistic, based on some scientific knowledge and an increasing wealth of experience in dealing with the southern African environment. Practical advice was increasingly offered, suggesting the type of crops and livestock to be produced, and the manner in which a profitable farm could be built up.

Settlers' accounts of the environment of southern Africa were sent back to friends and relatives in Europe and sometimes widely published. Usually no systematic approach was adopted; only the particular events were noted. Thus the misfortunes of the Albany settlers through drought, storm and plant diseases were widely disseminated, and it was generally the unusual which was written about, as well as the trials and tribulations which afflict all groups of pioneers throughout the world. Thomas Phipson in Natal (1851) wrote of the sterility of the soils:[17]

> At all events, though I had often been told that if I went a few miles further this way or that way than I actually have been, I should find a difference in this respect, I can only say that I have never yet reached the spot where a good supply of manure was not indispensible.

This image of the apparently poor natural resources and agricultural potential of southern Africa was transmitted to other colonies striving to obtain settlers. For example, a Melbourne newspaper in 1860, commenting on the prospects for increased production in Victoria, referred to the wild wastes of southern Africa.[18] But settlers' accounts do not appear to have had the impact that they had in Australia or North America, where appraisal became involved in the political outlook of the settlers, although they probably did little to encourage agricultural settlement. Neither did the travellers' accounts, which dealt often with strange, even bizarre, events. They tended to show southern Africa as a land of rugged mountains and vast plains, with hostile inhabitants and wild animals — not a picture likely to encourage immigration, but they did, as they had in the past, comment upon signs of precious metals and other indications of wealth. Carl Mauch spoke of gold in the eastern Transvaal, and this gave rise to a minor gold rush, while other evidence of gold workings in Mashonaland undoubtedly influenced the course of development. After discoveries had been made, there emerged a flood of literature on the state of mining and commerce, and the likelihood of similar developments elsewhere in the subcontinent. The publicity given to the discovery of diamonds and, later, of gold opened a new phase in the perception of southern Africa. Assessment as a field for agricultural settlement lessened in importance, except in Rhodesia, and attention was increasingly given to the mineral resources. No greater contrast could be found than in the emigration figures for the period 1815–1914. During the first fifty-five years only 50,000 out of 6,759,000 emigrants from England, came to South Africa (0.7 per cent). In the following forty-five years some 808,000 out of 15,856,000 arrived in South Africa (5.1 per cent).[19] Thus the attraction of southern Africa lay not in the field of agriculture, but rather in the sphere of mining and commerce.

The Transvaal and the Orange Free State escaped much of the promotional literature of the nineteenth century, as they were totally opposed to attracting massive immigration from Europe. Although 'immigration' appeared in the arms of the Orange Free State, no attempt was made to encourage settlers from outside South Africa, and it was only in 1900 that literature appeared on any scale, as a result of unbounded optimism in the future of the new colonies.[20] Undoubtedly an awareness of the lack of water remained one of the dominant features in the perception of the Transvaal in the early twentieth century.[21] Although official ideas were more geared to ranching than they had been fifty years before, by 1906 the first flush of enthusiasm concerning the agricultural potential of the Transvaal was over.

By 1910 South Africa, if not Rhodesia, was no longer regarded as a field for agricultural immigration, and the literature devoted increasing attention to the economic opportunities open to intending settlers. Comments on the physical attributes of the subcontinent were limited to emphasizing the salubrity of the climate, particularly the sunshine, and increasingly accurate climatic statistics could be used to show how much more favourable the physical conditions of South Africa were than those of western Europe: they had no other function. For those engaged in agriculture, the wealth of information produced by agricultural departments, experimental stations and farmers' associations provided the detailed guidance they needed in selecting crops and animals and combating pests and disease, but such literature had only limited circulation and plays little part in building up a mental image of southern Africa.

The British South Africa Company, and later the Southern Rhodesian government, issued a great many manuals and handbooks between 1907 and 1960 exhorting intending emigrants to start farming in Rhodesia, with statements such as 'The climate of Southern Rhodesia leaves little to be desired.'[22] Generally, however, independent twentieth-century opinions concurred with Monica Cole, who has written 'Agriculturally South Africa is a relatively poor country enjoying few advantages and suffering many disadvantages both of a physical and of an economic nature.'[23]

Environmental Deterioration

The seriousness of impoverished pastures, apparently the result of declining rainfall, was recognized in the second half of the nineteenth century. Although in North America and Australia it was hoped to improve the climate as material progress in other directions proceeded, no such optimism was present in southern Africa. It was long-term climatic change which exercised most minds. In the 1870s, deterioration in the Transvaal was recognized as water supplies dwindled:[24]

> Land is next to useless, to blacks and whites alike, without water, and stream and water courses shown on maps rarely exist though the dry beds remain to show where, not so many years ago, there was water enough and to spare. The little that does remain near the fountain heads is usually monopolized by the Boer farmer who has carefully selected his farm round the spring. . . . It must be remembered that the water supply is still annually decreasing.

The recognition of the significance of short-term fluctuations was more belated. Rainfall variability is such that rivers might only come down in flood every few years, completely changing the normal appearance of the country. John Moffat in 1885 commented on this state of affairs when one traveller in Bechuanaland found that the land was of the greatest value from an agricultural point of view, though in reality in most years it was 'a region, the dryness and consequent barrenness of which baffles conception'.[25]

In the period following the discovery of gold, from 1886–95, there was markedly higher rainfall than average. This resulted in considerable increase in agricultural expansion, and ended with the drought of 1897, which caused large-scale rural dislocation. Drought, however, was still regarded as a temporary phenomenon, until that of 1919 shattered this illusion, and the degree of deterioration was recognized. [26] The Drought Investigation Committee could write in 1923:[27]

> Since the white man has been in South Africa, enormous tracts of country have been entirely or partially denuded of the original vegetation with the result that rivers, vleis and water holes described by old travellers have dried up or disappeared.

Periodic droughts, followed by overgrazing which prevented regeneration, are the key to the study of the vegetation, and hence the grazing possibilities in southern Africa. Acocks (1953) plotted the estimated vegetative changes since the arrival of the Europeans and predicted further desert encroachment: this has been amply confirmed by satellite photographs.[28] Although rainfall figures tend to be inconclusive so far as any long-term fluctuation in climate is concerned, short-term fluctuations are substantial.[29] What is more important is that, through changes in the vegetation and increased demand for water, droughts appear to be more severe than in the past.[30] Vegetative degradation has been confused with climatic change, but as Kokot (1948) has stated:[31]

> The historical record proves conclusively that the idea that a fertile well-grassed and well-watered land welcomed the early white settlers is entirely incorrect. Droughts and dry river courses are recorded from the very earliest days, and when we make due allowance for the damage done by man himself there is no justification for deducing, from the signs of desiccation, any change in the rainfall, either in respect of total quantity or in character.

This opinion has been borne out by later investigations, which show fluctuations within a settled climatic pattern. The deterioration of the vegetative covering, the lowering of the level of subterranean waters, and the drying up of springs and rivers cannot be disputed and they are serious hazards to agricultural and pastoral farming.

Animals, Pests and Diseases

Vegetation and climate are only part of the environment. Depending upon the time of the year, travellers and explorers commented upon the abundance of wild animals in the subcontinent. Plains teeming with antelope, zebra, and other animals appeared unending. Forests and bush-land abounded in elephants, hippopotamuses and lions. Settlers, it was believed, could live off the animal life by hunting, and need not trouble unduly with their own livestock and lands.

This wealth of animal life was periodically emphasized by the mass migrations across the Karroo. In 1849 such a movement through the town of Beaufort West was described by Sir John Fraser:[32]

> As far as the eye could see they covered the country, grazing off everything eatable before them, drinking up the water in the street furrows, fountains and dams, wherever they could get at it. It took about three days before the whole of the trekbokken had passed and it left the country looking as if a fire had passed over it.

As late as 1896 a mass migration of several million buck of various species, covering an area 140 miles long by 15 miles wide, was witnessed in the Prieska district.[33]

Commercially, the vast herds of animals provided trade in ivory and skins, and often this trading was the first European activity in an area. Big-game hunting followed, as the nineteenth-century explorers penetrated the interior of the subcontinent. Depletion was rapid, and by the end of the century some species had become extinct. The speed at which the extermination proceeded resulted in the first moves towards conservation in the 1890s, so that some of the wildscapes, with their fauna, might survive the last stages of colonization. Game reserves and national parks were established to protect the remaining wild life, and by 1960 some 52,000 square miles of southern Africa were so protected, providing a focus for the rapidly expanding tourist industry.

A more intangible factor was the restriction which disease and pests placed upon settlement. The first major encounter was with malaria in the Transvaal, in the 1830s. Retreat from the lowlands below the Great Escarpment took place as the population was attacked. The route to the sea from both the Transvaal and Rhodesia was hazardous and in Rhodesia itself only the highlands were found to be malaria-free; this strongly influenced the earliest settlers. The unhealthy nature of much of the tropical part of southern Africa was emphasized by the Transvaal census of 1904, which described the northern two-thirds of the colony as unsuited in large part to permanent colonization.[34] Large-scale settlement was thus only possible with the advance of medical knowledge.

If malaria was deadly for man, the tsetse-fly, constituting a major hazard for cattle and horses in the lower altitudes of lower latitudes, was equally deadly for his animals. Large tracts of Natal, the Transvaal and Rhodesia were affected by it, and stock-farming was thereby impossible. The progress of settlement was also diverted by fly-ridden areas. At the time of the Great Trek (1836) a body of explorers investigated Rhodesia as a possible area of settlement, but rejected it because of the effects of the fly on their horses, thereby delaying the European settlement of the country by fifty years.[35] The northern Transvaal was thus a cul-de-sac rather than a way to the interior, with settlement limited by the lowlands of the Limpopo River.[36] The tsetse-fly areas fluctuated according to climatic variations and the presence of big-game animals. Thus both the elimination of wild animals and the concerted effort of the authorities has resulted in significant reductions in the tsetse-fly areas during the last one hundred years. Other diseases created periodic epidemics. The rinderpest outbreak of 1895 was probably the most serious, decimating cattle and horse populations in some districts, and reducing the inhabitants to poverty.

Plagues of insects, particularly locusts, also appeared periodical-ly, destroying grazing lands and crops; and diseases, such as rust on wheat, and swollen shoot on sugar cane, could also upset the economy of substantial groups of settlers, whose European agricul-tural experience proved to be of limited value. Through the intro-duction of new strains of crops and new breeds of animals, agricul-tural research sought to overcome the attitude that the environment could not be changed, but by 1901 southern Africa was no longer a promised land. The Commission on Immigration warned settlers that 'the injury inflicted by locusts and by the varying pests and diseases which, in South Africa, affect almost everything in the animal and vegetable world, make the occupation of farming an exceedingly precarious one.'[37]

The Indigenous Population

From the early years of the Cape settlement, the indigenous inhabitants were an important element in the European economic structure for they provided herdsmen and servants, while the importation of slaves by the Dutch from 1657 onwards emphasized and entrenched the division of labour in colonial society. Thus the use of slave and cheap Coloured labour almost immediately pre-vented certain categories of manual labour from being undertaken by Europeans, and was particularly significant for the younger sons of farmers, who had little or no inheritance. In the early eighteenth century the long-term advantages of European as opposed to Col-oured labour were debated, but they were always outweighed by the short-term costs of European settlement.[38]

The scientific and travel accounts of the eighteenth century abound in descriptions of the indigenous peoples of southern Afri-ca, but these had little impact upon settlement, beyond making Europeans aware that such people existed, whereas the Frontier Wars led to an awareness of the dangers inherent in the presence of a large African population. By the early nineteenth century the fear of danger assumed substantial proportions, for the depredations of the Africans were held to make settlement extremely hazardous. One of Cruikshank's anti-emigration cartoons (1819), showing cannibals burning a settlement, bore the caption 'The Blessings of Emigration to the Cape of Forlorn Hope is to be half roasted by the Sun & Devoured by the Natives!!' Surprisingly little attention was paid to these possibilities, despite substantial European loss of life in the various nineteenth-century wars fought in southern Africa.

The theme of abundant black labourers recurs regularly in official and other literature. It developed two major arguments: the availability of cheap labour, and the undesirability of labouring-class European immigration, as[39]

> ... there are already in that country large bodies of natives, whose labour can, it is supposed, be obtained on much cheaper terms than the labour of Europeans, and as therefore the persons wanted are rather those who should direct the labour of Natives than those who should labour themselves.

Discouragement of labourers and men without capital was fairly constant. Sample budgets were produced to show how little money was needed to establish settlers on the land, but few writers thought even £200 sufficient for the purpose, while many gave £1,000 as nearer the mark.[40] Agricultural labourers were not required as settlers, and this was bluntly stated in 1911 by the South African Committee on Closer Land Settlement: 'white labourers without means cannot be economically settled in South Africa.'[41]

At the same time the presence of cheap labour was seen as a mixed blessing in the progress of the agricultural industry. One official noted that the poor gentleman can[42]

> ... vegetate in a sort of way, with his few head of stock, his patch of 'forage' or 'mealies', his cheap acres and his kafir servants. There is a certain ease in Natal life, an absence of the stress and strain, the hard unremitting manual labour which is the immigrant's lot in more bustling communities.

Similarly, emigrants to Rhodesia could 'sit back and leave it to the Africans', to the detriment of technical innovation, but 'there is no doubt that, partly owing to its climate and partly owing to its supply of coloured labour, Rhodesia is a far more comfortable country than Canada for the average settler.'[43]

Thus the indigenous population was attractive to a certain class of settler in providing cheap labour, but this was achieved by refusing entry to most unskilled working-class European settlers, for whom southern Africa had no place.

2

The Dutch Foundation

THE FIRST EUROPEANS to settle permanently at the Cape of Good Hope were the Dutch. Originally the Portuguese, and later the Dutch and English, had found the land unattractive, but by the 1640s the United Dutch East India Company's station at St Helena was no longer able to provide the necessary food and stores for ships plying between the Netherlands and the Dutch East Indies. In 1649 a report showed that the Cape was not so inhospitable as had been believed. Fresh water and fruit and vegetables were to be found, and furthermore it was discovered that the indigenous people were not cannibals.[1]

In 1651 the Council of the United Dutch East India Company approved a plan to establish a station at the Cape of Good Hope where water, meat and vegetables might be procured, and where the sick might recover from the ill effects of the journey. On 7 April 1652, the commander of the Company's expedition, Jan van Riebeeck, went ashore at the site of Cape Town, to establish the refreshment station. Largely because the Company did not wish to become involved in conflict with the indigenous inhabitants, who, it was hoped, would supply all the livestock required by the station, its aims were strictly limited to the maintenance of a small, confined settlement and little profit was foreseen from the station, which was placed under the control of the East Indian administration.[2]

From the Company's point of view, the settlement was far from ideal. It proved expensive to run, and consequently little was expended on its development; in addition, it was not in a satisfactory position, as ships outward bound for the East Indies had to deviate from their course to reach Cape Town, while gales were a serious hazard in the open roadstead of Table Bay and claimed

many vessels. Attempts at finding an alternative proved to be
fruitless, although after 1741 Simonstown became the port of call
for the winter fleets.[3] Nevertheless, the Cape was able to supply
water and provisions, the volume of which may be gauged from the
situation in 1659, when Dutch ships received sufficient fresh vegetables and fruit for two meals a day during their stay, together with
six to eight oxen and ten to twelve sheep.[4] They left with at least two
weeks' supply of vegetables and about fifteen live sheep. This was
all the more remarkable when it is considered that between 1652
and 1699 an average of thirty-three Dutch ships called at the station
each year. The number rose in the eighteenth century, but a smaller
number of foreign ships was provisioned. It was the necessity of
supplying these quantities and maintaining the station itself that led
to the initial European colonization and settlement of southern
Africa.

Cape Town

Cape Town was founded in 1652 as a fort to guard the projected
garden of the Dutch East India Company. The fort was located near
to the main streams flowing down Table Mountain, where they
might be diverted around the fortifications in a series of canals
(Fig 2). It was originally an earth and wood construction, but
later, under the threat of English and French attack, it was replaced
by the brick and stone Castle. The fort formed the core of the initial
settlement. Around it the Company constructed the hospital, store,
cow and sheep sheds, bakery and mill. Beyond the fort was the
Company's garden, which covered a substantial area (35 acres) and
was designed to provide a wide range of fruit and vegetables for the
supply of passing ships. It was, for much of the Dutch period, the
Colony's major asset in terms of trade. No town was contemplated,
as Company servants lived within the fort, but in 1656 the Company authorized the establishment of two inns. Two more were
built in the following two years. The establishment of the free
settlers on agricultural plots in 1657 resulted in their obtaining
permission to build houses near the fort, and by 1660 the first
elements of a town plan had appeared. Van Riebeeck was apologe-
tic over this development, replying to criticisms levelled at him:[5]

> Our idea of laying out a town here had always been very little. We can
> very well feel the burden of freeman exclusive of agriculturalists and
> therefore will allow no more than there are already, for which, should
> they build any houses here, we have, so that they might be erected in

Fig 2 The Cape of Good Hope, 1752. View showing the Castle (left) the town and the Gardens above the town. Beyond the core of the settlement a somewhat exaggerated number of large houses and their gardens are depicted.

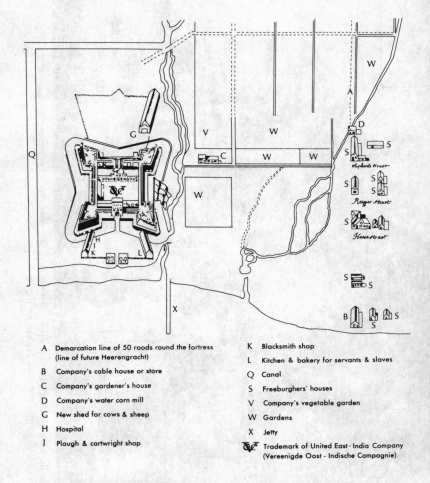

A	Demarcation line of 50 roods round the fortress (line of future Heerengracht)	K	Blacksmith shop
B	Company's cable house or store	L	Kitchen & bakery for servants & slaves
C	Company's gardener's house	Q	Canal
D	Company's water corn mill	S	Freeburghers' houses
G	New shed for cows & sheep	V	Company's vegetable garden
H	Hospital	W	Gardens
J	Plough & cartwright shop	X	Jetty
		ꝜꞒ	Trademark of United East-India Company (Vereenigde Oost-Indische Compagnie)

Fig 3   The initial layout of Cape Town, 1660

proper order, as an incipient town, marked off 500 roods outside the Fort's walls, so that it has at present more the name than the reality.

No private buildings were allowed within 600 feet of the Fort (Fig 3). A straight line was drawn that distance away, at right angles to the shoreline, and the first houses were constructed along this line (later the Heerengracht), along three streets at right angles to it. The grid pattern had thus been introduced, although the pattern of plots had still to emerge.

Growth was slow. In 1658 the population amounted to only 360, and in 1679 it was still only 460, including 171 slaves. However, during the governorship of Simon Van Der Stel substantial improvements took place. The gardens were redesigned and moved back from the sea by some 750 feet, allowing for a more extensive town grid; new streets were laid out, canals were dug, and the characteristic oak trees were planted, to provide vistas within the city. The city blocks were small — generally 300 feet square, with plots of 1/6 acre. Roads were narrow — 60 feet wide for those running parallel to the stream, and 40 feet for the cross streets; such a restricted layout has resulted in major problems in the age of mechanical transport. A church had been built in 1665, and a new hospital followed on part of the land added to the town from the re-organization of the garden. The site of the original fort was turned into a large parade ground (14 acres), which, apart from one small square of two acres, provided the only formal open space in the town until the late eighteenth century.[6]

Initially, Cape Town houses were built of stone, wattle and daub, and porous, locally produced bricks. Imported materials were expensive and erratic in supply, and because of the poor material available, buildings had to be plastered and whitewashed (Fig 4). Lack of roofing tiles made thatch the normal means of roofing.[7] But the town changed appreciably in appearance as prosperity increased in the course of the eighteenth century, the most significant change being the gradual disappearance of thatch and gables, and their replacement by flat roofs and generally straight parapets. The elimination of thatch was in large part due to the fear of conflagration, particularly after the fire of 1736, and the construction by the more prosperous inhabitants of two—and even three—storeyed houses. Brick remained generally of poor quality, and Dutch imports were limited to finishing only. Thus the general style of building, as in the country, remained plastered brick and stone, but with some pretension to European styles. The gable, a feature of seventeenth-century Dutch architecture, disappeared in eighteenth-century Cape Town, but survived in the countryside.[8] The rebuilding was such as to excite favourable comment from visitors around the year 1800: 'It is often remarked by Englishmen, that there are a greater number of well built houses for its size at the Cape than in any town in England.'[9]

As a result of the increase in external trade and the expansion of the Colony's economy, steady growth took place throughout the eighteenth century; new streets and blocks were laid out, and the area between the Castle and the settlement was gradually filled in (Fig 5). Expansion away from the Castle tended to be for private

Fig 4   Green Market Square, Cape Town, 1764. The Town House stands in the centre surrounded by typical early Cape-Dutch housing

Fig 5 View of Cape Town, 1776–7. A more faithful depiction of the town showing the Castle (left), with the jetty and the Gardens (centre).

housing in regular blocks; that around it contained a new hospital and various public buildings on more irregularly sized blocks. By the end of the eighteenth century most of the land between the town and the Castle had been built upon, and even the parade ground had been cut down in size. (Fig 6). Whereas in 1712 there had only been 250 private houses in the settlement, by 1805 there were 1,258.[10]

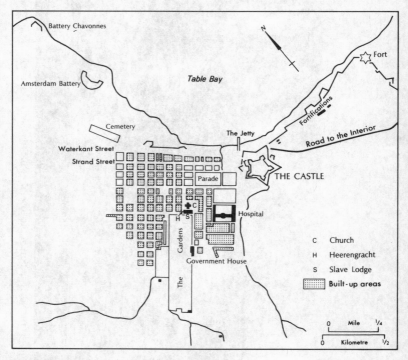

Fig. 6 Cape Town in the eighteenth century

Trade and commerce, the life-blood of the city, brought substantial warehousing activity in the streets nearest to the sea, although the jetty built in van Riebeeck's time remained the sole port installation until the 1830s. The silting of the Bay enabled the warehousing and industrial area to be expanded. Originally Strand (Beach) Street marked the seaward edge of the city, but by the early eighteenth century a further series of town blocks was created, and Waterkant (Waterside) Street became the new beach front.

The First Farms

The cultivation of grain by the Dutch East India Company's servants developed slowly. Farming along the lines envisaged by the
Company involved intensive cultivation practices, similar to those
employed in the Netherlands, and such a system demanded close
supervision and a substantial supply of labour. Company servants
proved to be unreliable, as they had no stake in the results of their
labours, while the Hottentots were not interested in working for the
Europeans. The result was neglect, and the grain crops fell below
expectation. Van Riebeeck realized that the Cape's deficit could be
wiped out by developing grain production on a commercial scale.[11]
Other sources of income such as whaling, sealing and mining were
investigated, but with little success. The agricultural potential of the
Cape Peninsula was considered to be substantial, and Van Riebeeck
believed that close settlement along the lines of the Netherlands or
the Dutch East Indies was possible, and that 1,000 families could be
placed on the land. In 1656 he undertook experiments in farming in
the Liesbeeck River valley, to the east of Cape Town, and the
results encouraged him to undertake the momentous step of establishing free settlers.

In 1657 the Company embarked upon such a scheme in the
Liesbeeck River Valley (Fig 7). The settlers received 28–40 acres
of land and undertook to cultivate certain crops, of which wheat was
the most important, and, significantly, to sell their produce to the
Company at fixed, often depressed, prices.[12] The land grant was
subject to conditions of improvement and residence, but these
generally proved irksome and were relaxed in later years. The
settlers faced considerable problems, and it was realized, from the
start, that they would need considerable Company assistance in the
form of credit and labour. An estimate suggested that an individual
settler would require 2,000 guilders (£160) to establish himself and
enable him to survive while the bush and trees were cleared, fields
prepared, fences erected, ditches dug, and farm buildings constructed.[13] The free settlers were released Company servants who
generally lacked capital, and they were thus heavily in debt to the
Company from the start of their farming operations. Furthermore,
because of the expense of free European labour, slaves were introduced from the East Indies in the same year (1657). They rapidly
became an integral part of the economic system of the Cape Colony,
in that their introduction effectively tied up much capital which
might have been otherwise employed, and determined the direction
of agricultural development along plantation lines.

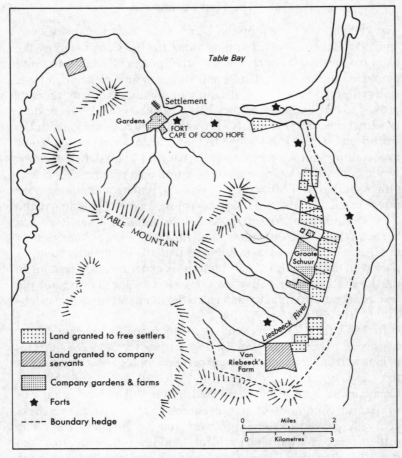

Fig 7   The first farms granted on the Liesbeeck River, 1660

The agricultural system, conceived on Dutch principles, soon deviated from expectations. The farmers, heavily in debt to the Company, required an immediate source of income in order to be able to make repayments. Labour-intensive methods of cultivation, as practised in the Netherlands — crop rotation, heavy manuring, and careful preparation of the ground — were abandoned. High yields were not required in a situation where land was plentiful and labour expensive. Thus in practice yields were low, sometimes barely bringing a return on the seed sown. With the introduction of extensive methods, fallowing became an established practice. Fodder crops, which the Company intended to play a part in rotation farming, were abandoned. Cattle were grazed on the natural pastures, and so manure was lost to the arable lands. Owing to the low nutritional value of the pasture compared with that in the Netherlands, large areas of common pasture were needed to support the livestock and, owing to the low returns obtained from small plots extensively cropped, the settlers sought other forms of income, mainly from stock raising. In the 1670s vines were successfully and profitably grown.

The agricultural settlement in the northern part of the Cape Peninsula was only partially successful. In 1661 there were only 31 free settlers, who owned 39 slaves and employed 41 European labourers. Approximately 1,000 acres had been distributed in farms, but a mere 300 acres had been cultivated. The settlers were located on 15 operating farms, situated entirely within the Liesbeeck valley and protected by a boundary hedge and small forts. The individual farms were small, but possessed a complex of buildings to house the family, slaves, implements and animals. Construction was unpretentious, with whitewashed stone walls and thatched roofs. In addition to the free settlers' farms there was the Company's farm, which, for most of the period before its closure at the end of the century, continued to grow more grain than those of the settlers. The Company established its 'Big Barn' (Groote Schuur) in the valley, to store its own grain and that of the settlers.

Expansion of the settlement was slow. Land continued to be granted, but by 1679 there were only 40 farmers, and a total free European population of 142, struggling to make a living on an area which only twenty years before had been considered capable of supporting a thousand families. The settlers remained comparatively poor, and clearly the Cape was not a place where fortunes were to be made. In addition, highly capitalized farming, such as that run by Van Riebeeck on his own account, had its limitations, as he had great difficulty in disposing of his property when he left the Colony. Without an example to follow, Cape farming developed along its own lines, with increasingly less reference to its European antecedents.

The significance of the first free settlement was not that it changed the Cape's economic situation, but that it provided the beginning of an independent farming community. The children of farmers required land, and after 1700 they exerted a constant pressure on that of southern Africa. It was largely through the natural increase of the European population that this recurring theme in the development of the subcontinent unfolded.

The Settlement of
the South-western Cape

The land beyond the sandy wastes of the Cape Flats had been left to the indigenous Hottentots, with whom the Company and individual Europeans traded for livestock. Although rights and contracts to supply livestock were issued, no permanent European settlement was founded beyond the Cape Flats until 1672, when a post was established at Hottentots Holland.

In 1679 it was felt that expansion was necessary to reduce the station's dependence on the Hottentots for the supply of meat. The new commander at the Cape, Simon van der Stel, was given free rein to decide upon the form of the expansion. He inspected the land between the Cape Flats and the mountains, and selected the site of Stellenbosch, on the Eerste River, as the centre for the new colony. He found[14]

> several thousand morgen fine pasture land, also, very suitable for arable husbandry, provided with a very delightful fresh river, decorated on both sides by beautiful high trees suitable for garden and fire wood.

Within the new settlement land was available on a first-come-first-served basis. Freehold title was available for all the land which could be improved within three years. Unimproved land remained the property of the Company and was used as communal grazing land. Survey was initiated from the start. Under such a system the water courses were immediately selected, and later arrivals found the land available to them impossible to water. In 1687 the settlement was considered complete, although a mere 6.5 per cent of the available land had been granted to settlers.

The closing of the Stellenbosch settlement led to the opening of the next, at Drakenstein. Its opening coincided with the arrival of a party of approximately 200 French Huguenot refugees (1688), who were mainly settled at Franschhoek (French Corner). The allocation of land at Drakenstein proceeded in a more orderly fashion than at Stellenbosch, and plots of 125 acres, with river frontages of 250 yards and lengths of 2,500 yards, were granted to settlers. Similar conditions prevailed further north as new lands were opened in the vicinity of Paarl in the 1690s. The Drakenstein settlement did not warrant a village, although a church was later established in the area: in the main this was due to the very extensive nature of the settlement, and the poverty of the settlers. Even under ordered layout, by 1699 only 7 per cent of the Drakenstein area had been granted, but it was apparently full, and all the suitable water frontages had been taken. Thus whereas the average size of grant was only 113 acres, effectively each farm had, with its portion of common grazing, 1,600 acres.

In 1699 the European population totalled 1,265, spread across some 1,500 square miles. If the population of Cape Town is excluded, there were approximately 1½ square miles per European man, woman and child. In terms of land granted or occupied, only 12,800 acres were opened up north and east of the existing settlements, so that the opening of the Land of Waveren in 1699 was very significant, as it lay beyond the first of the mountain ranges. Such expansion continued until 1717, when the limited immigration policy and the issuing of freehold grants ceased (Fig 8).

The limitation of the settlement was due to the development of agriculture in the new areas. Production outstripped demand, and exports were expensive. As early as 1685 the Colony produced sufficient wheat to feed its inhabitants, and thereafter there was sufficient for export.[15] In addition, wine production began seriously under the aegis of the Commander. Between 1680 and 1700 production rose from 6,000 gallons to 144,000 gallons. In all, some 1.6 million vines had been planted in the latter year. The rise of the wine farm was largely to satisfy the local needs of the population and passing ships, for there was little demand for inferior wine elsewhere in the Dutch possessions, and production was kept in check for much of the eighteenth century.

The western Cape settlement, based on arable agriculture, formed a distinct entity, its extent limited through physical and economic factors. The mountain ranges to the east effectively blocked expansion, until road improvements were effected by the British in the early nineteenth century. To the north, increasing aridity made crop farming a hazardous affair. Superimposed on the physical limitations was the problem of communications. Land transport of produce to Cape Town was expensive and placed obvious limits on the profitability of produce. Owing to the low population densities and lack of revenue, road improvements were few and far between. Hence for much of the eighteenth century the areas of arable land were limited, although within them major changes took place, particularly in the second half of the century, when production of both wheat and wine showed major growth under the favourable conditions of increased trade and the wars in Europe (Table 1)[16]

Table 1 INDICES OF GROWTH 1662–1806

| Date | Population | | Production | | Livestock | |
	European	slave	wheat (tons)	wine (000 galls)	cattle	sheep (nos 000)
1662			36			
1682	318		173			
1700	1,265	891	387	144		
1711	1,756		1,147	138		
1721	2,101	2,485	1,004	149	18	74
1731	2,920	4,303	1,666	206	24	124
1741	3,866	5,336	2,976	130	32	152
1751	4,941	5,587	1,713	376	33	161
1760	6,155	6,487	1,487	359	34	204
1770	8,088	8,220	1,428	503	38	258
1780	10,500	11,692	1,948	641	64	356
1795	14,952	16,839	3,294	793	72	419
1806	26,568	29,861	13,800	1,220	208	1,254

Within the predominantly arable area expansion occurred, with increased planting of both wheat and vines. New areas were taken into cultivation at the expense of the waste, but there was no continuous wheat or vine belt. Substantial areas remained in grazing and unused bush, as most farmers possessed livestock. In addition, the system of agriculture was extensive and exhausting to the soil, with long fallow periods necessary to restore fertility. As early as the 1720s complaints were made about soil exhaustion and the need for larger farms. Overgrazing similarly disturbed farmers, although after 1720 this was partially relieved by sending flocks and herds over the mountains to the interior for the summer months.

The agricultural system was operated by slave labour, and this continued to have a profound effect upon the whole economic state of the Colony. After the Hottentot smallpox epidemic of 1713 slave importation increased rapidly, so that by 1721 there were more slaves than Europeans in the Colony, and this situation was maintained throughout the remainder of the Dutch period of administration, although the rate of importation of slaves slackened in the 1740s.

The use of slave instead of free white labour retarded economic development, as slaves lacked purchasing power and the ability to enter the money economy. The large landholdings were worked as plantations, in the style of tropical colonies. Dispersion, which was the keynote of the Cape settlement, was maintained by slavery in a way that free European settlement would not have done, as free labour, slowly accumulating money, could have bought land, and

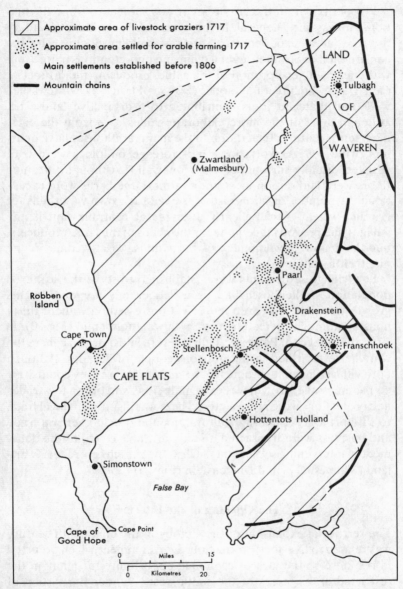

Fig 8 The settlement of the South-western Cape

thereby created a more egalitarian society.[17] It is noteworthy that throughout the eighteenth century the number of arable farms possessing more than ten slaves increased, while those with under six markedly declined.[18]

Prosperity within the arable areas was subject to some fluctuation, but was fairly general. In the course of the eighteenth century the rural areas experienced a series of building booms, with the construction of farmhouses of a plain and unpretentious nature, but with increasing elaboration of the gable, producing the distinctive Cape-Dutch architectural style (Fig 9). Plastered, whitewashed walls and thatched roofs contributed to a distinctive landscape, although most of the more elaborate gables date from the early nineteenth century. In addition to the main farmhouse, slave quarters, wine cellars, workshops and storeage buildings were constructed, usually surrounded by a low wall.[19] Although threshing floors were laid out on most grain farms, large barns were exceptional. A number of farms also possessed their own watermills for grinding wheat, because early attempts at centralization in the villages had proved inadequate for the needs of the large producers, but the major development of farm mills was to come in the nineteenth century.

Few village settlements were established to serve the scattered population. Stellenbosch had been deliberately founded, but its growth was slow, and even in 1753 it possessed only about thirty houses, although thereafter its growth was more rapid (Fig 10). In 1763 the villages of Paarl and Tulbagh were laid out, adjacent to the churches established in the previous couple of decades. Athough both villages lay on the routes to the interior where they could draw on passing trade, growth was extremely slow, and only a few trades and professions were represented. There was insufficient local trade to support a great non-agricultural population, and general trade and business were transacted directly in Cape Town, to the detriment of intervening settlements such as the church centres of Zwartland (Malmesbury) and Drakenstein (Fig 10).

The Opening of the Interior

The territorial expansion of the Colony in the eighteenth century was related to livestock production, a development which occurred in response to the lack of economic opportunity for many in the restricted arable areas of the south west.[20] Under the system of divided inheritance operable in the Colony, families could soon be reduced to poverty, and it was only on the frontier of settlement that a man with a small sum of money could make a start in farming. At first livestock production was seen as a means of gaining capital to enter arable farming; later it became the dominant colonial enter-

Fig 9 Cape-Dutch farmhouse, Vendutie Kraal (Worcester District), slave bell (left), and vineyard. The present farmhouse dates from 1815 and illustrates the Cape-Dutch style of architecture, developed in the western Cape Province, and later transferred to other parts of southern Africa.

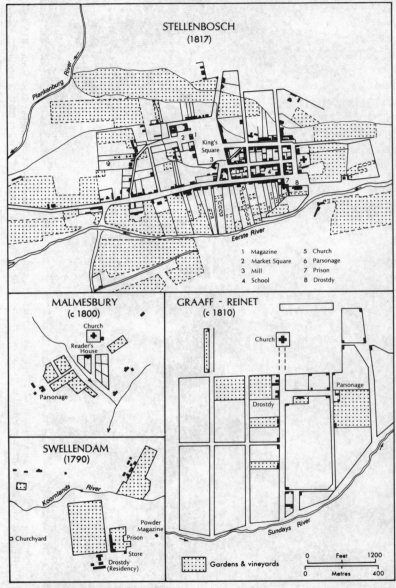

Fig 10   Village plans, 1790–1817

prise. As a result, whereas in 1716 only 9 per cent of all agricultural producers were stockfarmers, in 1770 this had risen to 66 per cent.

This dramatic change in the Colony, and in the Colony's extent, came about as a result of the continuing need for livestock by passing ships. Initial grazing experiments had led to the pasturing of flocks and herds at ever increasing distances from Cape Town. As early as 1692 official warnings were being issued against penetrating too far from established settlements, but the need for a steady supply of meat forced the Company to relax its control. In 1703 individuals were given permission to graze their livestock beyond the limits of the settled areas. At first permission was general, with several graziers entitled to use the same area, but in 1708 it was evident that exclusive rights were being issued, at first for a few months only, but from 1720 annual leases were offered.[21] Further extension of rights was granted in 1710 when holders were entitled to cultivate small quantities of wheat.

In 1714 the entire leasing system was phased on a regular basis. Grazing rights were leased, and the right to cultivate the 'loan place' was accepted as general. Furthermore rentals were to be levied at the rate of 12 Rd (£2.50) per annum, and there were to be tithes on grain. In 1732 this was raised to 24 Rd (£5), which declined in real terms as the silver rix-dollar depreciated in value. At first the majority of loan places were taken for the summer season by farmers from the settled areas, but settlement became increasingly permanent as greater numbers applied for licences, and stock was taken ever-increasing distances from the south-western Cape.

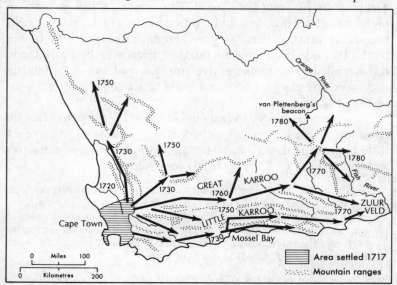

Fig 11   The spread of the graziers, 1717–1780

Expansion of the area settled by the graziers came in two marked phases, although these merged into one another (Fig 11).[22] The first, prior to about 1745, was the settlement of the lands adjacent to the early settlement, approximately within 200 miles of Cape Town. The main lines of expansion were over the Hottentots Holland mountains and into the southern coastal plains; into the interior through the mountains of the Land of Waveren, and then either southwards to the southern coastal plains, or on to the interior plateaux. After 1745 there was a more general movement eastwards and northwards — the latter constantly limited by aridity. The eastward movement entered progressively more attractive land, until in 1779 the first major clash occurred with the African tribes, who were solidly established along the line of the Fish River.

The livestock areas were only sparsely settled. This was in part due to the land tenure system. Loan places, unlike freehold lands, were not surveyed, and no specific area was defined for the farm, but it soon became the custom to select the centre of a new loan place at least one hour's horse ride from that of another man. The licencee then rode his horse at walking pace for half an hour in several directions from this central point (*ordonnantie*) to mark out his boundaries. Theoretically the loan place was thus a circular farm with a radius of 1¾ miles comprising 6,000 acres, which became accepted as its standard area.[23] The origin of this practice is undocumented and was only officially specified in the early nineteenth century. Inevitably the amount of land secured by this method varied substantially: in the areas nearest to the arable lands, farms tended to be smaller as overlaps occurred, but in the interior they were often larger and farms might be spaced two hours' walk, instead of one hour apart.

Loan-place tenure was highly insecure, and few frontier farmers considered their loan places to be lifelong possessions. As a result little improvement was made to the land, and housing standards were poor (Fig 12). Barrow (1797) commented:[24]

> The miserable hovels in which the graziers live are the pictures of want and wretchedness. Four low mud-walls, with a couple of square holes to admit the light, and a door of wicker work, a few crooked poles to support a thatch of rushes, slovenly spread over them, serves for the dwelling of many a peasant whose stock consists of several thousand sheep and as many hundred heads of cattle.

Standards were poor because of the difficulties of construction in largely woodless areas, the absence of the grazier for long periods

Fig 12 Karroo farm, Queekvalij (Prince Albert District), 1778. Pioneer farmers in the Karroo were able to achieve moderate prosperity. This farm with its arable fields, cattle pens and buildings would, however, have been unusual with regards to its scale of operations.

(depending upon the seasonal state of the pasture) and the general instability of the population.[25] The frontiersmen were even more isolated than the arable farmer. Education and specialized services were left behind. There were few slaves or artisans, as the population was too poor to afford them. By 1800, Cape Town was a journey of up to four months from the furthest frontier and only infrequently visited.

The problem of instability was appreciated by the Cape Government, and it sought to remedy the situation by offering more secure land tenures. In 1732 quit-rent tenure with fifteen-year leases was offered to established farmers: these, however, mainly allowed wheat farmers greater security in extending their acreage. In 1743 freehold conversion was offered for 125 acres around the farmhouse. Security of house, gardens and arable fields was felt to be desirable, but few took advantage of this offer: indeed, as time went by, there was an increase in the numbers of stock-farmers without any title. The frontiersmen (*trekkers*) divided themselves into two groups: those who found moderate prosperity and those who did not, and available statistics tend to suggest that in the eighteenth century the latter tended to exceed the former. Those who did prosper established themselves on their loan places in a state of semi-self-sufficiency, with enough income to secure some of the luxuries of life from passing traders or during periodic visits to Cape Town. Others continued to wander, becoming squatters on open land or on other people's loan places, sometimes as the employees of the successful. Squatting became steadily more common as time progressed, and it has been estimated that by 1800 possibly two-thirds of the farmers in the eastern and most remote part of the Colony possessed no title at all to their land.[26]

The low level of settlement intensity is emphasized by the fact that even in 1806 there were only 1,736 loan places, equivalent to approximately 17,000 square miles, while the area of the Colony at that stage covered some 150,000 square miles. Even in areas which were comparatively highly developed, such as the southern coastal plain, there were 30 square miles per loan place in 1770, when the area was considered to be occupied.[27] Densities of population of one person per 4–20 square miles resulted from the loan places being scattered over wide distances. Equally, livestock densities were low. The number of sheep in the Colony rose from approximately 75,000 in 1721 to 203,000 in 1760 and to 1.2 million by 1806; cattle numbers in the same years were 18,000, 34,000 and 208,000. In terms of livestock-unit densities, values of under half a unit per square mile persisted in at least one district until the beginning of the nineteenth century. The major increases occurred during the period of the first British administration (1795–1803), when both sheep and cattle numbers tripled.[28] Livestock continued to supply the Cape Town market. It was very largely the graziers in the western part of the Colony who supplied the provision trade, yet because of its size, butchers had to travel far afield. In 1796 it was estimated that each year the population and merchants of Cape Town required some 5 per cent of the cattle and 11 per cent of the sheep and goats of the Colony. Although the Graaff Reinet district possessed half the sheep and a third of the cattle by 1795, few could have been driven the 500 miles or more to market in Cape Town.

Within areas of such low population densities, village settlement was even less desirable than in the arable farming areas of the south west, and government officials became increasingly concerned about the isolation of the stock farmers. In 1743 Swellendam was established in the southern coastal plain, some 130 miles from Stellenbosch, and two years later it became the seat of a magistrate (Fig 10). But already the frontiersmen were settled far beyond the reach of this official, and it was not until 1786 that the next town was established at Graaff Reinet to control the eastern frontier districts. It was small, with only a few simple houses (Fig 10). Barrow, writing ten years after its foundation, described it as:[29]

> an assemblage of mud huts placed at some distance from each other, in two lines, forming a kind of street. At the upper end stands the house of the landdrost, built also of mud, and a few miserable hovels, that were intended as offices for the transaction of public business; most of these had tumbled in, and the rest were in so ruinous a condition as not to be habitable. . . . Its appearance is as miserable as that of the poorest village in England.

The last village founded by the Dutch was in 1804 at Uitenhage, near the disputed eastern frontier. This town was occupied by settlers who were offered free grants for living there, on condition that they were available for military service. Its expansion, as was indeed the case with most of the rural settlements, had to await the permanent British occupation two years later. All the villages in the grazing districts remained small, providing few services, and through lack of trade they were unable to attract potential artisans.

The Cape of Good Hope in 1806

In 1806 the Cape Colony passed permanently into British hands. It is therefore worthwhile examining its state after 150 years of Dutch rule. The first most noticeable feature is the small number of people living within its boundaries. There were still only 26,568 Europeans, 20,436 Hottentots and 29,861 slaves living in an area of some 150,000 square miles — an average density of approximately two persons per square mile (Fig 13). Equally noticeable was the imbalance in its distribution. Almost a quarter of the population lived in Cape Town, the only town in the Colony, and half in the two districts in the south-western Cape Colony (Cape Town and Stellenbosch), which accounted for only 5 per cent of the Colony's land area. The interior districts remained open and largely unoccupied, except on an occasional basis. The Tulbagh district possessed no more than one European per 30 square miles.

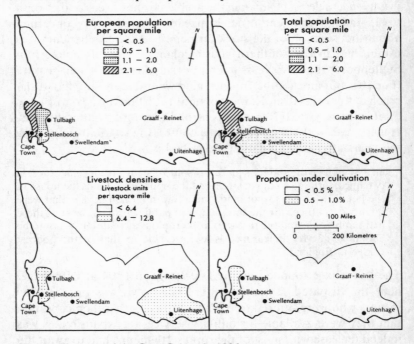

Fig 13   The state of the Cape Colony in 1806

The threefold division of the Colony — Cape Town, the south-western Cape, and the Interior, based on trade, arable-mixed farming and stock farming respectively — was still a close reflection of the origins of settlement. Little urban development had penetrated beyond the Cape Flats, while in the interior arable farming was minimal. Cape Town, a city of some 16,428 inhabitants, including

6,435 Europeans, was the only port in the Colony, and still a vital refreshment station on the Europe to India route. After a period of sustained European warfare, the town experienced considerable prosperity and growth, with major rebuilding programmes providing it with some of the amenities of Europe.[30] The town acted as the main market for the Colony where the produce of the interior was exported and to which the bulk of the imports were consigned. The administration, both civil and military, was heavily concentrated in the capital, and rarely penetrated the Cape Flats. Cape Town and its vicinity constituted an entity separate from the interior, and this separateness was reinforced by the presence of large numbers of officials, at first Dutch, later British, who had little concept of the nature of the interior.

Through the growth in the wine trade, the arable-mixed farming area of the south-western Cape was highly prosperous by 1806. Increasing wine exports, to passing ships, as well as the expanding internal trade, were augmented by successively larger garrisons stationed at the settlement. The number of vines more than doubled between the two British occupations. With prosperity went a wave of renovation and rebuilding: estates were improved, and in particular homesteads were embellished. The Cape-Dutch gable, the distinctive feature of many parts of the south-western part of the Colony, became a sign of wealth. Prosperity resulted in Baroque and later neo-classical features being extensively used, for, with a substantial slave population, including artisans from the East Indies, ambitious projects could be effected. [31] In terms of cultivated area, however, the vineyards probably covered no more than 12,000 acres, some 2 per cent of the south-western districts.[32] Extensive grain production probably occupied a further 7 per cent of the area, and thus nine acres in every ten in the arable-mixed farming district either remained as grazing land or were unused.

The interior districts, covering the remaining 140,000 square miles of the Colony, were sparsely occupied and devoted to livestock grazing, densities being greatest in the coastal districts, with three head of cattle per square mile in Uitenhage and Swellendam, one per square mile in Graaff Reinet, and only a third of that density in the western interior. Sheep numbers were greater, even in terms of livestock units. The Graaff Reinet district, with over half the sheep of the Colony, reached a density of one sheep per 50 acres, while Tulbagh possessed one sheep per 200 acres. The low level of development and the poverty of the interior was in marked contrast to the south-western portion of the Colony, and isolation remained the major problem of the frontier districts.

The Dutch heritage of southern Africa is of considerable importance, for the Afrikaner nation evolved after 1717 as a separate entity, as a result of isolation from Europe, and indeed, by the later eighteenth century from almost any form of governmental supervision.[33] Most important was the failure of any later immigration from Europe to outnumber the Afrikaners, who, through a high natural increase, were able to maintain numerical superiority over other groups of Europeans in southern Africa. Finally, political superiority ensured that it was this nation which shaped the development of the subcontinent. The Dutch heritage extended from the construction of towns and farms to a whole concept of land-holding and race relations which still exists. The initial towns were Dutch foundations, and their plans influenced later town planning. The ideas of land entitlement and farming built up in the eighteenth century were vital to later generations. In the field of race relations the influence of slavery lasted long after that institution had been abolished, to bedevil politics in the twentieth century. Thus in 1806, the Cape of Good Hope possessed a substantial, unique cultural landscape heritage to pass on to the future, to be preserved and adapted both within the boundaries of the Colony and beyond.

3

Agricultural and Pastoral Development 1806–1860

THE FIRST HALF-CENTURY of British rule in southern Africa was of major importance in the transformation of the subcontinent. The European population increased more than fivefold, to reach approximately 150,000 by the mid-1850s (Figs 13 and 14). Extensive new areas were opened up for European colonization and in all some 36,000 Europeans arrived in South Africa from Great Britain before 1860. Nevertheless only half of these remained permanently, and South Africa was able to attract only 0.7 per cent of British emigrants, compared with 14.1 per cent who went to Australasia. Thus the overwhelming majority of the European population of the subcontinent at any time was locally born, in contrast to the position in many other colonies.

With regard to the British government's relations with both European settlers and African tribes, the period was one of considerable instability. In 1806 the Cape Colony had been the only European political entity, but by 1860 it had been joined by two further British colonies, Natal and British Kaffraria, and two semi-independent republics, the Orange Free State and Transvaal (South African Republic), which lay beyond direct British administrative control, and therefore outside the area attracting British capital. This division, colonial and republican, may be regarded as the territorial expression of two schools of thought. The first, the Cape-Dutch school, envisaged minimal governmental control and virtually complete freedom to pursue grazing activity far into the interior of the subcontinent, regardless of African and Hottentot interests. The second, the British Imperial school, envisaged greater government control and limits placed on the settlers' wanderings and their relations with the indigenous peoples. Furthermore, the

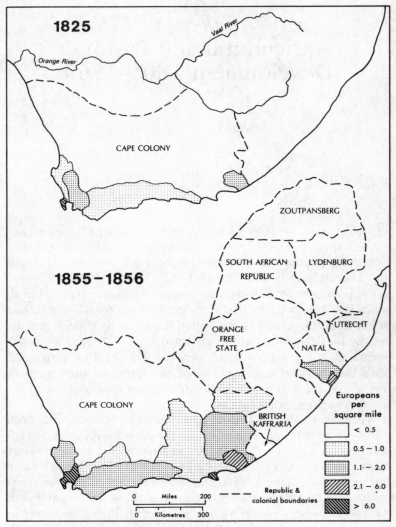

Fig 14   Distribution of European population, 1825 and 1855

Imperial government, through its policy of 'systematic colonization', was at complete variance with Cape-Dutch practice.

The period was one of turmoil amongst the African peoples, who in turn came into conflict with the Europeans throughout the sub-continent, but particularly on the eastern boundary of the Cape Colony. Between 1811 and 1853 there were five major frontier wars, and considerable uncertainty during the periods of 'peace'.[1]

Attempts at achieving frontier stability included close settlement, first by the British (1820) and later the Germans (1856). Insecurity on the long frontiers of settlement and the dispersed nature of the settlement were permanent features of the period, and only the

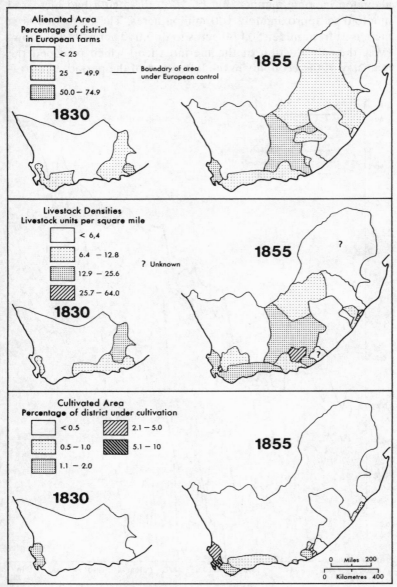

Fig 15   Progress in farming, 1830–1855

western Cape, with Cape Town, the metropolis, escaped this state of turmoil.

Against this background the achievements of the period are considerable (Table 2, Fig 15). In 1806 only 11 million acres were alienated in some manner, but by 1860 this figure had increased ninefold to approximately 100 million acres. The cultivated area increased from under 50,000 acres to 300,000 acres. It was, however, the introduction of the merino sheep which provided the mainstay of the economy in the latter part of the period. Unfortu-

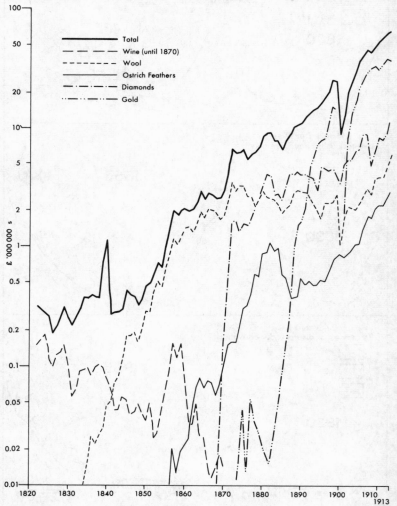

Fig 16   South African exports, 1820–1913

nately only Cape statistics may be regarded as in any way reliable, but from a few thousand in 1824 the number of woolled sheep rose to over 6 million in 1855. The increases in livestock densities attributable to this development, particularly in the eastern Cape Colony, were marked, and the development of the wool export trade had a major bearing upon the colonial economy. Exports, which had lagged after 1815, received a major boost in the later 1830s (Table 3, Fig 16). The growing volume of trade and dependence upon British markets was symbolized by the start of a regular steamer service between England and Cape Town in 1851, which cut the journey time from 80–90 days to 35 days. The rest of European-occupied southern Africa was not so securely linked. The inhabitants of vast areas existed at semi-subsistence levels, similar to those of the eighteenth century; their contact was through itinerant dealers, or periodic markets, where ivory, skins, etc were bartered for guns, powder, and a few luxuries.

Table 2 CAPE OF GOOD HOPE: INDICES OF
AGRICULTURAL & PASTORAL DEVELOPMENT 1806–1855

Date	Woolled sheep (000)	Other sheep (000)	Cattle (000)	Area cropped (000 acres)	Area alienated (million acres)
1806	14	1,240	208	50	11
1815	15	1,577	258		
1824	15	2,192	352		20
1830		1,906	312	135	
1839		2,339	307	164	32
1849	2,283	2,115	525	198	45
1855	4,828	1,626	451	198	48

Table 3 SOUTH AFRICAN EXPORTS 1810–1859

Period	Annual Average (£000)		
	wine	wool	Total
1810–14			111
1815–19			218
1820–24	165	2	230
1825–29	123	1	246
1830–34	81	5	277
1835–39	99	24	469
1840–44	58	73	567
1845–49	44	180	526
1850–54	36	386	808
1855–59	115	984	1,720

The Reform of the
Cape Land Grant System

The British administration at the Cape of Good Hope was faced in 1806 with a number of problems, of which the land question was one of the most important, controlling as it did the spread of settlement, and consequent conflict with border tribes. The initial administration regarded the British occupation as temporary, in the same manner as that of 1795–1803 had been, and it was only gradually realized that the Colony would be retained in any general European peace settlement, and consequently that changes could be made in its administration.[2]

The uncontrolled nature of the South African frontier under Dutch rule, associated with the loan-place system, was clearly unsatisfactory from an official point of view. The lack of permanence in the system, the ability of many to ignore completely the regulations on land holdings, together with the lack of revenue, all militated against the system. Impermanence resulted in reluctance to make improvements, as well as the farmer's inability to borrow money against the security of his farm. Avoidance of the regulations and subsequent squatting depreciated the value of Crown Lands, and so lowered revenue. Revenue from the system was such that, as a result of currency depreciation, each loan place could produce an annual rent of only approximately £2 by the 1810s. Owing to the inability of the government to collect the rents, the land revenue was indeed far smaller than even this low figure would suggest.

This state of affairs was at variance with the British government's concept of order, stability and progress. Constant movement meant that the administration, to be effective, would be costly. Reform of the land ownership system was difficult, owing to the scarcity of surveyors and of capital, and it was only with the arrival of Sir John Cradock as governor in 1811 that real direction was given to a permanent policy. He recognized that the Cape Colony was to remain a British possession, and therefore ought to be developed to a far greater extent than was then the case. In 1813 new land regulations were issued to deal with the interior districts, through which stability and agricultural improvement were to be achieved by granting land on permanent quit rent, after accurate survey. Increased revenue from re-assessed rents would enable public works to be undertaken in order to open up the interior, and permanence would, it was hoped, settle the constantly moving frontier population and reduce the possibility of frontier wars, while survey would enable boundaries to be recognized and illegal squat-

ting to be identified. It would also have the advantage of eliminating
the conflicting claims and the many errors which had crept into the
haphazard system during the Dutch period.[3]

The new regulations provided for the regranting of loan places
and other unsurveyed tenures as free grants, liable to perpetual
rent. Farms were to remain at the standard size of 6,000 acres
wherever possible, and certainly not to exceed it. The process of
survey was long and not without the very errors it was hoped to
avoid. In the main the surveyors attempted to lay out square farms,
though in the Swellendam district, where circular farms of long
standing existed, the original shape was retained. Between 1813
and 1823 some 443 of the 2,206 farms were regranted on perpetual
quit-rent tenure.[4] Only in the Uitenhage District did conversion
approach completion (58.8 per cent converted), while in the two
interior districts of Graaff Reinet and Tulbagh less than 10 per cent
were converted after ten years. The backlog was all the more serious
when it is remembered that new petitions for land had built up, and
that by 1828 over 2,990 claims awaited attention.[5]

Thus the immediate result of the legislative reforms, an increase
in squatting, was the reverse of that intended. The administrative
machinery, the First Land Commission, was clearly incapable of
dealing with the whole problem of adequately enforcing the law.
The requests for farms were traded in the same manner as farms
granted, although at lower value. Even if each applicant squatted on
only the regulation size, approximately 18 million acres were illeg-
ally occupied by 1828. Applications for new farms closed in 1832,
and later alienations up to 1844 may be regarded as the measure of
the amount of land occupied, or at least applied for, by 1832. By
1844 some 40 million acres had been granted in quit-rent tenure,
but this was not the end of the matter, as the problem was not finally
solved until the 1860s, after the introduction of two further sets of
land regulations. There were examples of extreme dilatoriness, such
as the search in 1850 for the memorial for the conversion of three
loan places lodged in 1817.

The whole question of the administration of the Cape of Good
Hope was investigated in 1828. The Report of the Commissioners
of Inquiry upon the Government Finances recommended the granting of larger holdings than the standard 6,000-acre unit.[6] It was
recognized that multiple-farm holding was administratively incon-
venient, and that restricted size limited the improvement of livestock. In 1814 some 162 persons held 604 loan places in multiple
units, although the remaining 1,602 (72.6 per cent) were held sing-

ly.[7] These larger units had several advantages. Farmers in the dry interior had effectively controlled larger areas through selecting sites on rivers and springs, and the government was thus left with the valueless dry backlands which, as a result of a lack of supervision, were effectively part of the farmers' holdings. If the loan place and the backlands were granted at once, administrative expense would be reduced, and the government could obtain some return for the land.

Thus in the 1830s and 1840s larger units were disposed of in the dry interior. In areas of low rainfall (under 10 inches per annum) farm sizes of 20,000 acres became more general, and a realistic basis was established for the settlement of the interior. The Second Land Commission under the Surveyor-General (appointed 1828), evolved a system of survey and evaluation which allowed for a wide variety of rents to be charged according to the expected returns from grazing. Thus the average size of grazing-farm grants (over 500 acres) between 1835 and 1844 (10,362 acres) was almost twice that of the previous decade (5,327 acres).[8] In the Beaufort District the average size in the latter decade was 18,000 acres. The more realistic appraisal of the interior undoubtedly assisted in the disentangling of existing claims and the spread of new settlement, as well as the regularization of the situation by encouraging the much needed improvements which had to take place if the country was to become a major wool exporting country. Once grants had been made, pastoral farmers had no fear of displacement, as was the case in many other parts of the world, such as the Australian colonies, and so the improvements which the government wished to see slowly materialized. Prosperity became possible, particularly with the introduction of the wool trade, which necessitated controlled breeding of the merino sheep.

The layout of farms assumed distinctive patterns according to the area and time of layout. The simplest method was to fit the existing properties together, thus eliminating all Crown Land which separated them, for example Klipfontein (Fig 17a) in the developing arable area of Malmesbury. Alternatively, in the mountainous areas only the valley floors were appropriated (Fig 17b). Where land was more plentiful, surveys attempted to produce regular figures of standard size, such as the circular farms of Swellendam (Fig 17c) or the squares of the eastern districts (Fig 17d). In the interior, Crown Land was appropriated to establish larger units (Fig 17e).[9]

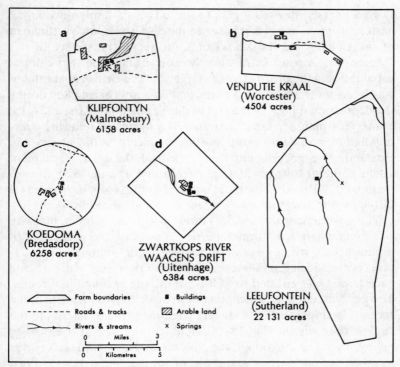

Fig 17   Farm plans in the Cape Colony, 1815–1835

The English Settlement of the Eastern Cape

In the years immediately following the British occupation, the eastern frontier of the Colony was highly insecure. Two frontier wars (1811–12 and 1818–19) forced the government to reconsider the whole question of frontier defence. In 1815 the districts of Graaff Reinet and Uitenhage contained only 11,650 Europeans, or approximately one European per 4 square miles, although growth in the European population of the eastern districts had been substantial, with an increase of two-thirds in the previous nine years. However, the land distribution system, even in its reformed state, would not result in the type of close settlement capable of resisting African attack; while the frontier farmers were incapable of producing sufficient food for the army stationed there, with the result that the state-run Somerset Farm was established in 1815 to supply the garrisons.

Faced with the problem of defence and supply, the Governor,

Lord Somerset, devised a plan to settle British immigrants on the
eastern frontier, as a buffer between the dispersed Dutch settlement
of the Colony and the Xhosa of Kaffraria. In pursuance of this
scheme, he wrote extravagantly concerning the agricultural
capabilities of the districts (see Chapter 1). The British government
was faced with rising unemployment and distress in England during
the depression following the end of the Napoleonic Wars, and Lord
Somerset's plan appeared desirable as a means of relieving overpopulation, and demonstrating official concern at the situation in
England. The government thus approved the plan, Parliament
voted £50,000 towards its implementation, and in 1820 an estimated 4,000 British settlers set out for South Africa, to participate
in the largest government-directed scheme of the century.[10]

The government did not deal directly with the settlers, but with
sixty gentlemen, who formed parties of settlers, and proceeded to
organize and, where necessary, finance them, although all emigrants possessed at least some means. Under the terms of the scheme
each family was entitled to 100 acres of land at a nominal rental.
The government land allocations were made to party leaders in the
form of locations, and the leaders were then free to distribute the
land as they wished (Fig 18). Undoubtedly most had been led to
believe that a re-creation of the English landscape and society was
possible, and one party leader spoke of 'my individual rights as Lord

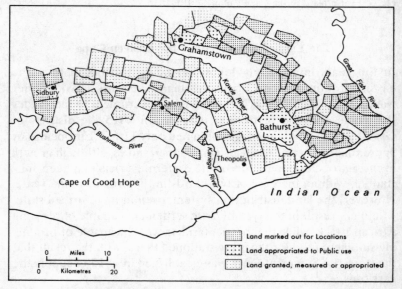

Fig 18   The Albany Settlement

of the Manor'.[11] Co-operative and joint agreements were entered
into between leaders and members of the parties, many of whom
were guided by high moral and religious ideals in planting the new
colony.

The organization of the parties and the attempts at reproducing
the better features of English rural society meant that the locations
were not necessarily divided amongst the settlers. In general the
leaders assigned only small individual plots and the remainder
became commonage or the leaders' estates. Village or hamlet settlement was envisaged, with central churches, schools and stores.
Occasionally a formal village was laid out around the church, but
more usually the settlers were housed on their own individual plots.
The layout of the schemes may be gauged from the largest, at Salem,
where the fifty allotments covered only 1,166 acres out of the total
11,828 acres assigned to the party (Fig 19): the (approximately) 20

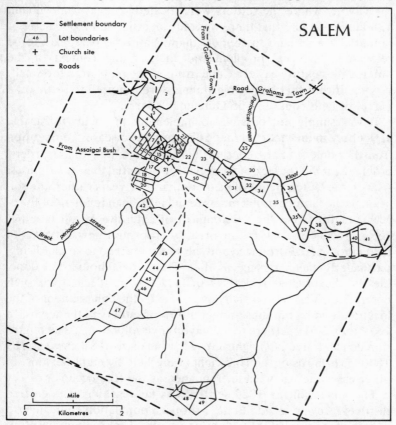

Fig 19   Plan of the Salem Settlement

acres per allotment was considered to be the limit which could be handled by a family as an arable farm. In addition, commonage rights were given to each settler, at the rate of ten head of cattle and ten sheep.[12] Arable allotments could be enlarged by withdrawing one head of cattle for every 5 acres enclosed. It should be noted that such acreages provided reasonably large holdings by the English standards of the time.

What the settlers could not have foreseen was the enormous contrast between rural England and the eastern frontier of the Cape Colony. The agricultural potential of the area was very limited, with large tracts of rugged stony ground covered by dense scrubby bush, incapable of cultivation; the climate had extremes of drought and flood, both of which took the settlers unawares. More deadly was the rust which attacked the wheat, which was the intended economic base of the settlement. These limitations extended to other parts of the Colony where the settlers were located: thus at Clanwilliam, 126 families found that there was only an estimated 2,000 acres of potential arable land to support them,[13] and the party had to be relocated. The real problem was that, in the context of the nineteenth-century eastern Cape frontier, the plots were too small: it is significant that sixty Englishmen were required to settle on a parcel of land equal to one Dutchman's farm.

It was simply not possible to implement the plans for arable agriculture in the face of climatic disasters and disease. Competition from the Somerset Farm continued until 1825, adding to the settlers' problems, as did the lack of an outlet for potential export surpluses. As with the Dutch free settlers more than 160 years earlier, the solution to the farming problem was found in an abandonment of European practices, and the development of extensive mixed farming. By a process of trial and error, new crops and new methods of cultivation were introduced and the settlers turned to stock raising, particularly sheep raising, as their Dutch neighbours had done. Clearly the original allocation of land was insufficient for such enterprises. This was partially overcome by the enlargement of the locations and by the substantial outflow of settlers to the towns. In 1824 only 1,619 settlers remained on their allotments. The migration concentrated land rights into a few hands, as at Salem where, by 1840, two-thirds of the land rights were held by eight persons. In other cases the party leader remained as the sole occupier.

The impact of the 1820 settlers was far-reaching. The eastern districts received an additional European population equivalent to a tenth of the total of the Colony as a whole. The resultant development transformed the eastern province, and helped to shift the centre of economic activity eastwards, although in 1825 there were still fewer than two Europeans per square mile in the Albany district. The infusion of capital had a marked effect upon the economy, once the community had established itself. Less than half the settlers were agriculturalists, and the remainder, when the settlements were badly affected by crop failure, were able to migrate to the towns and resume their trades as artisans and mechanics. This infusion into the urban life of the Colony was of the utmost importance in the following decades.[14] The advent of a solid body of British settlers was highly significant, doubling the numbers of British in the Colony, and leading to the essential British-Dutch dualism which has pervaded southern African life ever since.

The Great Trek

The actions of the British administration in Cape Town resulted in dissatisfaction amongst a section of the Dutch-speaking inhabitants. Problems such as those associated with the aboliton of slavery, African frontier policy, and the speed of issuing land titles assumed increasing importance. Government control, which had been slight before 1806, became ever more pervasive, and, as government institutions caught up with it, the free expansion of the frontier appeared to be coming to an end. In the 1830s a group of farmers decided to leave the Colony and establish their own government further afield. After careful exploration of the lands beyond the Orange River, some 15,000 *(trekkers)* emigrated from the Colony, and in the period 1836–40 several groups moved to the areas of the present Natal, Orange Free State and the Transvaal.[15]

European settlement had already taken place north of the Orange River (Trans-Orangia), as the more adventurous graziers searched for improved lands. Indeed, seasonal movement across the Orange River was widely accepted, and continued after the Great Trek. Thus it was noted in 1840 that the substantial increase in stock in the frontier districts of the Colony over that of 1838 was due to the return of animals from beyond the colonial boundary after drought.[16] This movement had been taking place since the late-eighteenth century, and in 1834 there were estimated to be approximately 1,500 European farmers north of the Orange River, many on a virtually permanent basis. The earlier occupants, the Griquas, welcomed the Europeans, and made land available to them on a loan basis, such as had been general in the Colony before

1813. Such a form of land tenure continued until the 1850s.[17]

Initially, however, it was not the Trans-Orangia lands which attracted the *trekkers*, but the more fertile land of Natal. Indeed, it was there that the *trekker* republic was established in 1838, and where the fundamentals of administration were worked out. Most significantly, the land question was solved, with considerable portent for the rest of southern Africa beyond the Orange River. In 1841 the republican parliament agreed that the fixed-area farms should be continued, with 6,000 acres as the standard size.[18] All citizens were entitled to a farm by right. Until the 1860s two farms each were allowed to pioneers, while later arrivals received only one farm. Officially the farms were registered and inspected, but the government lacked surveyors, and individual claims exceeding the prescribed 6,000 acres could not be detected.

The Republican government was inundated with claims for farms. By 1843 some 1,780 of these had been registered in Natal, but 1,000 of them could be regarded as purely paper claims. Claims extended beyond the Republic's boundaries, and some descriptions were so vague as to make location on the ground impossible. Often description referred to a locality, or to the place where some event had taken place.[19] Despite the attempt to create a democratic society on the basis of equality for all citizens in land matters, speculation appeared at an early stage. The Commandant, the chief republican official, had acquired forty farms by 1844, and other persons acquired large tracts of land at minimal prices of as little as ¼d (1/10p) per acre. An investigation made by a British official in 1843, in an attempt to disentangle the claims, revealed that only 198 farms had been permanently occupied and used for pasturage or cultivation.[20] The land question in Natal was finally settled by the Land Commission of 1848, which recognized all reasonable claims to land based on Republican legislation. Thereafter, no further 6,000-acre grants were permitted by the British government, which considered the land to be capable of subdivision into smaller farms.

In Trans-Orangia, farms were also laid out over much of the area between the Orange and Vaal Rivers in the period 1836–46. The British administration of the Orange River Sovereignty (1848–54) attempted to disentangle the conflicting claims by issuing Land Commission certificates, and where possible, by surveying the farms. The British government adopted a generous approach by allowing full farms, together with any discrepancies (Fig 20a), but comparatively little progress had been made with the survey by 1854, when British administration was ended, and the Orange Free

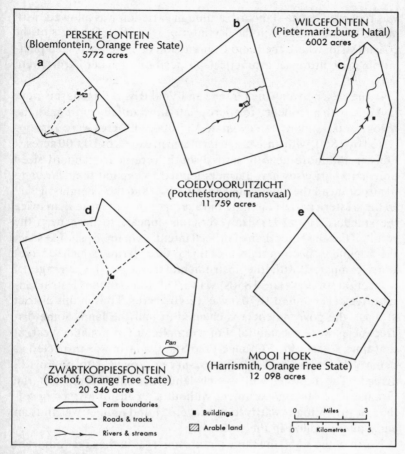

Fig 20   Republican farm plans, 1840–1850

State was established. North of the Vaal, the same pattern of standard 6,000-acre farms was perpetuated, with two farms for each of the pioneers (Fig 20b). No direct British control was exercised, but outside the early settled portion around Potchefstroom a reasonably efficient system of inspection was evolved.

The Great Trek thus resulted in a massive extension of European settlement. Although all areas were laid out in accordance with the regulations of the Pietermaritzburg parliament of 1841, the resulting farm sizes varied substantially, according to the degree of control exercised by the local administration. In Natal the British administration finally granted some 585 farms covering 3.3 million acres, an average of 5,674 acres per farm.[21] In general 6,000 acres was regarded as the standard, although variation was allowed, with an 8,000-acre standard in the dry interior (Fig 20c). On parts of the coastal strip, where the Land Commission of 1848 envisaged plantation agriculture as a practical proposition, smaller farms were surveyed.

In the area between the Orange and Vaal Rivers large farms were laid out, with a tendency to appropriate substantially more than the recognized standard. An estimated 25,000,000 acres were appropriated by 1860, with an average farm size in excess of 10,000 acres.[22] Only in the more densely settled south were near-standard-sized units laid out; elsewhere farmers tended to expand their farms to incorporate all the lands between their own and their neighbours'.[23] In the western part of the state the average size was more than twice the standard (Fig 20d). However, this appears to have been the result of deceit rather than of official intent, as in the Boshof District the original inspection reports of thirty-three farms (which survive) were compared with the instrumental surveys: the average of inspection surveys (late 1850s) was 6,311 acres, that of instrumental survey (1860s and 1870s) was 12,403 acres. Thus in this district at least, the government was cheated of half the land. Some discrepancies were substantial. For example, in Griqualand West, at that time a part of the Orange Free State, a farm was inspected as being 9,101 acres in 1860. Later survey proved it to be 26,122 acres.[24] The rapidity with which land was squandered left the Orange Free State government without a means of attracting settlers or providing rewards to its citizens. Land hunger was thus an early phenomenon in the state.

North of the Vaal, the same picture emerges in the areas adjacent to the Orange Free State or Natal. In the Potchefstroom district, the average size of a sample of farms approached double standard size, as a result of the promise of two farms to each of the early *trekkers.* The Transvaal was able to attract later settlers from both the Orange River Sovereignty and Natal after they came under British control, but in general the outer zones of the Transvaal, settled by the early 1850s, were under single-farm units. In both Utrecht and Lydenburg average sizes were approximately standard. Farm claims were pressed to the north far beyond the region of actual settlement, as the individual's right to two farms proved to be highly demanding upon the land resources of the state. The inspection system evolved in the Transvaal appeared to be effective in controlling excessive size, and therefore in conserving the land resources — in marked contrast to the situation south of the Vaal River.

The layout of the land by the European settlers, during and immediately following the Great Trek, resulted in greater isolation on the part of the pioneers. The large farms supported only a low density of population, with individual homesteads separated from one another by several miles of open waste land, and the position was aggravated in some cases by the presence of intervening abandoned farms (Fig 20e). Although the *trekkers* broke the power of both the Zulu and Matabele military monarchies, south of the Limpopo, the threat of African attack clearly made isolation a danger. The political control established by Europeans over this vast tract of land was to prove permanent, and infilling was to strengthen it. Thus by the mid-1850s, some 25,000 Europeans north of the Orange River had acquired 150,000 square miles — one European for every 6 square miles.

The Colonial Reformers
and Systematic Colonization

The movement for the reform of Crown Land disposal within the British Empire profoundly affected southern Africa.[25] Those colonial reformers who viewed the overseas Empire as a field for emigration and development considered the basic problems of settlement to be related to an imbalance of the three elements of land, labour and capital. They envisaged the regulation of settlement so that by control of land prices through the alienation of Crown Land, any imbalance could be corrected, and settlement would be made more profitable and socially beneficial. Land was therefore regarded as the key to colonial development, and its disposal needed to be carefully regulated. Colonial land regulations were mainly formulated with regard to Australia, but were applied generally, whether conditions warranted them or not.

The situation in southern Africa was such that land was plentiful and available at low cost, while European labour and capital were scarce and expensive. In the market conditions of the 1830s and 1840s almost any price set on Crown Lands available for disposal would have been excessive. Rentals on farms could be as low as £1 per 10,000 acres, and land could be purchased for as little as ¼d per acre. Thus the introduction of a minimum upset price for the disposal of Crown Land would effectively stop virtually all extension of the settlement. This was recognized when the Imperial regulations were issued, and they were in effect ignored. It was not until 1844 that the ideas officially adopted in 1831 were enforced at the Cape

of Good Hope.[26] Systematic colonization proved to be impossible,
and land sales were limited. The Imperial authorities ruled that 2s
(10p) per acre should be the minimum upset price, and that sales by
valuation and quit-rent grants should cease. Land alienation in the
Cape Colony, therefore, was virtually at an end until the abandonment of the Imperial code soon after self-government in 1853.

Natal presented a different picture. After the disentanglement of
the *trekkers'* land titles, there remained a substantial area of land
suitable for systematic close settlement. The Imperial government,
encouraged by the supposedly better conditions in Natal, raised the
price in that colony to 4s (20p) per acre in 1848. Substantial tracts of
the coastal belt remained in government hands, and were deemed
capable of supporting a close population by means of crop farming.
Several crops had been tried and cotton appeared to provide the best
results. Thus in the late 1840s, a sustained propaganda campaign
was launched in England to show the attractions of the new colony.
A series of promotional schemes was put into operation in the
period 1848–51.[27] Typical of the optimism and aspirations was a
passage appearing in the *Emigrants' Journal and Natal News* in
1850:[28]

> In Natal would be found a new country, with a virgin soil of unsurpassed
> fertility, well watered and endowed with a magnificent climate; and
> there the inhabitants do not labour under a large weight of debt con-
> tracted by their ancestors, as we did here.

The result of a combination of such factors was that approximately
5,000 emigrants came from the United Kingdom to Natal.[29] Settlements were planned and schemes laid to profit the promoters. The
government was content to deal with promoters who organized the
schemes and recieved blocks of land in return.[30] Land was provided
by the government on the basis of the number of emigrants sent out,
and settlements were devised in which each immigrant received a
town plot, a rural holding, and the use of a commonage, on the
model of the English village (Fig 21a). Although plots were to be
small, no attempt was made to institute regular rectangular survey
on the American model, as had been done in parts of Australia. On
the major scheme organized by Joseph Byrne, the plots were generally rectangular, although occasionally long, narrow lots were surveyed (Fig 21b and c); they were 20 acres in extent for a single
man, 40 acres for a married couple, with 5 extra per child. Additional land could be purchased from the promoters if desired, and
the government was later forced to grant a bonus. Other schemes
were more generous, with 45 acres as the basic size, while occasion-

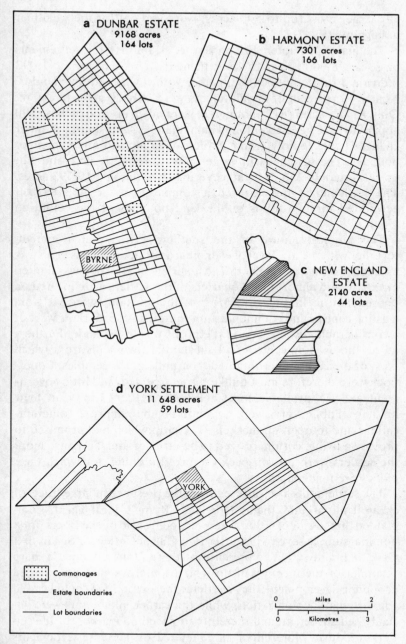

a DUNBAR ESTATE
9168 acres
164 lots

BYRNE

b HARMONY ESTATE
7301 acres
166 lots

c NEW ENGLAND ESTATE
2140 acres
44 lots

d YORK SETTLEMENT
11 648 acres
59 lots

YORK

Commonages

Estate boundaries

Lot boundaries

0   Miles   2

0   Kilometres   3

Fig 21   Plans of Natal settlement schemes, 1850

ally larger plots (up to 500 acres) were laid out for the wealthier immigrants (Fig 21d).

The major promoter, Joseph Byrne, established ten settlements on some 78,000 acres. These settlements were divided into 1,093 individual rural allotments, together with towns and townlands.[31] Nearly 40 per cent of all allotments were only 20 acres in extent. Only 45,475 acres (812 allotments) were taken up, and of these 190 appear to have been abandoned immediately. A substantial number changed hands rapidly, leading to consolidation and enlargement of holdings. The schemes with larger plots were more successful, but there were only 256 of them, covering an additional 19,593 acres. The settlements thus covered a comparatively small area, yet accounted for two-thirds of the land holdings of the colony in 1850–1.

The physical nature of the southern African environment, together with the low level of economic development, was in no way analogous to that of England. The luxuriant coastal belt was limited in extent, and almost three-quarters of the settlers were located on poorer land in the interior. Most of the locations were far from existing centres and communication routes, and so markets were at a considerable distance, and little profit was to be made. Furthermore, the existing centres had substantial townlands from which most of the inhabitants obtained their milk and vegetables. Conditions were therefore most unlike those expected, and little government aid was available to establish the settlers firmly on their holdings. Public works were not undertaken to improve communications and to open up markets. The crop which had promised to provide a living, cotton, proved to be unsuccessful, and once more the settlers were thrown back on mixed farming, for which their plots were inadequate.

The settlements also suffered from the presence of large tracts of cheap land around them; Moreland, Byrne's local agent, complained that 'farms of 6,000 acres were being sold by the Boers, for a nominal sum; in several instances for a Bag of Coffee, or Sugar, or a Cask of Brandy.'[32] The presence of these farms provided a sharp reminder of the inequity of the land disposal system, and retarded economic development; they restricted the areas which could be used for systematic colonization, while the earlier inhabitants were virtually self-sufficient, and therefore provided no market for the settlers' produce. More important, they led to the close settlements being located some distance from markets. All these problems resulted in Byrne becoming insolvent, and the scheme collapsed, with considerable financial loss to all.

The failure of systematic colonization in Natal effectively brought the expansion of the Colony to a halt. The low level of development deterred many from staying on their plots, so that when gold was discovered in Australia, substantial numbers emigrated. In 1852 some 3.4 million acres had been granted, yet only 22,000 acres were cultivated and, despite major attempts at agricultural development, only 71,000 acres were cultivated in 1860 as against the 5.1 million acres granted.

Two further attempts were made in Natal to bring in settlers to fill the empty expanses. The first (1856) was the introduction of military grants for persons willing to act in defence of the Colony, but the terms of the grants were considered too onerous and only twenty-three farms were granted. The second (1857) was a reversion to the practice of granting land on quit-rent tenure, but on stricter terms and with more limited sizes, from 300 acres on the coastal lands to 4,000 acres in the far interior. Quit rents also varied from 2½d (1p) per acre per annum on the coast, to ¼d (1/10p) per acre per annum in the interior. Such terms proved to be popular and a total of 657 grants were issued, covering 1.5 million acres. The resulting surveys produced a range of patterns, from rectangular blocks on the coastal belt to irregular-shaped areas in the interior. The regulations were, however, repealed by the Imperial Government, as they were not in the spirit of the Imperial land and emigration policies, and the resulting return to land sales at a minimum upset price of 4s (20p) per acre effectively stopped all expansion. It was not until 1893 that the Natal government received self-government and complete control over land policy.

The settlement of British Kaffraria provided the only other example of systematic colonization. The area was annexed in 1847 and settlement began soon afterwards in order to provide a dense European population capable of defending the frontier. Discharged Imperial troops (1854), German troops (1857), and German civilians (1858) were settled on plots of approximately 20 acres, with associated town lots. Extensive commonages, with regulated grazing practices, allowed for mixed farming. A distinctive landscape of close settlement emerged; it was probably the most successful in southern Africa, but it was exceptional, as the Germans were willing to accept a lower standard of living than the British in Natal.

The attempt at systematic colonization was largely unsuccessful in southern Africa, and there were few rural areas with close European settlement, although a significant number of settlers arrived. Finding conditions on their allotments impossible, they moved to the towns, so that surprisingly, it was the towns rather than the countryside which witnessed the impact of the movement. Nevertheless, certain rural areas, such as the Natal coastlands and British Kaffraria were successfully transformed, and new elements in the southern African landscape were firmly established.

The Rural Landscapes of the Cape Colony

The period from 1806 to 1860 witnessed a major transformation of the Cape rural landscape. European settlement spread over a larger area, and was intensified, as the filling-in of vacant areas began. But the pastoral frontier had still not penetrated deeply into the dry Karroo or Namaqualand, and only 40 per cent of the Colony had been appropriated by Europeans on some form of tenure. The number of livestock increased rapidly throughout the period, particularly the number of woolled sheep, but in 1855 there were only 9.3 livestock units per square mile, and only 0.1 per cent of the area of the Colony was under crops. Owing to problems of transportation, specialized farming districts had not emerged and, in general, districts still attempted to produce most of their agricultural needs themselves.

In 1855 some 47.8 million acres had passed into European hands, out of a total of 117.3 million acres. The distribution of the alienated area was not in one contiguous belt, but consisted of blocks of land with considerable acreages of Crown Land interdigitated Undoubtedly far more land was alienated than was occupied and used. Thus in 1855 only 20.5 million acres (17.5 per cent of the total area) were enumerated as lying in functioning farms. The highest proportions (over 60 per cent) were in the eastern part of the Colony in the Cradock and Somerset East districts, and in the west in the Malmesbury district. By contrast, only 0.5 per cent of the area of the Clanwilliam district was enumerated.

The establishment of divisional councils in 1855 involved the valuation of all property in the Colony, in order to levy rates, and the assessments thereafter give some indication of the level of rural land values and improvements. Land and improvements were valued at some £15.9 million in the period 1858–63.[33] Cape Town and Port Elizabeth accounted for £3.5 million of this sum, while little of the Colony outside the south-western Cape exceeded a valuation of £200 per square mile.

In terms of other rural assets, livestock may be valued at a further £8.7 million, but commerical livestock production was valued at only £0.4 million, compared with £1.5 million for crop production. But in the export trade, it was wool which predominated by the late 1850s. Most crop production was used locally either as fodder or for human consumption, and so its value needs to be regarded as an adjunct to livestock production, except in the south-western part of the Colony.

In 1855 a mere 198,000 acres were under cultivation. Their distribution was uneven, with a marked concentration in the south-western Cape, where 41.6 per cent of the cultivated land was found on 4.1 per cent of the land area of the Colony. Crop farming had increased slowly in the previous quarter of a century, with only an extra 47.0 per cent under cultivation between 1830 and 1855. In terms of land use, wheat remained the major crop, covering 37.3 per cent of the cultivated area, followed by oats (27.4 per cent), barley and rye (9.7 per cent), and maize (8.1 per cent). Vines, despite their economic significance, covered only 6 per cent of the cultivated area. The crop-combination regions thus show the dominance of wheat, with maize of importance only in the eastern districts of the Colony.

The viticulture districts of the Cape exhibited comparatively little change between 1806 and 1855, with approximately 11,000 acres under vines. In 1855 the Stellenbosch-Paarl Districts accounted for 59.1 per cent of the total vineyard acreages. The value of vineyard production in 1855 amounted to some £408,000 — more than that from wool. It provided the only major crop export, in the form of wine and brandy. The access which the Cape Colony gained to British markets after 1806 led to a major expansion of production, but the protection it received waned after 1820. In the period 1822—7 wine exports amounted to 53.5 per cent of the Cape total; by 1841—5 it had declined to only 17.5 per cent of exports by value, and in monetary terms to two-fifths of that of twenty years before. The wine economy remained dominant in the Stellenbosch-Paarl districts, where 81.5 per cent of the value of agricultural and pastoral production came from the vineyards.

Two changes were noticeable between 1806 and 1855. The first was the emancipation of the slaves in 1832. Thus instead of slave lodges attached to the farms, separate villages for the Coloured population grew up. After initial labour problems, the economy continued with comparatively little change, except in settlement patterns. The second change was a major wave of rebuilding and

improvement, occasioned by the high prices ruling early in the
century. Many of the major Cape-Dutch houses with their elaborate façades date from this period of prosperity, giving the landscape its present characteristics.

North and south-east of Cape Town, the Malmesbury and Caledon districts were similarly dominated by arable farming, in this
case wheat and oats. Crop farming was the major source of income
of all the coastal districts, largely as a result of the high grain prices
ruling at the time. In the Malmesbury District wheat amounted to
60.9 per cent by value of all agricultural and pastoral productions;
in the eastern part of the coastal belt, maize assumed greater importance, reaching 37.7 per cent of production value in Victoria East;
throughout the coastal belt cattle and woolled sheep were present in
the pastoral economy, resulting in variations of mixed farming.
However, in terms of cultivated area only, approximately 1 per cent
of the coastal districts was under crops.

The progress in land alienation and communications was such
that substantial transformation had occurred in the period between
1806 and 1860. New houses, often mixtures of Cape-Dutch and
British (mainly Regency) styles, had been erected on many farms,
and the emergence of the Albany district as a distinct entity was one
of the major features of the period. By 1823 a return showed that
after three years the settlers had built 107 houses (65 Devonshire
cobb, 32 stone or brick) and 267 wattle and daub huts. Frontier
wars introduced another architectural feature into the Eastern
Cape: the fortified farmhouse. These massive towered structures
were meant to protect the families of the farmers in case of attack.
Some 1,381 acres had been cultivated — half of it down to wheat.[34]
The closely knit communities envisaged had largely disintegrated
by the late 1850s, but at the same time the German military settlement of British Kaffraria was attempting to establish a similar kind
of village society.

The interior districts presented a different appearance. The pastoral element was dominant and there was little cultivation — a
mere acre per 4 square miles. In the eastern interior, over half the
area had been occupied, if not improved, but in the western interior
as little as a fifth had been occupied, and only a fraction of this had
been improved. The pastoral frontier was highly irregular, with
large holdings extending down the main rivers towards the Orange
River, and much of the backlands still unoccupied. Isolated farms
existed far in advance of the pastoral frontier, although the central
Karroo and Namaqualand had been largely avoided. The pioneer

Fig 22 Stuurmansfontein farm (Carnavon District), Karroo. The treeless Karroo environment presented many problems for the pioneer, not least that of house construction. Initial stone corbelled structures were later superceded by more conventional stone houses with corrugated-iron roofs.

thrust into Namaqualand late in the eighteenth century was not maintained, owing to the unsuitability of the area for woolled sheep; instead it formed part of an indeterminate area of nomadic pastoral activity, as much of the northern and central Cape Colony had done at the beginning of the nineteenth century.

The interior districts had begun to achieve some prosperity as a result of the development of the wool industry, but the major period of transformation had not yet occurred. The initial pioneers had found the lack of timber a severe disadvantage in building, while the more modest means of the graziers had led to their abandonment of many of the more elaborate building designs of the south-western Cape.[35] Construction with limited timber resources resulted in the emergence of distinctive styles, such as the corbelled houses of the central Karroo, which were built almost entirely of stone (Fig 22). In some cases more substantial rectangular thatched houses were constructed, but during the 1850s the rural pioneer's home was still a modest one.

The basis of much of the interior economy was the woolled sheep, which had been slowly adopted in the southern and eastern parts of the Colony, where they largely replaced the indigenous fat-tailed Cape sheep. The graziers of the interior thus began to produce for the export market. Wool exports increased markedly after 1830, exceeding 100,000 lbs in 1834 and 1 million lbs in 1841. Between 1846 and 1855 a spectacular transformation occurred as merino flocks spread across the Colony (Fig 23). In 1855 the Cape Colony produced 8.2 million lbs of wool and exported 12 million lbs, including production from areas outside the Colony and amounts unaccounted for in the official returns. However, in terms of numbers, the density of livestock was still low. No interior district

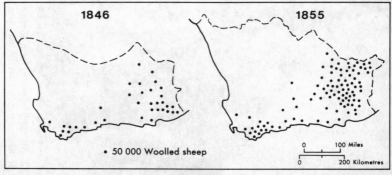

Fig 23   Distribution of woolled sheep in the Cape Colony, 1846 and 1855

exceeded 35 livestock units per square mile, and the farm value of pastoral production was equally low — approximately £240,000 from the interior districts.

Owing to problems of communications and the comparative poverty of many interior holdings, areas were cultivated for the local needs of both men and livestock, and not for the export market. The importance of crop farming, even on so limited a scale, may be gauged from the farm value of crop production in the interior districts at approximately £165,000 in 1855. It is possibly worth recalling that the vineyards of Paarl and Stellenbosch produced £205,000 worth of products in the same period. Thus the landscape of farmsteads, each with small fields, a small reservoir, and enclosed walled paddocks surrounded by several thousand acres of open land, remained predominant in the interior throughout the period: the main variation lay in the increased areal extent of the holdings towards the drier part of the interior.

The Rural Landscapes of the
Orange Free State and Transvaal

The interior republics, owing to their unsettled state and comparative isolation, showed little active sign of improvement as late as 1860. The European populations were small, as indeed were the African and Coloured populations, within the zones of actual European occupation: in 1856 the Orange Free State recorded 12,859 Europeans, of whom approximately 500 lived in the towns.[36] The European population of the Transvaal was probably smaller. Broadly, the republics could be divided into three zones, based on degree of occupation: none could be described as settled, in the North American or Australian sense of the word. First was the zone actually occupied and settled; second was the area subdivided into farms, but housing only a scattered European population, often of a semi-nomadic nature; and third was the area occupied exclusively by Africans.

Nowhere in the Republics did the European density of population exceed 1 per square mile, and only in the Caledon Valley on the Orange River did a density of more than 1 European per 2 square miles occur. This compares with 1 European per 10 square miles in the Harrismith District. Densities in the Transvaal were probably generally lower.

In terms of landscape transformation, often the only change was the beaconing of farms, and this continued apace. At first rough houses, similar to those in the frontier districts of the Cape Colony, were built (Fig 24). [37] Simple shelters based on 'A-frame' principles or with barrel-vaulted roofs were common, and such houses survived until the 1880s. However, permanent buildings of stone and sun-dried bricks were soon constructed, as in the Cape Colony, to provide houses of modest proportions. The roofs were generally thatched, and not made of stone or slate, and outbuildings were generally few, although a wagon shed was essential, in view of the importance of this form of transport, when farmers might be over 100 miles from their nearest town. Housing for servants and labourers varied. House servants generally lived in the house, while field labourers would be lodged in buildings of the local African style — a group of round thatched huts, organized by the farmer, or, more generally, a pre-existing African village which had been allowed to remain after the land had been appropriated.

Cultivation tended to be of a very limited nature. Evidence suggests that arable patches were small, and maintained only for on-farm consumption. In general only a few acres per farm would be cultivated. Thus in an area of 370,000 acres south-east of Bloemfontein, surveyed in the years 1851–2, there were only 540 acres (0.15 per cent) of cultivated land.[38] Dry-land farming for maize and wheat was supplemented by farm gardens for vegetables, but diets tended to consist almost exclusively of meat, so that the demand for vegetables was small.

Grazing was the main farming activity. In the Orange Free State there were by 1856 already over 1 million woolled sheep, concentrated in the main in the south of the state, but their importance decreased northwards as that of cattle increased. Densities of livestock also decreased northwards. Even in the Caledon valley there were only thirteen livestock units per square mile, while in the Harrismith District there was fewer than one. No figures are available for the Transvaal, but it would appear that densities were low and cattle dominated: the area was remote from the wool markets and except in the south, the land was not suitable for the animals, so that wool played a minimal part in its economy

Throughout the republics, in the absence of fences, large herds of wild animals roamed at will, the game providing both a means of livelihood and sport. Trade in ivory, skins and hides was one of the major sources of income to the farmers on the frontier, bringing sufficient income to allow the purchase of necessities such as guns and ammunition, together with such luxuries as coffee and sugar. Game resources were integral to the frontier economy, as the

Fig 24 Early Transvaal farmhouse. Pioneer houses in the interior of southern Africa were simple stone structures, with few of the elaborations found in contemporary houses in the more prosperous parts of the subcontinent.

animals provided food for the farmer and his servants, so that few inroads were made into the pioneers' cattle, which were required for transport and a means of reinsurance — much the same parts as they played in the traditional African economic system.

Thus the rural landscapes of the republics had changed to some extent since the *trekkers* found them in their unoccupied state. Farmsteads appeared, if at considerable distances from one another: even if all the claims-farms were occupied, farmsteads would be spaced at four- to five-mile intervals. (As late as 1880 only half the farms in the Transvaal were thought to be occupied.) [39] Generally settlement was patchy and distances were greater than this, and indeed it commonly happened that in a day's ride there would not be any sign of habitation.[40] Even in the occupied areas no systematic bush-felling or cultivation was undertaken. Physical changes were thus few.

The Rural Landscapes of Natal

Natal had been partially devastated during the wars of Shaka Zulu in the early years of the century. The initial impression gained by the *Voortrekkers* was of an open country, with few inhabitants or signs of habitation. But under the stable conditions after 1845 many Zulus reappeared and once more settled permanently in Natal. Their numbers were such that special areas had to be set aside for them and, within these, distinctive African landscapes either continued or were created. Outside these areas, large numbers of Africans were settled on the European farms, and exerted a powerful influence upon the evolution of the landscape.

It is difficult to re-establish the intial *voortrekker* landscape, as few records or descriptions survive. Even the survey plans give little indication as to topographical detail. The extant inspection reports for the period 1846–8 covered 67 farms, 346,000 acres in extent, [41] and of these some 23,000 acres (6.7 per cent) were assessed as being capable of arable farming. However, these were assessments only. Only 5 farms had cultivation areas measured. Some 26 acres (0.1 per cent) were actually cultivated, against 5,200 acres (21.9 per cent) deemed capable of cultivation. The assessments were gauged from the point of view of the southern African grazier, not that of the tropical planter. It would appear therefore, that *voortrekker* settlement made only a slight imprint upon the landscape, which was not unlike those of the interior states. Some farmers built temporary houses, while others erected permanent structures of stone and occasionally brick, with thatched roofs similar to those in the Cape Colony. A few even boasted gables.

The distinctive appearance of the Natalian landscape was imported by the British settlers, who looked to Britain and to the tropical colonies, particularly Mauritius, for their models. Their impact was largely restricted to the coastal counties and a few selected areas of the interior. However, development was slight, and owing to the substantial tracts of land assigned to African occupation, only 10 per cent of the coastal counties were in private European hands in 1860. Furthermore, nearly half this area was in the hands of speculators, and such land played an important role in the slow progress of development in the colony for, inevitably, such areas were largely occupied by African squatters, who paid rent to the owners.

The development of the sugar industry had proceeded apace after the first experiments by Edmund Morewood (1850–2). [42] (Other crops such as indigo, cotton and arrowroot had been tried, but they had failed.) By 1860 some 6,341 acres were under sugar cane, but a measure of the low level of development may be gained from the fact that only 1.1 per cent of the area of Victoria County, and 2.0 per cent of Durban County, were under sugar cane. The sugar belt was thus a misnomer, although its influence upon the landscape was considerable, for a large number of small mills was established during the initial formative years. In 1860 some forty-one mills were in operation, twenty-six to the north of Durban. The first mill, at Compensation, had already ceased production, and many others had small capacities and short working lives, particularly the fourteen driven by ox, water or hand power. The general euphoria of the sugar industry may be gauged from an article written by a leading planter in 1856: [43]

> It was . . . by many deemed a matter of speculation: it is now acknowledged by all to be a well ascertained fact. The experiment has been made, the speculation tested, and the result is most satisfactory.

The structures erected by the English settlers were similar at first to those erected elsewhere; they made use of wattle and daub, but other building materials were soon utilized, including corrugated iron. In general most of the houses erected before 1860 were small cottages similar to those built by settlers in many parts of the world, although an attempt was soon made to reproduce contemporary English styles: in particular, the desire to emulate the country seat in neo-Gothic style produced a marked variation from pioneer and Cape-Dutch styles. [44] Natal thus provided an almost complete range of the contemporary rural landscapes of southern Africa, based on English and Cape-Dutch traditions transplanted to a new environment.

4

Urban Expansion 1806–1860

THE PERIOD FROM 1806 to 1860 was one of major development in urban activity, in terms both of numbers of towns and their size. It must be noted, however, that the period prior to 1835 was comparatively stagnant, reflecting the basic problems of the Cape Colony's economy. After that date, as a result of a series of economic booms and the establishment of a commercial agriculture and new colonization movements, progress was rapid. Throughout the period less than half the European population lived in towns, but the proportion increased from a quarter to a third. Town foundation was such that the number of towns increased tenfold (Fig 25), and if 'paper towns' are considered, an even greater gain was registered, although the urban network was far from complete by 1860.

Town foundation formed an essential part of the frontier process. In common with other frontiers, the urban centre appeared early, and provided a living for a substantial proportion of the population. There was a need for new administrative centres, new ports, new markets and church centres, as well as for forts and mission stations. Towns were founded by both the governments and private individuals: often they were over-ambitious and impractical, and more towns were built than were actually needed. Although there were occasional official investigations into the desirability of establishing new centres, no over-all plan was in operation, and towns were established as the need for them became apparent.

In a predominantly pastoral economy, towns were looked upon essentially as administrative and commercial centres. Administrative activity under the British government was distinctly more pervasive than it had been under the Dutch, and the fivefold increase in the size of the civil service between 1815 and 1860 amply illustrates

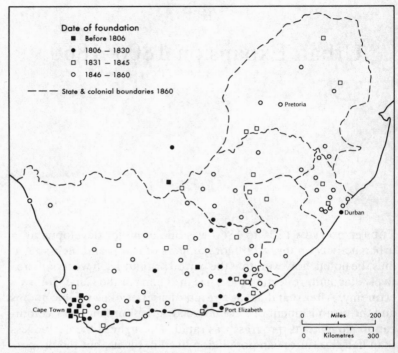

Fig 25   Town foundation prior to 1860

this. Administration involved not only the collection of taxes (far more efficiently than before), but also the establishment of systems of justice, education, and spiritual welfare: effective government was believed to be essential to maintain a civilized society. Thus in the Cape Colony alone the number of administrative units rose from 6 in 1806 to 9 in 1835, but thereafter rapidly to 20 in 1850 and 43 in 1860 (Fig 26). Furthermore the predominance of administrative staff in Cape Town was lost, with a tenfold increase in administrators outside the capital. Elsewhere, as a result of the Great Trek and the settlement of Natal, further administrative centres were established, and by 1860 Natal had nine districts, with a like number in the Republics. Thus in a period of twenty-five years (1835–60) the number of administrative units in the subcontinent increased sevenfold — an unparalleled development.

In the Cape Colony the increase in the number of administrative areas was largely the result of the division of existing units. Although the vast areas of the 1806 Graaff Reinet and Tulbagh districts, with over 50,000 square miles apiece, were reduced, even in 1860 two districts exceeded 20,000 square miles in extent. The

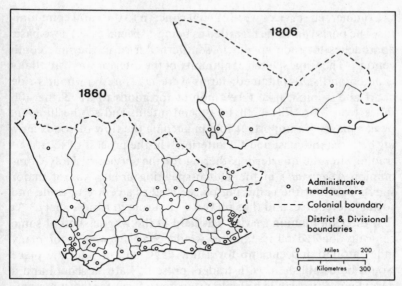

Fig 26   Administrative areas of the Cape Colony, 1806 and 1960

Cape Colony as a whole was regarded as an unwieldy unit, and, following the introduction of representative government in 1853, a movement took place for the separation of the Eastern and Western Provinces. The Eastern Province had continued its rapid rate of European population growth, and by the mid-1850s possessed nearly half the total European population. The separatists gained some government officers, such as a lieutenant-governor and a deputy surveyor-general, but no real separate administration was built up in Grahamstown. The improvement in the administrative services of the Cape Colony was not emulated by the other states until the second half of the century.

In Natal only three towns were given administrative functions by the Republic. The British administration divided the Colony into counties, but later into divisions and districts as in the Cape Colony, and the republics possessed only rudimentary administrative machineries prior to 1860. The experience of the inhabitants was that of the Cape Colony, and the basic framework of that state was applied to the new republics, but as few services were provided, there was little need for the elaborate structure of the Colony. In predominantly rural areas the payment of farm rentals, legal disputes, and marriages, required minimal attention, and it was little wonder that initially, in many areas, all these services could be provided by one man.

Commercial services were of vital concern to the rural community. (The ports can be disregarded as being a special case.) Two basic approaches to trade appear in southern Africa in the nineteenth century. The Cape-Dutch community of the interior was essentially isolated and self-contained: farms were measured an hour's ride apart and it might take three months for goods to travel the 400 miles from Port Elizabeth to Bloemfontein, and so the itinerant pedlar played an important role in keeping the flow of goods moving between the coast and the interior.[1] In the process of locating a trading site, the quarterly gathering for the service of Holy Communion (*Nagmaal*) in the Dutch-speaking areas, was of major significance, for the gathering-place acted as a centre of trade and social intercourse, and thus played a vital role in rural society.[2] At first the Communion service was held in the wagon shed of some centrally located farm; families would come by wagon for many miles around and encamp for a few days, and in time the place would be established, with traders present. Later a school and a permanent store would be built, providing a focus for the community, and then at some stage a church would be constructed. Later a small township would be laid out by the farmer or the church. Once founded, a town acquired a degree of stability, as a trader or two established themselves, or a permanent church minister was inducted. Other functionaries would follow, and finally a magistracy would be established, but as a rule the town remained small in terms of size and population. This progression became increasingly important as the rural areas filled up and European population densities increased, and although few towns had by 1860 passed through all the stages outlined, there was a number of church and store sites which was to grow in the latter forty years of the century.

A second approach to the provision of market, service and ecclesiastical centres was associated with the British settlements in the eastern Cape and Natal. Close rural settlement was complementary to village and urban development. Town and country were planned as a whole, a concept generally at variance with southern African practice. In the Eastern Province in 1820, most of the major parties planned villages on English lines, although few grew to any size. Centres such as Sidbury and Salem provided for the basic facilities needed, with church, school and shops (Fig 27). The resident population was small, for few rural plot-holders chose to live in the village, as in some cases had originally been planned. The same idea was repeated in the settlement of Natal in the period 1849–51. Villages were laid out for all the main settlement schemes,

Fig 27 Sidbury Village, 1849. Sidbury was established as the centre for one of the parties of 1820 settlers. Some thirty years after its foundation it consisted of a dozen houses, a church, a school, and a store.

with a town plot for every rural landholder on which, it was hoped, he would live. In many cases this did not happen, and only the church and school were erected, while the settlers moved to their rural holdings and there built permanent dwellings in the course of the early 1850s.[3] The final stage of the planned rural-urban settlement concept was in British Kaffraria in the 1850s, where town plots and rural holdings were offered, and these settlements proved to be more successful, owing in the main to the perseverance of the German colonists who settled there.

Foundations for specific purposes, other than for port facilities, included the forts of the eastern province and Natal, and the mission stations. Both constituted settlements which had little economic relationship with their surroundings. The forts, with a specific function, occasionally grew into towns, as the squatters and camp followers became organized, but the removal of the military forces usually led to their abandonment. At most a store would survive. In the period before 1860 there was little military withdrawal, and the forts constituted a major source of income for neighbouring farmers and for traders. The missions, designed to protect and civilize the non-European inhabitants, grew rapidly. A number of church societies established chains of missions throughout southern Africa and built up planned and organized towns, often of several thousand inhabitants.

Southern Africa developed no industrial towns in the period before 1860. Mining, quarrying and manufacturing were essentially carried out on a small scale, and were widespread, in most centres providing services to the local inhabitants.

Owing to a lack of information, the urban industrial base in the early nineteenth century is difficult to establish. Towns were centres of agricultural processing industries, but manufacturers were not noted with any degree of accuracy. The number of persons engaged in trade and industry was small: in 1835 only 7,000 persons were so enumerated, half in Cape Town and a fifth in the Albany district.

Through the remainder of the Cape Colony, industry was relatively unimportant. Mills and tanneries were universal as the major industrial enterprises, and undoubtedly the number of such enterprises was substantial (Fig 28). It is probable that some 70 mills and 25 tanneries were operating, and these figures exclude farm-operated enterprises. Other industrial activities associated with hatters, candlestick makers and brewers, appeared in most towns, and so did tile and brick works, owing to the expense of importing these materials.

Fig 28 Milbank Mill, Fort Beaufort, erected 1859. Owing to high transport costs, agricultural processing industries were widespread in the nineteenth century. Mills achieved a certain degree of sophistication as may be witnessed by the 17ft diameter water wheel.

The situation changed as a result of the economic upswing in the second half ot the 1830s.[4] Banks were founded from 1837 onwards. Credit became available, and although much of this was spent on imports, agricultural and industrial development proceeded rapidly. This is not to overemphasize the growth of the towns. In 1855 probably a third (47,000) of the approximately 141,000 Europeans in southern Africa were resident in the fifty towns which housed 100 Europeans or more. Of these, forty-five were in the Cape Colony, two apiece in the Orange Free State and Natal, and one in the Transvaal. The physical size of the towns was small: in the Cape Colony only twenty-six possessed 100 houses or more. However, the degree of urbanization is striking when it is considered that the subcontinent was overwhelmingly agricultural, with no important known mineral deposits or industrial development. It would appear to be following the pattern of other European settlements where the urban frontier was of great importance to agricultural settlement, rather than a later growth.[5]

The Ports

Port development was of major significance during the first fifty years of the British administration, as a result of the subcontinent's increasing reliance upon overseas trade. The port of Cape Town continued to increase its trade, while Simonstown was extensively improved as a base for the Royal Navy — one of the vital links in the chain between England and India. The development of new areas in the interior and along the coast to the east of Cape Town resulted in a quest for new port sites and the foundation of a series of towns as trade centres. The expense and difficulty encountered in land transportation before the construction of the railways resulted in a multiplication of port sites, often with small hinterlands, and increasingly the expansion of the Colony's trade took place, not through Cape Town, but through the new ports situated closer to the areas of production. Thus by 1860 Port Elizabeth, founded in 1815, had overtaken Cape Town in the value of its trade (Fig 29 and Table 4).

Table 4 TRADE THROUGH THE MAIN SOUTH AFRICAN PORTS 1821–1860

Period	Cape Town	Simonstown	Port Beaufort	Mossel Bay	Port Elizabeth	East London	Durban
1821–25	652	24					
1826–30	539	16			141		
1831–35	630	11			113		
1836–40	1,596	28			161		
1841–45	1,017	12			262		23
1846–50	1,192	8			500		75
1851–55	1,520	24	58	5	887	3	144
1856–60	1,910	22	56	24	2,091	86	301

Annual Average £000

Source: Cape and Natal Blue Books, and Government Gazette. Averages are based on 2–5 years totals.

No figures are available for Port Elizabeth prior to 1829, Durban prior to 1843, East London prior to 1848, Port Beaufort and Mossel Bay prior to 1854.

Cape Town remained the largest city throughout the period under consideration, but its growth-rate was less than those of most other centres. The city's share of the European population of the Cape Colony fell from a quarter to a seventh in the period 1806–55, a remarkably low proportion for the established capital of a nineteenth-century colony of settlement. Indeed, in terms of total population, growth was very slow, particularly in the period 1806–35 (Table 5). The causes of this relative decline are to be found in the actual decline of the trade of Cape Town's hinterland, particularly the wine trade, and the rise of new areas. Wine exports, which accounted for half the value of exports in the 1820s, diminished in value in the following decades, as preferential tariffs were withdrawn. Wool, the new staple product, was based in the eastern portion of the Colony, and was exported through Port Elizabeth, although in terms of tonnage of shipping entering harbour, Cape Town remained supreme as the South African port, with three times as many vessels calling in there in 1860, as in Port Elizabeth (Fig 30). It was with the supply trade and government stores that the port remained buoyant, and undertook the construction of new jetties in the 1830s, to supplement the existing antiquated installations. No major works such as breakwaters were undertaken to overcome the exposed position of the Table Bay anchorage, where ships had to wait while being loaded or unloaded by lighter, though on the landward side, access to the interior was greatly aided by the construction of a hard-topped road across the Cape Flats in the years 1844–7.

Table 5 POPULATION GROWTH 1806–1855

Year	European population of Cape Colony	European population of Cape Town	% of European population of Colony in Cape Town	Total population of Cape Town†	% increase between dates
1806	26,568	6,435	24.2	16,428	
1815	37,264	7,715	20.7	15,552	− 5.3
1825	53,040*	8,806	16.6	18.662	+20.0
1835	68,148	10,429	15.3	19,513	+ 4.6
1845	81,600*	12,569*	15.4	22,543	+15.5
1855	109,921*	15,500*	14.1	25,189	+11.7

* Estimates based on available information
† Excluding suburbs (1855-3,683 Europeans; Total 7,550)

The slow growth of Cape Town resulted in comparatively few outward changes in the city between 1806 and 1855. (compare Figs

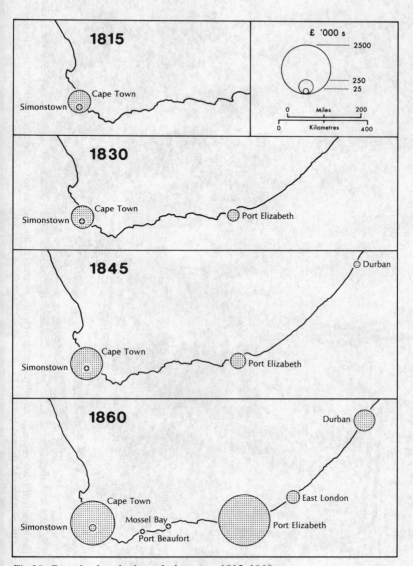

Fig 29 Growth of trade through the ports, 1815–1860

5 and 62; Fig 31). Rebuilding occurred, and suburbs gradually expanded up the valley to Table Mountain, while a few small settlements appeared on the road to Simonstown (22 miles to the south). Internal social and economic zonation, however, began with the emergence of a commercial core and a wealthier European area around the Gardens. Distinct Coloured and Malay quarters were

Fig 30 Cape Town Docks. The growth of trade necessitated substantial port improvements in the second half of the nineteenth century to cope with both the increase in southern African trade and ships in transit.

Fig 31   Adderley Street, Cape Town, c1840. A steady rebuilding of the towns occured in the nineteenth century, substituting an English colonial style for the Cape-Dutch. Regency styles became an important element in the townscape of many South African towns, and persisted for longer than in England.

built on either side of the old core, as slavery slackened and was finally abolished in the 1830s. The town remained less than 2 miles across even in 1860, and still retained much of its eighteenth-century character. Its importance and relative size are well illustrated by the 1855 building statistics. A third (3,891) of the private houses and shops in urban areas in the Cape Colony were situated in the capital, compared with only 938 in the next largest city.

The search for new port sites along the coast east of Cape Town was continuous throughout the period before 1860, and numerous schemes were proposed of which comparatively few were successful. The major port for the eastern Cape was at Port Elizabeth on Algoa Bay. In 1799 a British garrison had erected a fort to protect the landing beach, but it was only in 1815 that a township was laid out, and after 1820 that real sustained growth began. The town was limited by its site at the foot of a bluff, leading to the emergence of a long linear street settlement, with houses and shops lining the road route from the market square, near the landing beach and jetty, to the interior. Growth was rapid, as a result of the rise of the wool industry and the settlement of the eastern frontier districts. Thus by 1855 it was, with 4,793 inhabitants, the fourth largest settlement in the Colony, and its trade, which even in 1850 amounted to little more than half that of Cape Town, had by 1860 exceeded that of the capital.

Port Elizabeth was, however, some eighty miles from Grahamstown, the administrative and commercial centre for the 1820 settlers, and even further from the frontier itself, and so the quest for a more convenient port site continued. The mouth of the Kowie River (later Port Alfred) was developed in 1820, but proved to be incapable of handling the volume of trade. Later still, in 1855, Colchester on the Sundays River was planned as an export point, but failed to live up to expectations in the face of competition from Port Elizabeth. East London in British Kaffraria (1845) was also developed as a port for the frontier districts, leaving the eastern Cape wool trade securely to Port Elizabeth by 1860.

The eastern Cape's prosperity was only part of a general rise in production levels. On the southern Cape coast several ports were developed to facilitate the internal trade of the Colony. Thus Port Beaufort (1816) was developed to serve the Swellendam district, Knysna (1817) the southern forest regions, and later Mossel Bay (1848) the southern coastal districts. In addition, fishing ports such as Saldhana Bay and Lamberts Bay increased in use. In 1855 Port Nolloth was constructed for the export of copper ore from the

Namaqualand mines: this was one of the first mining outlet points on the subcontinent, and necessitated considerable ingenuity in the construction of the wagon way from the mine to the port, through an inhospitable and lightly populated part of the Colony. One of the features of all these ports was the lack of major portworks. Jetties were as much as most of them undertook; breakwaters were too expensive, although plans were numerous.

Durban's position differed from that of the other ports. It was founded in 1824 on the large semi-enclosed Bay of Natal, by a group of traders who wished to gain access to the ivory and skin trade of Zululand and the interior of southern Africa. The port lay outside official jurisdiction until the Republic of Natal was established, although the town possessed a surveyed township and local government before 1838. As a private commercial venture the port grew slowly, and it was only after the British annexation in 1843, and more particularly the start of the British colonization six years later, that trade, and with it the town, expanded. A measure of this may be gauged from the decline in the relative importance of ivory exports from 53.9 per cent in 1850, to 15.1 per cent in 1860. The small scale of the foundation, a mere 195 plots, and townlands of only 7,000 acres, was to prove disadvantageous to orderly growth.[6] The port also suffered from the swamps which separated it from the interior, and the sand dunes which separated it from the mouth of the Bay, for the entrance was originally partially blocked by a bar which at times reduced the depth of water to a few feet.[7] The hazard of crossing the bar was a serious one, causing larger vessels to remain out in the roadstead and to be off-loaded by lighter. Those vessels which did enter landed their goods not at the town, but at the bush free-landing stage some two miles distant. The difficulty of the journey to the town across the sand dunes led to the building of southern Africa's first railway in 1860.

In appearance the town remained a trading post until the influx of 1849–51, after which the wattle-and-daub buildings began to give way to others of brick, stone and corrugated iron.[8] Such materials were luxuries at first, owing to transportation costs, and brickworks were soon established to the north of the town. Particularly important was the appearance in 1850 of corrugated iron, which was found to be highly satisfactory, as it was resistant to white ants and other insects which attacked alternative forms of construction. In terms of population, the town remained small and junior to the capital, Pietermaritzburg. In 1853 there were 1,175 Europeans and probably a smaller number of Africans in Durban.

New Towns in the Cape Colony

The lack of towns was immediately felt by the British officials on
their arrival in 1806. As a result, a series of new government
foundations was established to facilitate trade, commerce, and particularly administration. Unlike the foundations of the Dutch
period, which had tended to be small and which grew by the laying
out of new streets and plots as the need arose, the British established, at least on paper, substantial and complete towns. These
were almost uniformly laid out on a grid pattern, with streets
intersecting at right angles, and each block was divided regularly
into a series of rectangular housing plots (Fig 32), but no model
town layout was ever devised, with the result that each foundation
differed in some manner from its contemporaries.

The standard grid was open to various interpretations. The size of
plots varied substantially, but by modern standards tended to be
large. One acre was a general conformity, but sizes between ¼ and
2 acres were adopted at various stages. This resulted from the
demand by townsmen for not only a house and a garden, but also a
paddock, stables, byre and other outbuildings. Thus most town
plots were organized as small farms supplying the owner with much
of his food. In addition most towns constructed an irrigation system,
allowing each plot to obtain water from a furrow for both domestic
and agricultural use. Apart from residential plots, sites were usually
retained for a church and a substantial market square, which had,
during the period of trading, to accommodate not only the goods
and stalls of the traders, but also the ox-wagons of all who came to
market (Fig 33). Thus from five to twenty acres might be set aside
in the centre of the town for this purpose. Surprisingly, after 1825,
land was rarely reserved for administrative purposes: government
buildings were usually restricted to a couple of town plots, and
commercial sites were unknown. A business was conducted from a
house and its outbuildings and even in the larger centres, residential
and business premises remained inseparable until the late
nineteenth century.

The form of the town was approximately rectangular, with the
plots ending along demarcated lines. Beyond lay the townlands or
commonage. The sizes of commonages varied as much as the towns
themselves, depending on the amount of Crown Land available
between existing farms, or the extent of the farms appropriated for
the purpose. Several thousand acres were deemed necessary to
support the town. The townlands provided grazing for the community's livestock, a source of firewood, clay for brick kilns, thatching

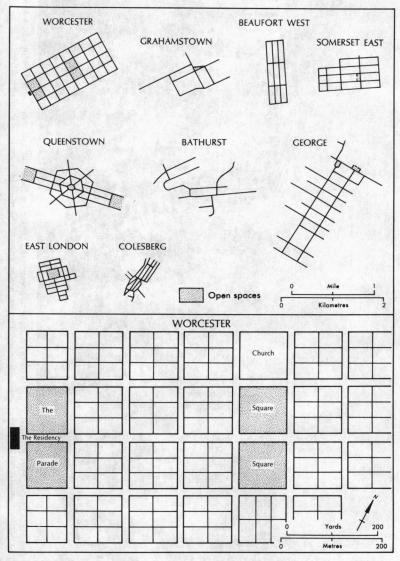

Fig 32 British town plans in the Cape Colony, 1806–1860

reeds, and sometimes stone. Thus to a high degree the town could become self-supporting, and needed to import only more specialized goods and services.

Town planning within this rigid framework achieved some degree of distinction in the period 1815–25, when the ideas of visible

Fig 33 Market Square and Main Street, Port Elizabeth, c.1860. Port Elizabeth became the centre for the export of wool, and developed on the proceeds of the trade. The market, illustrated with its characteristic wool bales, became one of the most important in southern Africa.

authority and order were imprinted upon the new urban landscapes. Lord Somerset, the governor of the Colony, placed significant emphasis on the vista as an element in town design: avenues closed on churches, *drostdys* (residencies), magistrates' offices, and even gaols. In this manner an enclosed urban landscape akin to those of contemporary England was achieved. The lack of terrace façades was compensated for by avenues of trees with lines of houses fronting on to the road. Little could emphasize the importance of the government more clearly than the plan of Worcester, where the main street vista closed on the *drostdy* with the parade ground in front of it (Fig 32). Other towns such as George, Somerset East and Beaufort West were laid out with similar plans in mind: even their names recalled the King and his governor.[9]

On some sites the search for regularity proved unsuccessful. Thus Bathurst was laid out on a more informal basis, with streets following contours (Fig 32). Colesberg, despite the survey of a central axis aligned to provide a vista, was situated in too rugged an area to allow a grid to be set out (Fig 34). Even Grahamstown, the main centre of the eastern districts, assumed an irregular plan as a result of building speculation and irregular topography. The vista of the Grahamstown *drostdy*, however, was complemented by the cathedral at the opposite end of the High Street, producing one of the most English of urban landscapes in South Africa.[10]

The eastern frontier of the Cape Colony and, later, of British Kaffraria experienced a series of wars and unsettled times throughout the period under discussion. As a result a substantial Imperial garrison was stationed in the area, and forts and roads were constructed to protect the farming community. In several cases the establishment of a fort was followed by the layout of a township. Thus Fort Beaufort, established in 1822, became the centre of a township fifteen years later. Centres such as King William's Town, Alice (Fort Hare) and (Fort) Peddie were established as forts, and later became towns with administrative functions, although by no means all the military posts which were established developed into townships (even if they were in apparently suitable positions), owing to their proximity to neighbouring centres. Thus Fort Brown on the Fish River, at the crossing of the main military road from Grahamstown to the north, received no attention.

In British Kaffraria many Imperial and German Legion soldiers received their discharge, and were settled near the forts and in new fortified villages, established for the purpose. Throughout the eastern frontier districts after 1825, town plans were more rigidly

Fig 34 Colesberg, 1844. The small country towns of the Cape Colony, Orange Free State, and Transvaal were influenced largely by Cape-Dutch architectural styles, particularly the large gabled house (left) and the smaller ubiquitous flat-roofed version (right).

regular, and generally they lacked the grand features of earlier foundations. Strict adherance to grid patterns was almost universal. Although many of the towns of the eastern frontier owed their origins to military planning, few layouts were conceived in military terms: Queenstown, with its six roads radiating from the centre, fulfilled the ideas of a defensive centre, but it appears to have been a unique experiment (Fig 32).

Republican Town Planning 1836–1855

The *Voortrekkers* were faced with the problem of selecting town sites and laying out towns in the areas they occupied after 1836. Owing to the small number of Europeans involved in the Great Trek and the consequent low densities of population, town foundations were few, and small in terms of population. If Natal is excluded, it is doubtful if any of the *voortrekker* foundations possessed a thousand inhabitants by 1856. Bloemfontein, the largest settlement in the Orange Free State, could number only 660 souls, including 229 Europeans, in that year. No figures exist for the Transvaal.

Most town sites were carefully selected, with a view to ensuring adequate water supplies. Strong-flowing rivers and springs were considered essential for a town of any size. Offical inspection was a feature of the first towns, although increasingly ecclesiastical authorities and private individuals became influential in town-site selection, once the initial administrative framework had been established.

In the first phase of development (1836–49) the plans varied substantially, but the cadastral plans reveal considerable generosity with regard to size of plot and provision of townlands. The basic grid of streets, with blocks divided into rectangular housing plots, was adopted throughout the lands north and east of the Orange River (Fig 35). Nevertheless, the impréssive vistas of Cape town planning in the first decades of the century were ignored, until Pretoria was established in 1855. To a large extent towns were envisaged as semi-self-contained units in terms of food supply, and so plot sizes were in general over 1 acre, and townlands averaged over 20,000 acres (Table 6).[11]

Table 6 TOWN FOUNDATIONS BY THE VOORTREKKERS 1836–1849

Town	Date of foundation	Number of plots	Size of plots (acres)	Width of road (ft)	Area of Squares (acres)	Area of Townlands (acres)
Pietermaritzburg	1838	485	1¾	100	14	26,000
Weenen	1838	132	1¾	100	—	19,000
Winburg	1836	85	¼–2	60	8	18,000
Bloemfontein	1848	156	¼–1	50	2	20,000
Potchefstroom	1838	408	½–2	50	17	23,000
Ohrigstad	1844	500	2/3	100	30	22,000
Lydenburg	1849	184	1¾	70–75	10	19,000

Town development in the Orange Free State

In the area between the Orange and Vaal Rivers the European immigrant farmers established the town of Winburg (1836) to act as the administrative centre. The plan was modest, with a considerable range of plot sizes; this was at variance with the general practice of providing plots capable of supporting a family with garden produce. The plan of 1848 showed only eighty-five plots including sixty-two at ¼ acre, the remainder being larger (up to 2 acres), mostly with river frontages. The most noticeable feature of the plan was the presence of a large square containing the church and the public offices, bordered by four terraces of small plots, evidently intended as shop sites.

Major Henry Warden, British Resident in the Orange River Sovreignty, considered Winburg too inaccessible, and in 1846 he chose the site of Bloemfontein for a new administrative centre. This was nearer the Cape Colonial boundary and closer to the Orange River, where many of the more settled inhabitants, who had entered the territory before the Great Trek, resided. Bloemfontein town was laid out in 1848 and consisted of only 156 plots covering some 89 acres. The general size of the plots was again only ¼ acre, although some riverside plots reached 1 acre in extent, and the pattern was a modified grid, interrupted by the river, and with a focus on the church site.

A number of other towns was planned and laid out in the 1850s, all with grid patterns and larger plots of ½ to 1 acre. In most cases the town was established in an area already settled, with the result that the government had to acquire the land. Towns were established on the Natal border at Harrismith (1849), also at Fauresmith (1850), and Smithfield (1848) to provide a basic network of centres to administer the territory. The towns of Jacobsdal (1858), Boshof

(1856) and Kroonstad (1859) were established by the republican government to cater for the northern and western districts, while Reddersburg (1857) was a church foundation. In all cases modified grid patterns were adopted, and substantial townlands of one or two standard farms were set aside.

In the south of the territory a number of mission stations, founded before the Great Trek, continued to act as places of refuge for the small indigenous population. Towns such as Bethulie (1838), Philippolis (1821) and Bethany (1834) owed their origin to the mission stations, although the laying out of a township was often not undertaken till later in the century.

Town foundation in the Transvaal

In the Transvaal the *Voortrekkers* laid out three major towns soon after their occupation of the area in the period 1838–45. The most important was at Potchefstroom (1838), which was established as the capital of one of the republics. It was laid out on the usual grid, but the plots were not all of the same size, varying from ½ acre to over 2 acres: of the 408 plots, 326 were of the largest size. Church and market squares, each of 8.5 acres, were included in the plan, and the site selected was amply provided with water, and allowed for future expansion. More important, it was centrally placed in one of the major areas selected for settlement in the Transvaal.

The two other early towns did not fare so well. Ohrigstad (1844) was established in the Eastern Transvaal on the edge of the Great Escarpment, where it was hoped to establish contact with Lourenco Marques as an independent way to the sea. The town was laid out on a restricted site, and consisted of 500 plots of two-thirds of an acre apiece, with three large squares. However, it was later abandoned owing to the prevalence of malaria and tsetse fly, which afflicted men and livestock, and a new settlement was established on higher ground at Lydenburg (1849). Lydenburg was laid out on the lines of Pietermaritzburg, although it was smaller. It consisted of 184 plots of 1¾ acres apiece, together with two squares of 5 acres each. Again, occupation appears to have been limited, as the survey of 1874 records buildings on only twenty-eight plots.[12] In the northern Transvaal, Schoemansdal (1848) was established by a *trekker* group in the Zoutpansberg Mountains. The agricultural prospects for the area were poor and the death-rate extremely high. The inhabitants made their living from hunting and the ivory trade, and the town was destroyed in 1867 by African tribesmen and never re-established.

In 1855 Pretoria was established by the authorities of the South African Republic, on a site which was thought to be capable of uniting the various disparate elements in the Transvaal. It became the capital in 1860 and was planned as such, with a church square at the intersection of the two main streets, a noticeable departure from standard practice. Unlike those in Lydenburg and much of Potchefstroom, the plots did not stretch from street to street (Fig 35), and as a result they were smaller — 1 acre apiece, but the number surveyed (861) made it the largest town planned outside the Cape Colony. A whole block of twelve plots was for a long time used as the market square. In common with other early republican towns, Pretoria owed much in architectural style to the Cape Colony, and whitewashed, thatched, stone, single-storeyed buildings, without pretensions, remained the general norm until the 1870s.

Other towns were established in the 1850s, as in the Orange Free State, in order to cater more closely for the now settled population of the territory. Towns such as Utrecht (1853), Potgietersrus (1858) and Wakkerstroom (1859) followed the patterns established by the earlier towns, except that plots in excess of 2 acres were not favoured — the general size being 1 to 1½ acres. As in all the other towns, extensive townlands were provided, the average size of those in the seven towns mentioned (excluding Schoemansdal) being 19,000 acres — the equivalent of three standard-sized farms.

The Voortrekkers in Natal

The *voortrekker* imprint upon the urban development of Natal, although restricted, was highly significant. Durban was replanned and two new towns, Pietermaritzburg and Weenen, were laid out, and the village of Congella was established. Although the European community of Natal in the republican period was at most 5,000, the urban network was adequate, particularly when it is remembered that most citizens possessed a plot in town as well as a farm. The two interior towns were situated in the prospective main grazing areas.

Pietermaritzburg was designed to be the capital of the *voortrekker* republics, and as such set a high standard of town planning in its spaciousness. The site was carefully selected on a fairly level portion of land in the Umsindusi River valley; the river bordered three sides of the town, providing a steady supply of water and, if necessary, a defensive position. The town was laid out on a grid, with 485 plots of approximately 1¾ acres apiece, together with a market square of 14 acres (Fig 35). Surrounding the town, townlands of 26,000 acres

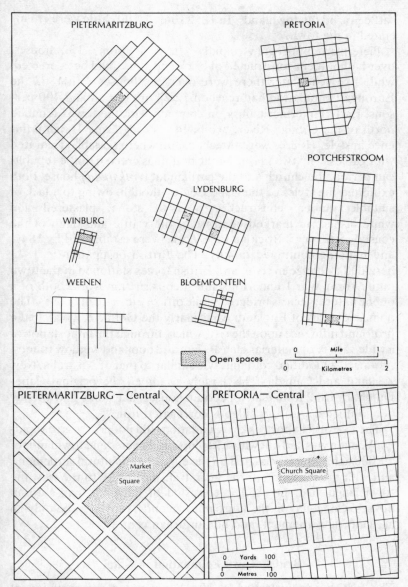

Fig 35   Republican town plans, 1836–1855

were demarcated. The settlement was designed to be as self-sufficient, agriculturally, as possible — a distinct disadvantage for the future British settlement schemes. The plots were large enough to grow all the town's requirements of vegetables and fruit, while cattle grazed the townlands. In 1852 some 1,700 cattle were enumerated in the town.

Pietermaritzburg grew rapidly. In 1844 some 132 houses, over half of them constructed of brick and stone, had been erected, while five years later there were over 200 houses.[13] In 1852 the European population had reached 1,524 out of a total 2,400 persons. Early Pietermaritzburg, in common with the towns founded north of the Orange River, exhibited a strong Cape-Dutch influence in style. Houses were thatched, and where possible decorated with gables. The two major public buildings erected in the republican period, the church and the parliament (*volksraad*) house, both exhibited the styles of the Cape Colony though, owing to a lack of suitable timber, construction was of stone, plastered and whitewashed, in marked contrast to the wattle and daub of the coastal settlement. Brick and tile works were established by 1840, and building continued rapidly. The British occupation in 1843 heralded a change in style, and British forces stationed in the town until World War I undertook much construction work, both of a public nature, such as bridges, public offices etc., and of houses. The domestic styles of England, particularly the Gothic Revival, had a profound influence upon the city, which, through the importation of a wide variety of material such as slate and door and window frames, produced a modified colonial style similar to that of Australia, New Zealand and Canada. This largely swamped the original Cape-Dutch. In 1852 it was said of certain houses that 'some had already been inflicted with the hideous corrugated iron.'[14]

The two other voortrekker foundations did not progress so rapidly. Weenen was laid out with 132 plots of 1¾ acres and townlands of 19,000 acres, but it was sited on the edge of agricultural settlement, and with the diversion of the main transport route to the west the town languished. In 1853 it consisted of no more than a dozen houses. Congella, on the Durban townlands, proved to be only an agricultural settlement, and not an urban centre.

British Town Foundation in Natal

The British administration of Natal considered the provision of towns to be inadequate, and appointed a commission to investigate the matter. In 1848 this commission suggested that the Colony be divided into six divisions (later counties), each with a town, and that several villages be established.[15] The sites selected were generally at river-fording points on the main routes to the interior, or along the coast. The commissioners suggested that the towns and villages should possess a cattle enclosure, market place, church, school and magistrate's office, arranged within palisades for defence. The need for townlands was also stressed, in view of Durban's cramped conditions. The suggested sites were mostly adopted, but the proposed pattern was much modified by the large-scale immigration of 1849–51, which led to the establishment of a number of other towns.

In the period 1848–50, the government foundations attempted to maintain the broad principles of town planning adopted by the *Voortrekkers* and the Cape Colony — large plots, generally 1 acre in extent, with some form of grid pattern for the streets. Market squares were provided, usually of one complete town block of 10 to 15 acres. Townlands were also generous with two of them — Ladysmith and Newcastle — receiving over 15,000 acres apiece.

Towns attached to the immigration schemes were to serve a different purpose from those established by the government. It was intended that the rural land-holders should live in the schemes' towns and villages, with the result that the number of urban plots was high compared with those in earlier towns. In order to save land, the plots were smaller, generally ½ acre, and townlands were in most cases restricted or non-existent. These towns ranged in size from Richmond (731 plots) to York (58 plots). The plans of the settlement-scheme towns were mostly grid patterns, with a market place provided in some cases, although in others an unused block was taken as a temporary site (Richmond) (Fig 36). Otherwise provision was more limited than in government foundations, for example, York (2 acres). However, two interesting variations were planned. Thornville provided for a market street closed at one end by a church, and Mount Moreland was planned with a crescent and terraces in view of its expected importance.

The towns were generally unsuccessful, and the plots were abandoned as the settlers relocated themselves on their holdings, or left Natal altogether. Towns like New Glasgow and Mount Moreland disappeared completely; others such as Byrne and York survived with one or two buildings, such as churches and schools, while those on main routeways, such as Richmond and Verulam, prospered and grew. The settlers who moved to the towns, whether the capital, the port or one of the more prosperous small centres, were more likely to succeed.[16] The result was the emergence of a high urban proportion to the European population, in common with most frontier societies. In 1855 over 40 per cent of the European population of

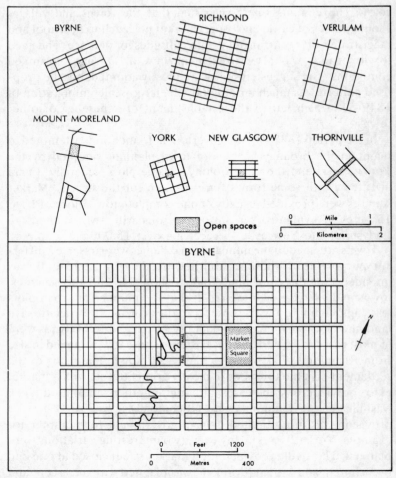

Fig 36   Natal town plans associated with the 1850 settlement schemes

Natal lived in the two main centres of Durban and Pietermaritz-burg.

The Mission Stations

The establishment of the missionary societies in southern Africa in the course of the nineteenth century introduced a new element into the urban pattern: that of mission stations. In the first half of the century these were of considerable importance and size, both within the Cape Colony and far beyond its borders, and in their endeavour to convert the heathen, the missionaries were often only a short distance behind the hunters and explorers.

The first mission station was established by the Moravians in 1737 at Genadendal near Swellendam.[17] Although it soon closed, its acitivities were resumed in 1792, and in the following two decades the Moravians established a series of stations across the entire length of the Colony. In 1799 the London Missionary Society began its work, and it was followed by the Wesleyans, American Methodists, Lutherans and others.[18] In the main the Government provided generously for these societies, despite colonial opposition. At first the stations were for the protection and enlightenment of the Coloured and Hottentot populations, but in 1820 missionary work began amongst the African tribes of the eastern frontier region.

The stations were designed to achieve a high degree of self-sufficiency, through improved cultivation and animal husbandry, and the promotion of local crafts and industry: thus outside influences could be kept at bay. A considerable degree of control was exercised, both in the layout of the settlements and the regulation of their activities. Generally a grid of streets was laid out, but plots were small (10 to 20 per acre). Houses were designed to a standard plan, built of stone, and thatched. In addition each station possessed a church, parsonage, workshops, and usually a mill. The result was a distinctly Cape-Dutch village in terms of architectural style. The growth of a station beyond its capacity to support the population usually led to division and the establishment of a further settlement. Those stations serving the African population tended to be African in appearance, with little control, and no attempt at laying out a settlement with streets and uniform housing. Usually the only recognizable features were the church and the parsonage. Significantly, the mission station usually survived the colonization of neighbouring lands by Europeans, and this resulted in the maintenance of islands of high density settlement, surrounded by European farms.

The population of the stations was substantial. As early as 1799 Genadendal possessed 1,234 people in 228 dwellings, making it the second largest centre in the Colony. In 1855, with a population of 3,540, it was comparable in size with Graaff Reinet (3,662) and Paarl (3,800). In 1855 the four listed mission stations contained almost 6,000 inhabitants. It is probable that there were at that time, as many as 20,000 living on the more than thirty stations, or nearly one sixth of the non-European population.[19]

5
Closing the Agricultural and Pastoral Frontier 1860–1914

THE MAIN OUTLINES of European rural development had been drawn by 1860, but the processes of filling in and closing the farming frontier took place in the half century before World War 1. The spread of settlement to Rhodesia and the Kalahari Desert margins constituted the final phase of colonization from the Cape of Good Hope hearth of European endeavour. The movement north of the Zambezi was slight, and regulated more stringently than further south. The latter half of the nineteenth century also witnessed the breakdown of the semi-self-sufficiency of the rural areas, first in the coastal colonies and later in the interior states. Production for export, which had become increasingly important in the first half of the century, became dominant by 1914, and specialized farming for wool, feathers and sugar played its role in linking southern Africa more securely to the world economy.

The period was one of substantial advance as the area of European farms doubled between 1860 and 1911 (Table 7, Fig 37). By 1911, approximately 227 million acres out of a total of 586 million had passed into European hands, supporting a substantially increased European population, but although the total European population increased from approximately 150,000 in 1855 to 1,300,000 in 1911, the rural component fell from 60 per cent to 47 per cent in the same period. Although much of the new land was relatively poor, and hence sparsely settled, the intensification of settlement in the areas occupied prior to 1855 was such that the number of Europeans per farm square mile increased markedly _ver that of the first half of the century (Fig 38).

Table 7 AREA IN EUROPEAN FARMS 1860–1911

Province or Colony	Area 1911 (million acres)	1860		1911	
		Area of European Farms (million acres)	Percentage in European Farms	Area of European Farms (million acres)	Percentage in European Farms
Cape of Good Hope	178.2	51	27.6	125.7	70.5
Natal	21.5	5	23.7	10.3	47.9
Orange Free State	31.9	25*	78.4	30.4	95.3
Transvaal	70.2	20*	28.5	32.8	46.7
Bechuanaland	176.0	—	—	3.8	2.2
Rhodesia	96.2	—	—	21.9	22.8
Swaziland	4.3	—	—	2.0	46.5
Basutoland	7.5	—	—	—	0.0
TOTAL	585.8	101	17.2	226.9	38.7

* Areas approximate

Allied with the growth in rural European population and farm area was the expansion of livestock numbers, the cultivated area, and the export trade. Wool exports rose from 23.2 million lbs in 1860 to 177.0 million lbs in 1913, although by value the increase was only from £1.5 million to £5.7 million. Apart from ostrich feathers, no agricultural export commodity sold more than £1.0 million worth in any year between 1860 and 1913. In terms of livestock, the number of woolled sheep increased approximately fourfold between 1855 and 1911, while the cultivated area increased more than twentyfold in the same period, to reach almost seven million acres in 1911 (Tables 8 & 9, Figs 39 & 40).

Table 8 WOOLLED SHEEP IN SOUTHERN AFRICA 1855–1911

	Cape Colony	Natal	Orange Free State	Transvaal	Southern Rhodesia
			(000)		
1855	4,828	38	1,012		
1865	8,370	198			
1875	9,986				
1880		373	5,056		
1890/1	13,631	799	5,917		
1904	8,465	505	2,437	413	16
1911	11,052	1,105	7,355	2,330	58

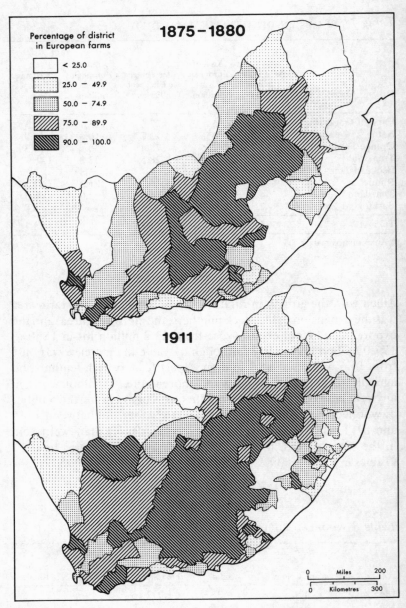

Fig 37   Progress of land alienation in South Africa, 1875–1911

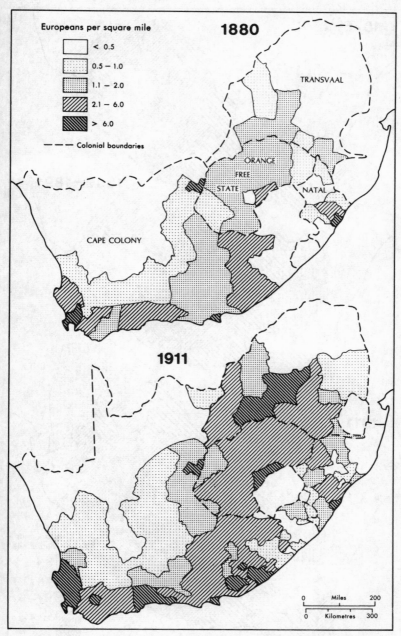

Fig 38   Distribution of European population in South Africa 1880 and 1911

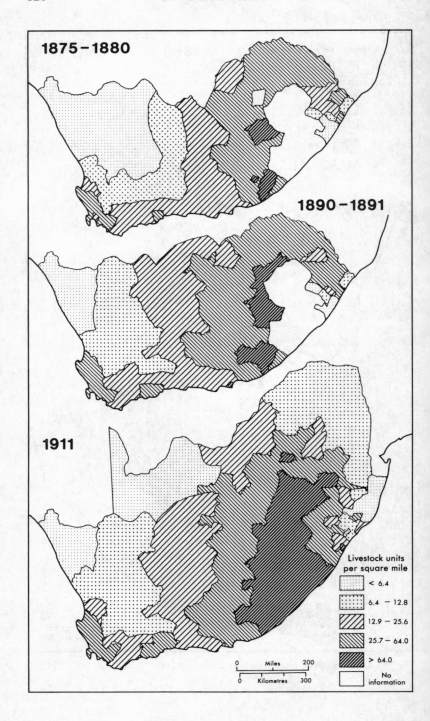

1875-1880

1890-1891

1911

Livestock units
per square mile

< 6.4

6.4 — 12.8

12.9 — 25.6

25.7 — 64.0

> 64.0

No
information

Miles   200
0
0
Kilometres 300

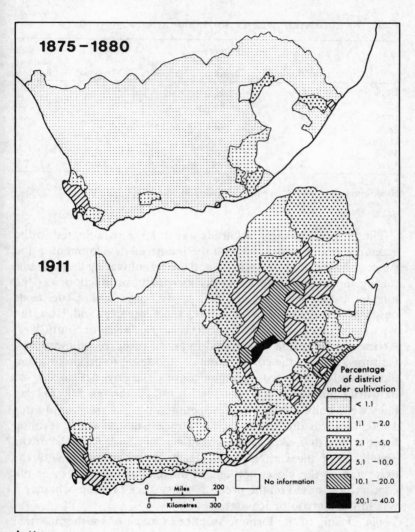

▲ Above

Fig 40   Cultivated areas in South Africa, 1875–1911

◀ Opposite page

Fig 39   Distribution of livestock in South Africa, 1875–1911

Table 9 CULTIVATED AREA IN SOUTHERN AFRICA 1855–1911

	Cape Colony	Natal	Orange Free State	Transvaal	Southern Rhodesia
	(000 acres)				
1855	198	11			
1865	461	44			
1875	580				
1880		63	122		
1890/1		85	252		
1904	410	538	563	952	
1911	2,062	1,020	1,846	2,021	183*

* 1914 figure
Natal figures prior to 1904 are open to considerable doubt.

The progress in the rural areas was in large part related to the economic boom associated with the industrial development of the subcontinent. Intensification of land use by cultivating larger areas, raising more stock and generally increasing production was the long-term response. In addition, a well-organized cattle trade developed by the mid-1870s, linking the Kimberley and, later, the Witwatersrand markets to the cattle surplus areas of South West Africa and Rhodesia.[1] Increased financial resources allowed new ventures, notably the colonization of Rhodesia, to be undertaken. Significantly improved communications, largely developed for industrial purposes, benefited agriculture, although few railway lines were built specifically for opening up rural areas until after 1900. This was due to the lack of any substantial arable farming frontier like that, akin to the wheatlands of South Australia or the grainlands of the United States. Each of the advances, with the exception of the closer settlement movement of the turn of the century, was based on the premise of livestock farming, whether it was in the Karroo or Rhodesia.

The closing of the farming frontier in much of southern Africa before World War I resulted in a number of major problems, including a growing land hunger associated with rural overpopulation, both European and African. Although this was serious in parts of the subcontinent by 1911, renewed economic prosperity was capable of postponing until later the realization of the extent of the problem.

The Settlement of the Karroo

The Cape Colony was granted representative government in 1853, and three years later the unpopular imperial land regulations were abolished.[2] In 1860 the Crown Lands Act provided for a new land disposal system which retained auction, but not the high minimum price. Land was sold in variable sized blocks of up to 50,000 acres, with assessed rentals.[3] The object of the Act was to allow legal occupation of the semi-arid lands of the interior, and the new flexibility enabled the Cape Colonial Government to dispose of neglected areas. A rapid alienation of land began, with the result that by 1911 little Crown Land, outside Namaqualand, remained south of the Orange River, and even in that district over 40 per cent had been appropriated, although 6.8 million acres remained unclaimed — largely in areas with rainfalls of less than an average of 5 inches per annum.

The 1860 legislation recognized that vast areas were necessary for sheep-farming in a semi-arid environment, and the making of large grants was in marked contrast to the general approach to land legislation elsewhere in southern Africa, where few farms in excess of 10,000 acres were granted after 1860. Even greater flexibility was provided with the introduction of the Agricultural Lands Act of 1870, which made provision for the disposal, on freehold tenure, of such lands as were deemed suitable for arable farming. These lands were restricted to a maximum size of 500 acres per applicant.

The rapid alienation of land resulted in the introduction of large numbers of colonists, and the interior districts between the southern coastal belt and the Orange River, which in 1855 had only one European per 5 square miles, had by 1904 achieved one European per square mile. The rate of increase was slightly greater than that of the Colony as a whole. The census of 1904, however, marked the maximum rural European population in many parts of the eastern Cape, where colonization had first taken place, and where intensification was impracticable.

The increase was associated with the rise of the wool industry. The number of woolled sheep rose rapidly from 4.8 million in 1855 to 8.4 million ten years later. A peak number was reached in 1891, with 13.6 million, but thereafter numbers fell to 11.1 million in 1911 as a result of drought, grazing deterioration and falling world wool prices. The concentration of sheep was most marked in the eastern half of the Colony where densities in excess of one sheep per 2 acres were reached. Production of wool increased from approximately 12.0 million lbs in 1855 to 55.8 million lbs in 1911, when the Cape Province accounted for under half of South Africa's wool production. Wool occupied the most important place in the Cape

Colony's export trade, reaching 85.5 per cent of exports by value in 1869, when £1.9 million of the £2.2 million export trade consisted of wool. Indeed, most of the rise in the Cape Colony's export trade between 1830 and 1869 may be accounted for by the wool trade. After 1869 minerals assumed the major role, but the value of wool exports hovered at £2–3 million until 1909, although it was affected by the disaster of war in 1899–1902.

Settlement, even south of the Orange River, was not continuous. Areas such as Namaqualand received few settlers as, owing to drought and remoteness, conditions were unfavourable for farming. In order to further settlement, the government issued temporary grazing licences after 1870, enabling stock to be grazed on the land in good seasons, but not committing the licencee to permanence. Thus migratory farmers (the *trekboers*) were free to move as they wished, until permanent alienation took place later in the century, and fencing began.[4] Settlement did not occur in the form of the classic continuous wave frontier thesis, but rather through the picking out of the most desirable lands — those possessing surface water — and then a more gradual filling in of the interfluves. Government surveyors attempted to overcome the worst features of peacocking, by surveying large blocks of land (10,000 acres or more), and by attempting to prevent a small number of farmers monopolizing the water supplies.

The spread and intensification of settlement was assisted by a number of important technical inventions. The windmill pump was probably the most significant, allowing water to be raised from subterranean sources to the surface in places where, previously, surface storage had had to suffice. Windmills enabled apparently waterless areas to be settled, and stock to be grazed on previously inaccessible interfluves (Fig 41). Nowhere was this more noticeable than in the dry north-west Cape Colony. Unfortunately, however, South Africa lacked the vast artesian basins which had so changed Australian interior farming. The introduction of barbed-wire fencing also had a profound effect upon livestock farming, and livestock improvement became easier, while controlled grazing practices also enabled farming returns to be increased. Although the inventions were made in the 1850s and 1860s, and knowledge thereof was widely disseminated through the press and enterprising traders, the degree of use was limited. By 1911 only 30 per cent of the area of the Cape south of the Orange River was fenced. In addition, only 7,162 boreholes had been sunk in the same area, mostly under 150 feet in depth, and only 2,246 of the boreholes

Fig 41 Windmill and Merino sheep, Karroo. In the nineteenth century, technical innovations, particularly barbed-wire fencing and light-weight windmills for pumping water, enabled large tracts of land to be opened for grazing by woolled sheep.

were for windmills. In Namaqualand only one was recorded. Thus the level of technical advance by the pastoral farmers was still low in the years immediately preceding World War I.

Filling-in the Other States

The period between 1860 and 1880 in Natal and the interior states was largely one of consolidation and filling-in. Areas which had been less attractive to the pioneer settlers were occupied, and the general level of settlement rose. There was little outward expansion, although there were small groups who, like the *trekkers* in the previous hundred years, roamed far and wide. Some entered South West Africa and Angola in this period, while others made unsuccessful penetrations of the Kalahari Desert.[5] In the main the unoccupied lands had been settled, and the three states were faced with large African populations on their borders, presenting considerable problems to small groups of Europeans. In 1855 there were probably no more than 35,000 Europeans in the three states, but by 1880 this had increased to 127,000 and ten years later to 244,000. Inevitably such a rapid increase in population led to pressures to expand, and therefore to conflict with neighbouring African states.

Transvaal

In 1880 it was estimated that 43,260 Europeans and 773,700 Africans were living in the Transvaal.[6] Nevertheless, only part of the territory could be regarded as settled and organized. The two northern districts of Waterberg and Zoutpansberg, covering approximately 40,000 square miles, contained only 3,140 Europeans, or one European per 13 square miles, and even the five southern districts supported just under one European per square mile — a slightly higher figure than that for the Africans. Thus less than a fifth of the Transvaal could be described as 'settled', and grave doubts were expressed by the government over the long-term prospects of the territory as a field for European colonization. The population was almost entirely agricultural, with only 1,200 persons described as non-agricultural in 1878.

The discovery of gold in the Transvaal profoundly affected all aspects of the South African Republic's economy, including its agriculture. Money became available, and profits were to be made in supplying commerce and industry, but, although the country was linked more securely to the world economy, no major agricultural product was developed. The number of woolled sheep only reached

2.3 million by 1911. Maize appeared in the first decade of the twentieth century as a major export crop, but the results were erratic, and the maize industry was still essentially in its experimental stage before 1914.

In the period 1880–1911 the European population of the Transvaal increased almost tenfold. In the 1880s alone it increased by 176 per cent, and although much of this growth was urban, it was rapid also in the rural areas. Thus in 1911 there were 168,015 Europeans described as rural and indeed, if the Witwatersrand is excluded, some 67.1 per cent of the European population was still rural, and in over-all distribution little changed from 1880. Although settlement had spread into the African-dominated margins of the Transvaal, many farms were held only nominally by Europeans, who made their living from rents, leaving an essentially African landscape upon their holdings.

The gold discoveries provided an internal market, which had previously been lacking. In the years 1886–92 the farming community benefited from the increased demand for transport riding, agricultural produce, particularly meat, forage and grain, which the Transvaal could readily produce, and from the high prices paid by speculators for farms and options on farms. The period of prosperity was short-lived, as the arrival of the railways opened the country to competition and removed other sources of income, while in 1896 rinderpest destroyed many of the herds and took away much of the wealth of the rural population. The level of rural development was still low. In the mid-1890s surveys of the western Transvaal, later part of the 'Maize Triangle', showed that the cropped area on few farms exceeded 100 acres, and only 0.5 per cent of the total area was under cultivation after more than fifty years of occupation (Fig 42).[7] Surveys in the northern Transvaal showed an even lower level of improvement.

The build-up of rural population resulted in two processes. The first, involving subdivision of farms and the emergence of a squatter class, will be dealt with later (page 149). The second was an expansion of the settled area. The process of filling-in reached a critical stage in the early 1880s when most of the desirable land had been appropriated, since the initial entitlement of citizens to a farm of 6,000 acres, and, in many cases to two such farms, had led to rapid exhaustion of the land reserves. The Transvaal had also recognized the enlargement of farms to 8,000 acres, which was the area of a square farm of one hour's ride across.[8]

Land could be acquired in neighbouring African areas, and

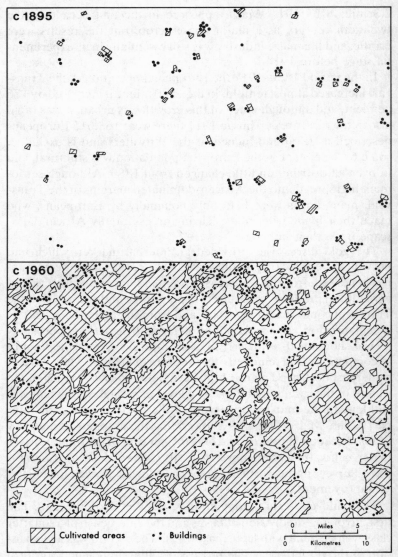

Fig 42 Land use in part of the Potchefstroom District c.1895 and c.1960

indeed many settlers obtained titles to land from African chiefs in the western margins of the Transvaal, but by the 1880s the instability of the African political structure allowed divisions to be exploited by groups of Europeans interested in creating new farms for themselves. Between 1880 and 1890 several small republics in

Bechuanaland, Swaziland and Zululand were established, and the land was apportioned amongst the conquering pioneers. Farms of 6,000 acres apiece were standard, although in Zululand there was insufficient land to satisfy the 800 applicants, so that farms had to be reduced to 3,500 acres apiece.[9] The layout of the new areas differed from that of many previous settlements, in that they were planned as a whole, with farms laid out in parallel strips, producing a modified grid pattern as opposed to the irregular shapes usually found in southern Africa. In addition, farms were selected by lot rather than by actual inspection, and the areas were open to massive speculation.

Each of these republics was later incorporated into the Transvaal, after dispute with Great Britain, although much of the Stellaland and Goshen Republics of Bechuanaland were later annexed by the British to form British Bechuanaland.[10] The New Republic of Zululand was cut down, and part of it was included in British territory, while the Swazi state was able to survive, if only under Transvaal protection.[11] The political difficulties involved in expansion were such that the Transvaal government was forced to consider the settlement of the north of the country.

In 1886 the Occupation Law was passed, allowing citizens to lease farms of 1,000–3,000 acres at a nominal fee. A number of people went north, but they were generally unable to make a living on the land: markets were too far away and mining did not develop as was expected. Malaria took its toll on the energy of the population, as it had done fifty years earlier. As the land was only leased, the occupiers could not mortgage the properties so as to effect improvements, and the result was abandonment, and large-scale purchases by companies and speculators, who in 1904 were able to convert leasehold properties into freehold.

The results of the leasing campaign were highly disappointing. In 1900, in the two northern districts, the government possessed 38.4 per cent of the farms, and companies a further 30.3 per cent.[12] Less than a third of the farms were held by private individuals and many of these were speculators. The movement to the north had failed. Indeed, between 1890 and 1911, the growth-rate of the European population was consistently below that of the Transvaal as a whole, despite a major campaign by the Lands Department to make the area more attractive. Even the borehole programme could not keep up with demand, and only 148 holes had been drilled in the two northern districts by 1911 (one per 278 square miles, compared with one per 66 square miles elsewhere in the Province).

Orange Free State

More successful in filling its territory with settlers was the Orange Free State. In 1856 the first census recorded 12,859 Europeans, while that of 1880 showed 61,022, and that of 1911 some 175,189. The state was largely appropriated by 1856, in terms of the land claimed. The only major territorial expansions were in the 1860s, when the Basuto were defeated and forced to cede land on the eastern boundary of the State, and in 1885, when the last African state (Moroka's Land) was occupied. The western boundary was fixed in 1874, after the establishment of Griqualand West as a British colony, although a proportion of the farms in that colony dated from the period of rule by the Orange Free State.

Standard-sized 6,000 acre farms were granted to settlers until the 1860s, when the areas conquered from the Basuto were settled. 'Half-farms' of 3,000 acres were laid out, as the area was assessed to be of greater value than much of the State.[13] Closer settlement in the conquered districts was noticeable even by 1880, when the density of European population exceeded two per square mile — the only area in the Orange Free State where this was the case. In 1890 densities in excess of four per square mile, and in 1911 in excess of six Europeans per square mile, had been reached on the Basutoland border, though densities decreased westwards and towards the north-east.

The problem of lack of land also affected the Orange Free State by the 1880s. Owing to the more favourable agricultural position of the State compared with that of the Transvaal, there was more possibility of subdivision: thus in 1900 the average size of farms was reduced to 2,600 acres.[14] In 1886 the Government began leasing its remaining lands, together with such lands as reverted to it, in small blocks, to persons who were otherwise landless.[15] In the period 1886–99 over 500,000 acres were leased, but the average size of lease was slightly less than 2,000 acres.

The Orange Free State proved to possess some of the best grazing lands in southern Africa, and numbers of woolled sheep increased rapidly, reaching over 5 million by 1880. Despite war, drought and falling prices, numbers rose to 7.4 million in 1911, when the State possessed 36.8 per cent of the South African total. It is a measure of the resiliance of the industry that numbers which were cut to 2.4 million in 1904 were able to make such a complete recovery. Wool production reached 19.5 million lbs in 1880 and increased slowly thereafter to 34.2 million lbs in 1911. The Orange Free State also possessed some good agricultural soils, which were increasingly exploited. Cultivation received considerable impetus after the mineral discoveries, and the moister eastern districts were extensively ploughed. By 1911 over 20 per cent of the area of the two districts on the Basutoland border was under cultivation, compared with only 2 per cent in 1880, and the 'Maize Triangle' was becoming more obvious.

Natal

Rural development in Natal between 1860 and 1880 was relatively unspectacular. Although the European population of the colony doubled in the period, most of the growth occurred in the towns, where by 1880 half the Europeans were living. This trend was continued between 1880 and 1911, when only one-third of the European population lived in the rural areas, the lowest proportion in southern Africa at that time. Fewer than half a million acres of land were settled between 1860 and 1880. High prices, coupled with the inaccessibility of most of the remaining Crown Lands, made Natal comparatively unattractive for new agricultural settlers. Where alienation did occur, it was usually in the form of peacocking, the selection of waterholes, springs and water-frontages, where considerable tracts of Crown Lands could be controlled with little capital outlay.[16] In 1880 new land policies permitted ten-year credit for purchases of Crown Land. Later, twenty years were allowed. As a result, between 1880 and 1900 some 2.3 million acres were purchased, effectively exhausting the remaining Crown Lands within the original colonial boundaries. In contrast to most earlier land grants, the new ones stipulated beneficial occupation, with the aim of fostering a permanent rural population, rather than allowing massive speculation.

In the interior, the rural economy became increasingly tied to woolled sheep, with sugar cane on the coastal belt; the interior landscape was similar in many respects to that of the interior states, although farm sizes were substantially smaller. Sheep numbers remained comparatively small (under 1 million) and the stocking ratios achieved before the droughts of the 1890s never equalled those of the Orange Free State or the eastern Cape Colony. Wool, however, remained the most important agricultural or pastoral export product throughout the period before 1914.

Sugar-cane production on the coastal lands excited most rural attention between 1860 and 1914. Initial experiments had proved the value of the crop, but the organization of an industry took some time.[17] The shortage of labour for a plantation economy was partially solved in 1860 by the introduction of indentured Indian labourers, a practice continued until 1910. Originally it was intended that such labourers would return to India on completion of their contract, but many chose to remain and work in Natal, where they were joined by free Indians who emigrated at their own expense. Some purchased or were granted land, so that by 1910 some 35,000 acres, mostly on the coastal belt north of Durban, were in Indian hands. The numbers involved were considerable.[18] In 1880 there were 18,877 Indians in the colony, compared with 25,271 Europeans, while in 1911 there were more Indians (133,419) than Europeans (98,115) in Natal. The Indian contribution to the landscape of Natal was profound, both through the provision of labour for the European-owned plantations, and through the intensive cultivation of the Indians' own land.[19]

It would, however, be inaccurate to speak of a 'Sugar Belt' before 1910. Even in the Inanda District, north of Durban, where almost half the area under sugar was found in 1911, only 23.6 per cent of the area was under sugar-cane cultivation, while in the next most intensively cultivated area to the north only 5.8 per cent was under sugar cane. Major reorganizations occurred with the emergence of milling companies which, through land purchases and major expenditure on mills and private railways, were able to control facilities. The number of mills in Natal south of the Tugela fell from a maximum of 74 mills in 1877–78 to 29 mills in 1911.[20] In the period 1865–82 there were over 60 mills in operation, many of a small nature. Production increased as yields were improved through selective breeding. Thus in 1860, with 6,000 acres under cultivation, the yield was only 0.2 tons per acre under sugar cane: by 1880, yields had trebled and by 1911 doubled again, with 72,654 acres under cultivation.

Of considerable significance, from the point of view of the landscape, was the development of the wattle industry.[21] The bark of the wattle tree provided tannin for the leather industry. Commerical plantation began in 1886, and by 1904 some 79,000 acres were planted to wattle trees. In 1911 some 266,000 acres were planted, and a fifth of the central district of New Hanover was under timber plantations. But as in the sugar industry, transport presented problems because of the bulky nature of the product, and railway lines with spurs were therefore constructed in the first decade of the present century, to serve the plantation areas.

The final stage of the colonization of Natal was the opening of Zululand to European settlement in 1904, following the demarcation of reserves for the Zulu population. Some 2.6 million acres became available, and in 1905 active settlement began.[22] Most of the coastal land was considered suitable for sugar-cane cultivation. The results were less encouraging than was expected, as by 1911, of the 315,000 acres surveyed, only 196,000 had been leased, and a mere 11,000 acres were under sugar cane, despite sugar cultivation clauses in the lease agreements. Attempts at establishing rubber plantations in the north, close to the Mocambique border, were unsuccessful.[23] The problems of communications and disease awaited solution.

Settlement of the Desert Margin

The Cape Colony north of the Orange River had been occupied early in the nineteenth century by the Griquas, a group of mixed-race people. [24] Their economy had been similar to that of the European *trekkers*, appropriating large farms of up to 75,000 acres.[25] From the 1820s onwards they had issued grazing permits to European *trekkers*, who selected standard-sized farms in the southern parts of the Orange Free State and Griqualand West. The discovery of diamonds at Kimberley in 1868, however, led to the annexation of Griqualand West by Great Britain in 1871, and its incorporation into the Cape Colony in 1880. Settlement accelerated around the diamond fields, and the unoccupied parts of Griqualand West were thrown open to occupation. Farms were of standard 6,000–8,000 acre size, but no restriction was placed on the accumulation of several farms, providing rents were paid. In the 1860s some 3,000 Griquas moved from Griqualand West, where they had sold much of their land, to Griqualand East around Kokstad.[26] New farms were laid out, but once more they were sold to Europeans, and Griqualand East became a European district.

In the early 1880s major advances towards the desert margins occurred. Within the Transvaal half-farms were offered, with singularly little success (Fig 43a), but, in contrast, the two republics of Stellaland and Goshen (1884) pushed contiguous farms far into Bechuanaland, leaving only small reserves for the Tswana peoples (Fig 43b). [27] In the second half of the decade the farming frontier advanced further into the desert, across what was to become the boundary with South West Africa. The Kalahari Desert Republic provided farms of twice standard size for its citizens in 1887, but two years later recognized that even this was not enough, and allowed farms of substantially greater size (Fig 43d).[28]

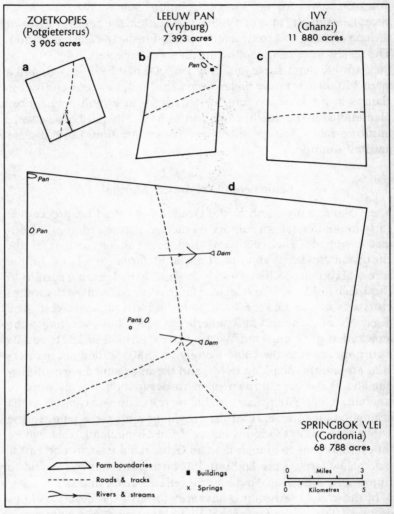

Fig 43   Farm plans on the desert margins, 1880–1900

The final stage of desert penetration was the colonization of parts of the Bechuanaland Protectorate, north of the Molopo River. The area to the south of the river (British Bechuanaland) was annexed to the Cape Colony in 1895. Within the Protectorate, the British South Africa Company acquired a number of blocks of land which were made available for European settlement, but the area was generally poor, with low and variable rainfall, and much of it was inaccessible until the railway from the Cape Colony to Rhodesia was built in 1897.

The inaccessibility of the central areas of Bechuanaland undoubtedly deterred many potential colonists. For example, the original settlers at Ghanzi reached their objective in 1895, after a journey of seventy-nine days (500 miles) from Mafeking, including a stretch of 83 miles without water.[29] Stock had to be driven across country to the railway line at Lobatsi, which became the major cattle depot. Bore-holes proved to be essential, both on the farms and along the cattle routes to the railway. (The farming blocks adjacent to the railway proved to be more fortunate, and they developed economies similar to those of the neighbouring farms of the Transvaal and Rhodesia.)

The farming blocks were more than half alienated by 1910, with some 3.8 million acres set aside for European farms.[30] The idea of the standard farm was now largely abandoned. At Ghanzi, in western Bechuanaland, 10,000-acre farms were offered (Fig 43c). On the Tuli Block, farm sizes ranged from 1,000 acres to 35,000 acres. The low level of the development may be gauged from the fact that only 32 farms had been formally granted in Ghanzi in 1910. In 1904 there were only 1,004 Europeans in the Protectorate; at the time of the 1911 census, there were 1,692 compared with 119,772 and 123,658 Africans in the respective years. The farms were largely taken as out-stations for farms elsewhere in southern Africa, as may be seen by the fact that as late as 1950 only a quarter of the surveyed farms were occupied.[31]

The Settlement of Rhodesia

Rhodesia was the last major area of European settlement which can be regarded as part of Cape Colonial expansion. To a large extent it was the outcome of the vision of one man, Cecil Rhodes, who foresaw a major agricultural and industrial colony north of the Limpopo River, under the British flag. In 1890 the British South Africa Company occupied Mashonaland, and embarked upon its exploitation. The initial pioneers were primarily concerned with the supposed mineral riches of the country, which was rumoured to be a second Witwatersrand, [32] and consequently they were more interested in the mining claims promised by the Company than in the half-farms (3,000 acres) which it also promised.[33] It was soon evident that the gold resources would not materialize in the quantities expected, and in 1893 Matabeleland was occupied. In this territory, in addition to mining claims, full 6,000-acre farms were

granted to pioneers, while agricultural immigrants, who were
attracted to Rhodesia from the southern African states, also
received full 6,000-acre farms, mainly in the better-watered lands
of the Eastern Highlands.[34]

The rate of alienation was high, with the result that 15 million
acres had been disposed of by 1896. In that year a general reorganization took place, and Cape colonial land laws were applied, with
some modifications, in an attempt to reduce speculation and to
introduce permanent settlers.[35] However, the British South Africa
Company continued to provide large tracts of land to major investment companies, in the hope that they would spend substantial
sums on the development of their properties. Thus by 1912 some
21.9 million acres had been alienated, of which seventeen companies held 9.2 million acres.[36] Indeed, one company received a
grant of over 2 million acres.

In an analysis in 1913 it was found that 74.2 per cent of the land
within twenty-five miles of the railway had been alienated, and that
there was comparatively little land available for immediate European settlement (Fig 44).[37] Much of the remaining areas were
below the 3,500-foot contour, which, because of disease, was
regarded as the lower limit of occupation. Nevertheless, an intensive drive for settlers from England and the South African colonies
was initiated in 1907, when the limited mining prospects were
realized.[38] The advantages of Rhodesia were emphasized, particularly for cattle ranching,[39] and all classes of pioneers, even 'gentlemen settlers interested in speculation', were welcome.[40] As a result,
the number of Europeans in Rhodesia increased from 14,007 to
23,606 in the period 1907–11. More important, the number of
Europeans engaged in agriculture increased from 1,174 to 2,140 in
the same period. In this manner approximately 10,000 acres had
been alienated for each member of the farming community.

One of the factors which assisted the colonization of Rhodesia
was the guidance offered by the British South Africa Company to its
settlers. In 1906–7 four central farms were established on the
Company's estates in various parts of the country.[41] On these farms
prospective settlers could be trained and taught about the country,
its crops and livestock, before they purchased their land and established themselves independently.[42] These central farms, together
with the Company estates, played an important role in the experimental work which helped to lay the foundation of the main farming
enterprises in Rhodesia (Fig 45).

The cattle industry was regarded as the backbone of farming.

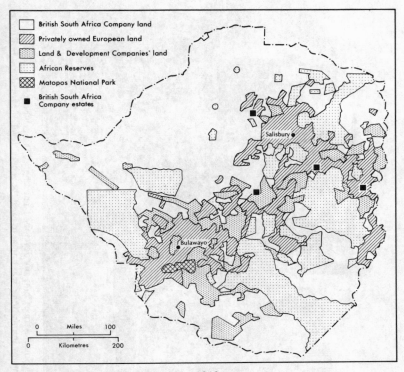

Fig 44   Land ownership in Rhodesia, 1913

After the war and the rinderpest outbreak, cattle numbers increased steadily, to reach 164,000 European-owned, and 300,000 African-owned animals in 1911.[43] The major expansion came with the establishment of a number of significant ranching enterprises (1912), and the commencement of cattle exports (1916). Sheep were regarded as generally unsuitable, and even the ostrich mania of the period 1906–13 made little impact on the country.

African maize production had been general before 1890, and at first the Europeans bought it from the indigenous population and little was grown on European-owned farms, where traditional southern African methods were employed. Thus in 1900 only 4,260 acres were under maize.[44] However, after the large-scale immigration drive, 161,268 acres were planted to maize in 1913–14, and exports ran at an average of 6,000 tons per annum.

Experiments in fruit growing began soon after the occupation, but were only beginning to show marked success by World War I,

Fig 45 Steam ploughing outfit, Premier Estate, 1905. The British South Africa Company developed a number of farms where new crops and machines were tested and adapted to Rhodesian conditions. Through Company innovation it was hoped to raise the general level of agriculture in Rhodesia.

largely as a result of the British South Africa Company's interest at Mazoe. Similarly, tobacco began its boom about 1909–10, with the establishment of the auction system and the Tobacco Planters Association. Other crops, such as rubber and groundnuts, were grown on a small scale, but little was accomplished by 1914.

North of the Zambezi, few farms had been claimed by 1912, when 0.9 million acres were in private hands, and a further 7.1 million acres alienated to companies.[45] Northern Rhodesia, with 40 per cent of the country infested with tsetse fly and 20 per cent set aside for African reserves, appeared to be unattractive to large-scale European settlement, and in 1911 only 1,497 Europeans had settled north of the Zambezi.

The Closing of the
European Settlement Frontier

The effective closing of the European settlement frontier in the first decade of the present century was an occurrence of major significance, as it had been in the United States twenty years before. Increasingly, European settlement had been hemmed in by settled African populations, the desert, international boundaries, and isolation. Each of these factors was responsible for preventing further expansion in the style of the previous two hundred years; major readjustments had to be made to southern African modes of thought.[46]

The dense African population zones had been avoided up to the 1860s. Where colonists had met an entrenched African population, they had moved in another direction. In Natal, the Transvaal and the Orange Free State conflict about land with large bodies of Africans, had been avoided as much as possible, but as expansion occurred on the fringes of the Transvaal and Orange Free State, it increased, and the problems of isolated indefensible settlement were also increased.[47] The sizes of grants were such that grouping was impossible. Continuous settlement broke down in Natal, the Eastern Cape and later in the Transvaal and Bechuanaland, since provision had to be made for the permanent settlement of Africans. In the Transvaal such provision was minimal, whereas comparatively large tracts of Natal and the Eastern Cape remained in African hands. In Rhodesia the problem of the division of land between Europeans and Africans was a source of constant trouble, and undoubtedly hindered settlement on the fringes of the European settled area.

By the 1880s European settlement had reached the desert margins. The paucity of water supplies in Bechuanaland and eastern Rhodesia made the land appear unattractive, even for large-scale ranching. Land grants increased in size as ideas of the standard farm were abandoned, in much the same way as the United States quarter-section had to be modified in the semi-arid West. Some attempt was made to open up the desert lands, but the lack of water proved to be an insuperable barrier, while the attack on the desert margin led to a deterioration of the vegetative cover and to the invasion of farmlands by inferior scrub plants and sand, so that retreat was inevitable.

The political partition of Africa in the 1880s, and particularly the acquisition of South West Africa by the Germans, also halted the traditional movement of the *trekboers*. Although some South Africans went to live under German rule, conditions were so unsettled through most of the German period that South West Africa no longer appeared to be the promised land.[48] It was only after the South African occupation in 1915 that South Africans settled in the territory in any numbers, and by that time the basic pattern had been drawn. Portuguese possession effectively blocked settlement on the coasts, although some *trekkers* moved to Angola in the 1870s, as a result of theological disputes in the Transvaal, and the Portuguese authorities tried unsuccessfully to attract colonists from the Orange Free State to Moçambique in the 1890s.[49] The scramble for Africa, with its attendant drawing of political boundaries, placed an effective limit on the southern African frontier, which could not be transferred to Kenya.[50]

Poor communications similarly placed limits, if not such definite limits, upon the frontier. The extension of settlement led to increased costs of transportation. Long-distance wagon carriage in Rhodesia, as late as 1895, cost approximately 2s 6d (12½p) per ton-mile.[51] Although the railways reduced costs appreciably, they were largely constructed to link the mines and industrial regions with the coast, with little consideration for the agricultural potential of the subcontinent. Thus in general crops could only be grown commercially in limited areas near the industrial centres, or along the line of the railways. Elsewhere livestock raising alone could provide an assured income. The cattle trade supplying the urban areas, together with the demand for wool, supported the southern African frontier, although often at only a little above subsistence level. Although large tracts of Crown Land remained unclaimed in 1914, their economic potential appeared to be severely limited by problems of inaccessibility and the poverty of the environment.

The Closer-Settlement Movement

The exhaustion of the best agricultural land is a constantly recurring theme from the 1870s onwards. Although vast tracts remained open for European settlement, most was clearly only suitable for pastoral occupation, and arable agriculture, if it was to be expanded, would have to be carefully planned on land already alienated from the government. Increasingly it was realized that some land granted for pastoral farming might, with improvements, be converted into crop land capable of supporting dense agricultural populations. The failure of previous attempts was attributed to a lack of planning, and in the 1870s both the coastal colonies launched intensification programmes. However, intensification meant irrigation, and irrigation prospects were decidedly limited, as a number of major investigations had discerned.[52] In addition, irrigation met with deep-seated opposition from a large number of traditionally-minded farmers, many of whom regarded it as sinful: 'We have been told that God made the rivers so that the water should run in them and hence it should not be taken out by artificial means.'[53] Such attitudes, expressed as late as 1909, represented a traditional approach born of a past era of unlimited land.

Natal

Although some 3.6 million acres of Crown Land remained in the colony in 1875, most of it was relatively inaccessible and capable of only extensive use. [54] If increased European settlement was to take place, more attractive lands would have to be found, and in effect this involved the expense of repurchasing land, the price to be recouped later through increased revenues from the immigrants. In 1879 the newly established Land and Immigration Board offered immigrants free passages to Natal, 100 acres for each family, and a commonage of 2,000 acres for every fifty families.[55] The price of land, 7s 6d (37½p) per acre, was hardly competititve with that in the United States, where free grants of 160 acres per person were available under the Homestead Act, but it was still more attractive than that in some of the Australian colonies.[56]

The first government scheme at Willow Fountains deserves particular attention, as it was the most intensively studied, and later officials possibly learnt from mistakes made there. The farm (5,471 acres) lay some 6 miles south of Pietermaritzburg, and was thus not so isolated as some of the Byrne settlements had been. Ample opportunities for irrigation were claimed, although in 1848 it had been reported that only 60 acres were capable of arable development.[57] The farm was divided into forty settlement lots (an average size of 85 acres), the remaining 2,090 acres constituting a commonage (Fig 46). The Land and Immigration Board paid £4,000 for the land, spending a further £4,321 on improvements, but the sale of lots would only have realized £5,008, the loss being regarded as a long-term investment in new immigrants.[58] The scheme was not particularly successful. Of the forty families expected, only twenty-three arrived. Three months before their arrival, the area had been swept by a grass fire, which destroyed vegetation and buildings, and as a result two families left immediately, and four more followed within the next five years. In 1882 the unoccupied lots were divided amongst the remaining occupants. The partial failure of the scheme was due to a number of miscalculations, several of which were remarkably similar to those attending the Byrne scheme of 1850. Only seven of the seventeen families at Willow Fountains in 1884 had agricultural experience before coming to Natal; the land was not easily worked, and the irrigation potential had been grossly overstated. Thus in that year only 150 acres were cultivated, and owing to the lack of local markets, the problem of what to grow arose, and was finally solved by the introduction of mixed farming based on cattle, sheep and pecan nuts. Understandably, the general lack of farming knowledge and assistance led to a wastage of money on the immigrants' part, to the detriment of the settlement.[59]

Later government schemes were better planned and were largely successful.[60] Greater preparation was evident in the construction of irrigation canals and weirs to supply settlement plots, and, where necessary, towns were laid out to act as service centres for the schemes. Thus by 1900 some 64,731 acres had been set aside for closer settlement, and 90 per cent were occupied.

The Anglo-Boer War was the turning point for closer settlement, as a result of increased interest in southern Africa as a field for colonization. Between 1902 and 1910 the Natal Government had acquired some 140,000 acres for closer-settlement schemes. Whereas in 1900 this had belonged to thirteen, mostly absentee, owners, ten years later it had been divided into 262 rural lots, townlands, and commonages. Several schemes depended upon irrigation channels and the provision of boreholes. The two largest schemes (over fifty lots apiece) were irrigated, with railway spurs constructed to export the expected produce, citrus fruit (Winterton,

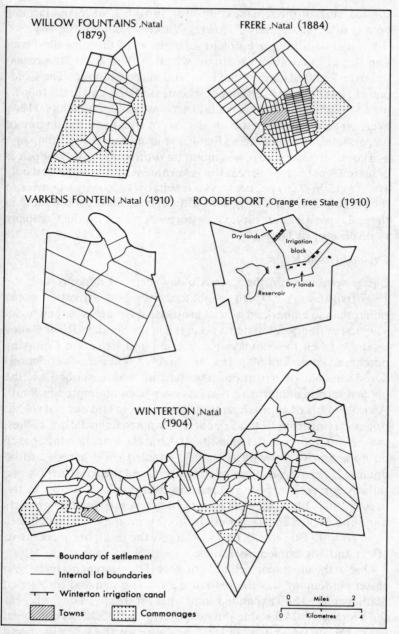

Fig 46   Plans of closer-settlement schemes, 1879–1910

Fig 46). Most of the schemes, however, provided for mixed farming on lots of approximately 700 acres (Varkens Fontein, Fig 46).

Parallel with the government schemes were those of the Natal Land and Colonisation Company, which by the mid-1870s possessed over 700,000 acres of the best land in the Colony.[61] The Company began its closer-settlement schemes in 1876, and in the following ten years laid out over 54,000 acres as immigrants' lots. However, on some schemes the lot sizes were small and the degree of preparation minimal (Frere, Fig 46), and moreover the Company, as a commercial concern, was intent on profits, and asked for prices of up to £3 per acre, whereas the government schemes charged only 10s–15s (50p–75p) per acre. As a result, by 1900 only a quarter of the prepared area had been sold, although sales were more rapid in the early twentieth century, as pressure was placed on the Company to dispose of its lands.[62]

Cape of Good Hope

Closer settlement in the Cape Colony received impetus with the 1877 Irrigation Act, which sought to assist private irrigation works rather than to embark on official projects, as Natal had hoped to do. The first major developments occurred in the Sundays River Valley in 1883, when the Sundays River Land and Irrigation Company purchased some 74,000 acres, of which 15,000 acres were considered capable of irrigation. The scheme was described as 'the boldest farming enterprise that has ever been attempted in South Africa'.[63] Lots of approximately 100 acres were laid out and sold at prices varying from £2 to £5 per acre. Owing to financial difficulties, the weir was not completed until 1910, but the irrigation lots, based on an extensive network of canals, enabled good harvests to be obtained. The introduction of citrus fruits and the construction of a railway for their export assured the future of the district in the period 1902–14. In the Fish River valley several irrigation projects were undertaken in the period 1906–09, raising the irrigated area from 80 to 7,000 acres.[64] This was largely the result of co-operative effort and government assistance.

One of the most spectacular agricultural developments leading to closer settlement was the ostrich boom. The demand for ostrich feathers after 1860 expanded somewhat erratically. Thus, whereas the average 1,404 lbs of feather exports in the 1850s had only been worth £8,749 per annum, in 1881 they were worth £1.1 million, and amounted to some 13 per cent of the Cape Colony's exports by value. The fluctuations in fashion resulted in several booms and slumps, up to the collapse at the beginning of World War 1, with prices ranging from 146s 2d (£7.61) to 27s 3d (£1.36) per lb.[65] In 1913, 1.0 million lbs of feathers worth £3.0 million were exported; they were the fourth most important South African export after gold, diamonds and wool.

The feather industry was highly organized and localized. Hunting had reduced wild ostrich numbers to such an extent that in 1853 attempts were made to domesticate the birds. By 1865 some 80 birds were in captivity: the number reached 154,880 in 1891, and 776,313 in 1913. It was found that only birds in excellent condition grew feathers to the standard required for the export trade, and consequently only the most suitable areas of the country were developed to produce high-grade plumes. It was also discovered that lucerne, which required an intensive irrigation system, provided the best diet for the birds, and so the Oudtshoorn district, with its extensive irrigation potential, became the established leader, although marketing was carried out in Port Elizabeth. Profits from the trade enabled substantial irrigation works to be constructed. With the introduction of controlled grazing through reinforced barbed wire fencing, it was possible for a pair of birds to live on less than one acre, compared with thirty acres in the wild.[66] Thus the landscape of ostrich farming developed an intensity of rural improvement equalled only in the vineyard areas of the western Cape (Fig 47).

Transvaal

Closer settlement, as envisaged in the coastal colonies, was alien to the whole concept of land distribution in the Republics. However, an important scheme was forced upon the Transvaal government in 1883, when, after a short war, a tribe of Africans, known as Mapoch's People, were dispossessed of their land. The area of land obtained was small, approximately 80,000 acres, and it could not provide standard farms for the more than 300 Europeans who had taken part in the war. Mapoch's Ground was, however, well endowed with a high rainfall, plentiful surface water and, by Transvaal standards, luxuriant vegetation. It was therefore eminently suitable for closer settlement, which was officially viewed as the only way of solving the land question. It was thus divided into 331 small lots of 17 acres apiece, with a commonage of over 74,000 acres (Fig 48). [67] No attempt at a rectangular survey was made; instead the small lots were situated along the main watercourses and in the swamps. Few Transvaal farms cultivated more than 17 acres

Fig 47 Ostriches, Oudtshoorn. The demand of fashion gave rise to one of the first major irrigation schemes in southern Africa, the lucerne fields of Oudtshoorn. The Ostrich Palace in the background is indicative of the wealth derived from the Ostrich Boom.

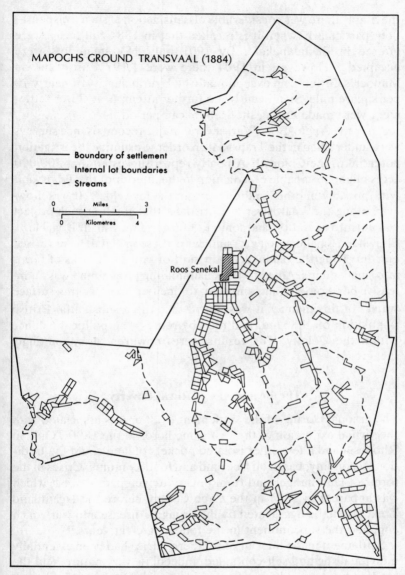

Fig 48   Plan of Mapoch's Ground, Transvaal, 1884

in the early 1880s, but the small lots were deemed capable of supporting a family, when use was made of the commonage for grazing. In addition a town (Roos Senekal) was surveyed, but apart from the building of a store and a church, it remained undeveloped.

Inevitably there was considerable dissatisfaction at such a dispensa-
tion, particularly when it is recalled that in 1884 full farms were
offered in Bechuanaland. By 1901 only 151 small lots were
occupied.[68] However, in 1904 there were 1,197 Europeans on
Mapoch's Ground, an exceptionally high rural density of nearly 10
per square mile. Significantly, no further attempts at closer settlement were made during the Republican period.

After the Anglo-Boer War, several major reconnaisance surveys
were undertaken in the Transvaal, in order to examine the irrigation
potential of the Colony.[69] An early report suggested that 500,000
acres might be capable of irrigation in the interior of the Transvaal,
with possibly another million acres in the lowveld.[70] It was, however, along the Vaal River at Christiana that the first such project
was put into operation, and some 17,000 acres were made irrigable.[71]
Elsewhere, smaller projects, similar to those in Natal, were carried
out, involving the planned subdivision of farms or blocks of farms
into smaller units. Allied to the small-holding programme was an intensive borehole-sinking campaign, to open up areas lacking surface
water. In this manner it was hoped to settle a substantial British
population on the land, and thereby redress the political balance
within the Colony. The results were, however, disappointingly
meagre.[72]

The Beginnings of Rural Poverty

The gradual closing of the settlement frontier was associated with
the virtual extinction of the vast game herds in the 1890s. Only in
Rhodesia and a few other isolated pockets of land could the traditional economy, based on free land and food, continue. Crises in the
forms of land hunger and rural poverty developed. Unrest, which
was apparent in 1894 in the Cape Colony before the Ngamiland
Trek, was to be aggravated by the drought, disease and war which
engulfed the subcontinent in the following eight years.[73]

Settlement in the interior of southern Africa had been essentially
individualistic and self-contained: indeed, its very nature held the
seeds of future problems, as was evident to the Transvaal Indigency
Commission of 1908, which stated:[74]

> Two features of the early conditions in the Transvaal must be noted: the
> isolation of the lives of its white inhabitants and the large size of farms.
> The daily life of the early Transvaal farmer consisted mainly in supervis-
> ing the work of natives in the mealie lands or among the stock, in tending
> his animals, in shooting game for the pot and in an annual trek to the

Low Veld for winter grazing. The land owner could not cultivate the soil because there was no market for agricultural produce. He did not even farm to supply his own wants. Except for the small supply of mealies which he grew he lived almost entirely on the game which fell to his rifle. His stock was not so much the source of his food supply as the only form in which he could accumulate wealth. He did not use them for food but grew rich or poor as their numbers increased or diminished. His homestead was usually some miles from that of his nearest neighbour; and there were few strangers with whom he ever came into contact. It was, therefore, but natural that his outlook was both circumscribed and essentially uncommercial.

Pressure of rural population grew in most settled parts of southern Africa in the second half of the nineteenth century. The large farms had to support an increasing number of persons, as children and grandchildren, with little possibility of obtaining land on the frontier, remained on the family farm, and the traditions of divided inheritance among the Dutch-speaking population resulted in multiple ownership, which, by the first decade of the twentieth century, was widespread. In the Transvaal in 1900, of the 6,976 privately owned farms, 757 were owned by six or more persons.[75] One farm was owned by fifty-three! The problem was most severe in the older-established regions. Thus in the Potchefstroom District 37 per cent of the farms were owned by six or more persons, and in the Cape Colony, the process had proceeded further, with shares in farms reaching meaningless proportions. Examples were quoted of one farm of 5,348 acres with shares such as $\frac{1}{48,141}$ and $\frac{296,387,007}{4,705,511,234,760}$![76] Where physical subdivision did occur, the results were often grotesque. In the Transvaal for example, a farm of 11.7 square miles had been subdivided with 140 miles of property boundaries. One holding of 148 acres was encircled by a boundary of 12 miles (Fig 49).[77]

In addition to those with the rights to land, there was a class of squatters (*bywoners*), who obtained permission, often only verbal, to pasture their animals and cultivate land in return for some assistance. Inevitably their position became progressively more insecure as population pressure built up. After the Anglo-Boer War reconstruction aid assisted owners rather than squatters, the able rather than the weak. Again the rinderpest outbreak of 1895–6 had decimated herds, and the squatters lacked security for loans to make good the losses.

Multiple ownership and squatting were detrimental to any attempt to improve agriculture, for a large part of a farm became a commonage where rights-holders and squatters pastured their ani-

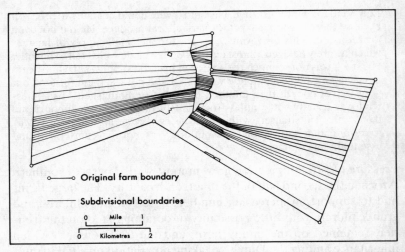

Fig 49   Farm fragmentation, the farm Nooitgedacht (Marico District Transvaal), 1908

mals together, so that scientific breeding, as required for both the wool and beef industries, was clearly impossible. Not only was fencing prohibitively expensive, but also most holdings were too small for grazing purposes, and many families were thus caught in the vicious circle of deteriorating conditions and circumstances, without the traditional means of escape — trekking to new land.

Rehabilitation of families caught in the economic circumstances of the 1890s became the concern of both Church and State. In 1895 the Dutch Reformed Church began the first labour settlement in the Cape Colony at Kakamas.[78] Families were leased 12-acre irrigation plots with access to common grazing. The land was obtained free of charge, and approximately a third of the costs was borrowed from the government. The major feature of the scheme was the close supervision of the family, with the aim of helping the children, through work and education, not to become indigent. The scheme was limited in its extent, and careful selection was also necessary, as some evidence of energy and desire for improvement was required on the part of the settler. At Kakamas all applicants to join the colony had to work for two or three months at a wage of 3s (15p) per day, digging the irrigation furrow, before they were leased a holding: this acted as a kind of selective entrance examination.[79] Further church settlements were established in the Cape Colony, Orange River Colony and Transvaal in the period 1900–10.[80] The labour colonies were expensive, and were regarded as a temporary form of aid in the exceptional circumstances then prevailing, but they provided evidence that the problems of the poor whites could be solved, and that manual work need not be regarded as degrading.

At the end of hostilities in 1902, the government embarked upon a rehabitation programme for those with nowhere to go. Thus the Burgher Land Settlements were envisaged as closer settlements, where each settler recieved 10 acres of irrigated and 25 acres of dry land, together with access to communal grazing (Roodepoort Fig 46). Between 1902 and 1906 some 200,000 acres were acquired in the southern Transvaal for this purpose, with 1,411 families passing through. However, only 461 families remained in 1906, and only two settlements achieved lasting success.[81]

6

Industrial Foundations 1860-1914

BETWEEN 1860 and 1910 the processes of urbanization and town formation were closely associated with the development of a mining industry. Until the discovery of diamonds in 1867, comparatively little capital was invested in industry and commerce.[1] Thereafter, South Africa took a major share of British overseas capital investment, and by 1910 it was estimated that some £351.4 million had been invested in South Africa, the mining industry accounting for £125.1 million.[2] In addition £9.4 million was invested in railways, as must have been the bulk of the £97.4 million government investment. Even service industries such as gas, water and electricity received £5.0 million, and tramways a further £1.8 million. This massive investment, plus the re-investment of profits and revenue, boosted the towns in a manner no agricultural development could have done.

In a less spectacular fashion, the predominantly rural economy had been transformed through the introduction of a cash rather than a barter economy, as a result of commercial banking.[3] Between 1836 and 1863, some thirty-one local and district banks were established, mainly in the Eastern and Western Provinces of the Cape. In 1861 the first of the Imperial banks began operation, and through the provision of credit allowed freer trade and a sound basis of interchange. Money in circulation in the Cape Colony rose rapidly from approximately £0.9 million in 1855 to £2.4 million ten years later, and to £6.0 million in 1875. Prosperity in the rural as well as in the industrial community resulted in increased urban activity and flow of trade.

The transformation of the subcontinental economy may be gauged from export figures, which illustrate the importance of, first,

diamonds, and, later, gold, in providing an income for the states of
southern Africa (Table 10, Fig 16). It is of great significance that
the mining areas were situated in the interior of the subcontinent,
whereas most earlier development had been comparatively close to
the coast. Thus whereas in 1855 only one (Graaff-Reinet) of the
twelve largest centres was more than 100 miles from the coast, in
1911 eight of the twelve largest towns were so placed (Fig 50). The
rise of the interior towns is symbolized by Johannesburg's superces-

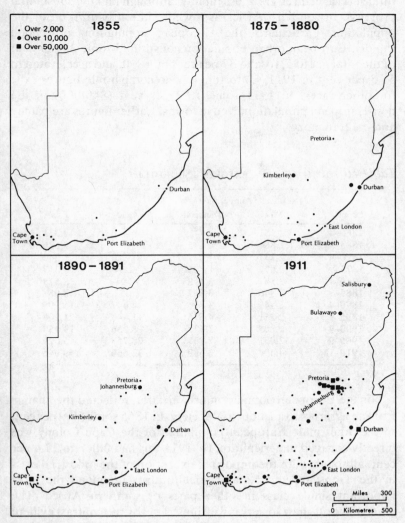

Fig 50   Distribution of urban centres, 1855–1911

sion of Cape Town as the largest urban centre in the first decade of the present century.[4] The relative instability of the urban hierarchy reflected the transformation of the economy (Fig 51). Thus of the twelve largest centres in 1855, only four remained in the top twelve fifty-six years later. Mining towns such as Kimberley and Johannesburg grew into major centres within a few years, and new administrative capitals such as Pretoria benefited from the mineral discoveries and the general expansion of trade. In contrast the agricultural service centres grew less rapidly, although making substantial progress. In southern Africa as a whole, the urbanization of the population, particularly the European population, proceeded rapidly. European urban population constituted some 32 per cent of the total in 1855, rose to 37 per cent by 1890, and accelerated to 51.5 per cent in 1911. Unfortunately no comparable figures exist for other races. In 1911 some 13.9 per cent (840,000) of the non-European population lived in towns. Earlier figures are patchy and contradictory.

Table 10 SOUTH AFRICAN EXPORTS 1860–1914

Period	Annual Averages (£000)			
	Wool	Diamonds	Gold	Total
1860–4	1,551	—	—	2,321
1865–9	1,886	5	—	2,626
1870–4	2,787	1,027	3	5,246
1875–9	2,679	1,905	34	6,317
1880–4	2,583	3,418	28	8,578
1885–9	2,446	3,717	653	8,982
1890–4	2,545	3,816	4,447	15,099
1895–9	2,251	4,516	11,440	21,208
1900–4	1,803	5,137	8,236	19,159
1905–9	2,931	7,231	28,753	45,027
1910–14	4,494	8,689	32,666	59,046

For the European population urbanization reflected the change from an agrarian to an industrial society. In 1865 some 50.9 per cent of the adult male European population of the Cape Colony was directly engaged in agriculture. By 1911 this had fallen to 27.4 per cent, although, with the important exception of the industrial class in the Transvaal and Natal, agriculturalists remained the most important single class in other parts of southern Africa. The emergence of a new society is well illustrated by the contrast evident in the 1890 Transvaal census, when 32 per cent of the Europeans on

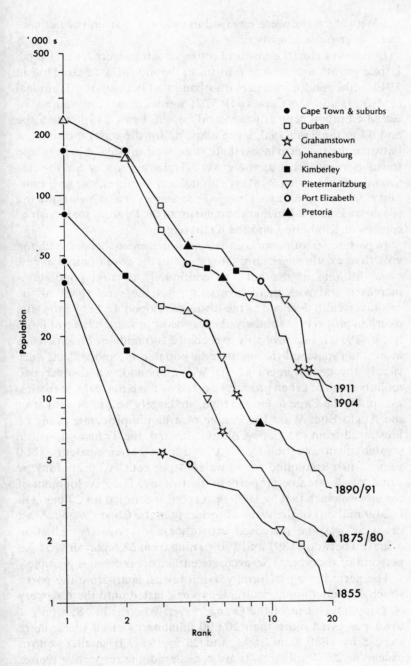

Fig 51   The urban hierarchy of southern Africa, 1855–1911

the Witwatersrand were engaged in industry, but only 4 per cent
were so engaged elsewhere.

· In terms of size, the towns of southern Africa were transformed.
Urban growth assumed new forms in the industrial areas. Thus in
1911, although the numbers of urban inhabitants in the Transvaal
(599,509) and the Cape (619,577) were similar, the number of
classified urban centres was very different, being 217 in the Cape
and 44 in the Transvaal. Even allowing for the difference in area
between the two provinces, there were almost twice as many Cape
towns per unit area, as there were Transvaal towns. Small-scale
urbanization, serving local agricultural communities, was an important element in the Cape, Orange Free State, parts of Natal, and the
southern Transvaal, in marked contrast to the large major industrial
centres of Kimberley and the Transvaal.

In part, town foundation and expansion were associated with the
growth of existing agricultural regions and the development of new
ones. Infilling of the network continued, as rural populations
increased and with them prosperity, but the rural share of the
colonial wealth declined as the towns developed. In 1860 the value
of urban property in southern Africa was approximately £6 million,
but by 1910 it had probably exceeded £140 million. This increase
more than matched the increase in population, and reflects very
clearly the development of the Witwatersrand, where over £40
million worth of urban property existed by the latter date. Statistics,
except for the Cape of Good Hope, are largely estimates until after
the Anglo-Boer War. The degree of urban improvement may be
illustrated from the Cape Colony, although the Transvaal, with a
greater urban valuation by 1910, is a more extreme case. In 1860
Cape Town accounted for some 18.4 per cent (£2.9 million) by
value, of all rateable property in the Colony. The development of
the city was such that by 1909 the capital accounted for 27 per cent
(£24.9 million) of the value of property in the Cape Colony. Most
dramatic was the increased urban share of property valuation
achieved between 1891 and 1909, rising from 28.6 per cent to 53.6
per cent of the whole. No accurate earlier breakdown is possible.

The period of agriculturally based towns, apart from the ports,
which depended on agricultural exports, lasted until the discovery
of diamonds, north of the Orange River. Whereas in 1855 only 1
town possessed more than 10,000 inhabitants of all races, there
were 5 by 1880, 7 in 1890, and 23 in 1911. If smaller centres
exceeding 2,000 inhabitants are considered, the respective figures
for the four years are 12, 20, 37 and 94. The large African rural

villages of Bechuanaland, of which six exceeded 2,000 inhabitants in 1911, are excluded from these figures.

Although diamonds generated trade and growth in many forms for the Cape Colony, it was the discovery of gold on the Witwatersrand in 1886 which revolutionized the southern African economy. Whereas in 1880 probably only 3 per cent of the European urban population of southern Africa was in the Transvaal, this rose to approximately 16 per cent ten years later, and in 1911 it reached 37.4 per cent. The stimulus of gold led to a major period of town foundation. Thus of the 40 registered Transvaal towns founded in the nineteenth century, 19 were founded between 1881 and 1890.[5] As always, booms led to oversupply. Thus by 1904 there were 46 towns situated outside the Witwatersrand and Pretoria, where only 16.2 per cent of the plots laid out had been built upon. Indeed, 7 towns possessed fewer than ten buildings. Even in Potchefstroom, the most 'developed' of the towns, only 595 of the 1,229 plots were built upon.[6]

The new industrial cities and the industrial suburbs of existing cities lacked many of the grand planning features of the rural-based towns. This may be illustrated by a comparison of mining-town plans and other towns (Fig 52).[7] Mining centres (e.g. Roodepoort, Barberton, and Molteno) were generally cramped, with approximately sixteen plots per acre. Grand plans as such disappeared, and either irregular patterns reflecting the layout of the original mining camp, or a rigid grid, usually of small blocks, accommodating as many persons as possible, took their place. This lack of adequate planning was often due to the feeling that the mining settlements would be abandoned within a few years, and it was only when they survived that major problems developed. Hence the large unimaginative towns and suburbs of the Witwatersrand grew up with little planning, amongst the mines and their waste heaps.

It must not be forgotten, however, that new lands were opened up and new towns were founded to fulfil administrative and commercial functions. The town plans of Bechuanaland and Rhodesia continued the tradition of the first half of the century, although grid plans were universal, and plot sizes were smaller than those distributed to the pioneers in the Transvaal or Natal in the 1830s and 1840s. Rarely did the church occupy the place allotted to it in towns such as Pretoria or Graaff-Reinet, where it acted as a focal point to the road system. Squares were smaller, roads narrower and townlands more restricted. In part this was due to an increased number of plots on the plans. Towns were expected to be larger, in terms of

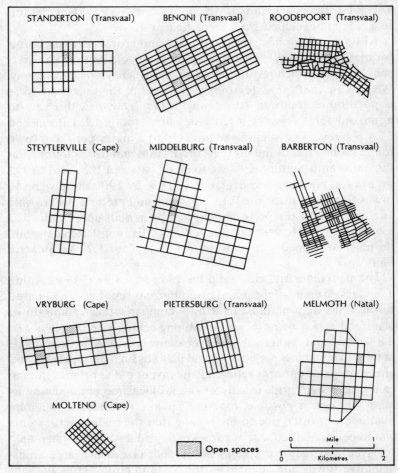

STANDERTON (Transvaal) BENONI (Transvaal) ROODEPOORT (Transvaal)

STEYTLERVILLE (Cape) MIDDELBURG (Transvaal) BARBERTON (Transvaal)

VRYBURG (Cape) PIETERSBURG (Transvaal) MELMOTH (Natal)

MOLTENO (Cape)

Open spaces

0   Mile   1

0   Kilometres   2

Fig 52   Town plans in the later nineteenth century

inhabitants, than they had been in the first half of the century, and at the same time increasing provision had to be made for Indians and Africans, usually in separate areas, such as the Asiatic bazaars of the Transvaal, or the African locations of Rhodesia or Natal. Plots in such areas were usually small, as once more the occupants were regarded as transitory. Only in Natal, and later Rhodesia, did true dual town centres (Indian and European) evolve.[8]

Towns now fulfilled greater functions. Whereas in 1860 only 62 towns possessed magistrates or commissioners (the basic government functionaries) in 1890 there were 141, and in 1911 there were

252 administrative districts in southern Africa. With them went a host of other officials, reflecting greater administrative concern and the provision of more services. Local penny postal systems began in Cape Town in 1860 and spread throughout southern Africa so that by 1914 there were over 2,500 post offices in the subcontinent, providing a network of rapid communication. The development of the telegraph system began in 1860, and by 1880 most of southern Africa was linked with Europe. In 1882 the first telephone exchange was opened. Thus in the second half of the nineteenth century the urban amenities changed rapidly, linking towns and breaking down the isolation which had existed in previous decades. There followed economic integration, and finally the political integration of much of the subcontinent.

Other services had to be provided. Water supplies in a land subject to periodic drought and to low rainfalls presented problems, especially on the Witwatersrand, where the siting of towns was not carried out with regard to springs and watercourses. Older towns, founded in the first half of the century, such as Bloemfontein, Pietermaritzburg, and Potchefstroom were sited near strong springs, which provided ample supplies until the present century, but by the 1870s the rapidly growing port cities faced water-supply problems of a serious nature. New engineering works to supplement sources were now sited at greater distances, and the search for water began. Gas and electricity services were introduced. Electricity was a comparatively late arrival; although part of Cape Town was lit in 1882, there was no general lighting until the following decade. By 1910 some twenty towns possessed electricity departments, and by the outbreak of World War 1 a further fourteen. In this manner the contrast between urban and rural living tended to be more marked in 1914 than it had been in 1860.

In appearance most towns remained relatively open and uncrowded before World War 1. Buildings of stone, brick and iron occupied only parts of the town grids, and houses varied from purely utilitarian corrugated-iron dwellings to fanciful stone mansions with elaborate wrought-iron work. Cape-Dutch styles lost popularity in the second half of the nineteenth century, and were replaced by British colonial styles which would be as much at home in Australia or Canada as in South Africa. The late nineteenth and early twentieth centuries were the age of the catalogue and pattern book. Entire buildings could be chosen from catalogues, with every element and ornament pre-selected. In general, economic limitations necessitated the choice of cheap and therefore simpler pat-

terns for colonial houses, but this was not always the case, as some of
the mansions in the main centres testified.[9] Possibly the flamboyant
ostrich-boom 'palaces' of the Oudtshoorn District provided a fitting
climax to the Victorian and Edwardian eras. But styles were not
uniformly British colonial. Pretoria, as the seat of the Transvaal
government during the height of its prosperity, looked to the continent of Europe for inspiration, with the result that Lord Milner was
to observe in 1900: 'Pretoria is a lovely little spot – of water, trees
and gardens, ruined by the most horrible vulgarities of 10th rate
continental villadom — German architecture of the Bismarckian
era at its worst.'[10]

Increased prosperity and changing fashions later allowed for the
construction of larger and more impressive buildings. Public buildings became more numerous and tended to create focal points in the
towns, and commercial concerns — first the banks, and later the
shops — were built in order to impress customers. All the styles of
Victorian and Edwardian England, plus some German and Dutch
styles were used, and whereas in 1860 a height of three storeys was
the maximum, even in Cape Town, by 1914 structures of up to eight
storeys had begun to mark the emergence of central business districts, displacing private houses from the main streets of the larger
cities.

Other important changes included the paving of the main streets
in the major centres, and in both wet and dry seasons there was far
less mud and dust in the streets, while sewerage systems and refuse
collection altered the aspect of larger cities, if not of the smaller
ones. Depressing descriptions of Cape Town in the 1850s and 1860s
referred to mud, refuse and smells: yet by 1909 civic improvements
were such that a brochure entitled *Cape Town for Health and
Pleasure All the Year Round* could be issued, extolling the virtues of
the city.[11]

The transformation of urban southern Africa was the result of the
discovery of diamonds and gold, which in their turn brought railway
development, other types of mining, particularly that of coal, the
opening of Rhodesia, and the vast expansion of the coastal towns.

Diamonds and Development in the Cape

Industrial development was slow in the Cape. Some processing
industries had been established in the ports, but mining and manufacturing were lacking, and it was not until 1852 that the copper
deposits of Namaqualand were at last exploited.[12] They did not,

however, give a major boost to the economy, providing, up to the discovery of diamonds, little more than 5 per cent of the Colony's exports. Copper reached a peak of £0.86 million in 1888, but thereafter declined significantly.

The discovery of diamonds was an event of the utmost importance, and the acquisition of the diamond fields by the Cape was an essential prerequisite to the development of the Colony. The intitial strikes of alluvial diamonds attracted diggers from all over the world, the first activities being on the terraces of the Harts and Vaal Rivers, where the 'Star of Africa' was found in 1869.[13] The discovery of the main diamond-bearing pipes, however, led to the major rush in the vicinity of Kimberley. By February 1871 there were 10,000 diggers in the area.[14]

Mining claims, 30 by 30 feet, were pegged out over wide areas, but it was in the restricted zones of the main pipes that problems arose. As mining activity penetrated deeper, the different rates of progress on the different claims and the means of raising the mined material to ground level presented substantial difficulties. Flooding of the deepest claims and the collapse of those with little activity increasingly demanded unified control (Fig 53). The earliest streets across the mines were gradually quarried away, until access could only be obtained by ropeways. The workings of numerous claims also necessitated a vast number of ropeways and an equally large number of spoil-heaps, after the material had been sifted for diamonds. At the Kimberley mine there were originally over 400 claims, but these were gradually amalgamated. Eventually the 'Big Hole' was dug. Deeper workings meant that more capital was required, and gradually a number of major firms emerged, until in 1888 De Beers Consolidated Mines Ltd gained virtually complete control of the industry. By then the individual digger had ceased to be of major importance, and he was relegated to the alluvial workings.

The diamond fields were the subject of dispute between the British and Orange Free State governments, but this was resolved by British annexation, and the establishment of the Province of Griqualand West. The resulting flow of money into the Cape of Good Hope may be gauged from the increase in exports. In 1872 diamond exports were worth £1.6 million, or over a quarter of the Cape Colony's exports: after reorganization, production value increased steadily from 1877, until in 1887 diamond exports (£4.2 million) amounted to over half the Cape's exports. The flow of money which this generated enabled major public works, such as

Fig 53 Kimberley Mine, c.1875. The 'Big Hole' was excavated by a large number of miners working his own claim at different rates of progress, giving rise to a chaotic landscape depicted. The diamondiferous rocks, once mined, were raised to the surface on ropes to be crushed and sorted.

the interior railway line and port improvements, to be undertaken at a time when the value of wool was declining.

The town of Kimberley, in the heart of the diamond fields, was the first modern industrial city in southern Africa. The mining camp, originally partially sited on what became the 'Big Hole', was a chaotic pattern of tracks and streets with no over-all planning (Fig 54). Roads were deviated to avoid obstructions, whether mineral

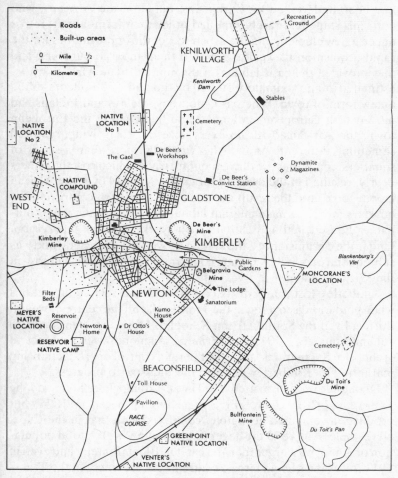

Fig 54   Plan of Kimberley, 1899

workings or spoil heaps, and no attempt was made to introduce the ubiquitous grid, until the satellite town of Beaconsfield was laid out. Plots were small and buildings generally covered most of the plot

(Fig 55). Tents gradually gave way to prefabricated iron structures, which became almost universal. Substantial brick and
stone houses were later erected in new suburbs, and the same
materials were used for prestige buildings such as the town hall and
club. In 1877 Kimberley, with a population approaching 20,000,
was the second largest town in the subcontinent.

It was unusual in its organization of mining. The initial diggings
had been undertaken by Europeans, but soon the Africans, who
until this stage had rarely supplied other than farm labour, introduced a new element into the urban scene; the opportunities for the
rapid acquisition of wealth attracted them in large numbers, and
they provided the basic labour on the mines. [15] The African influx,
estimated at approximately 10,000 by the mid-1870s, necessitated
a new form of town. Whereas Coloureds, Malays and Indians had
moved with European settlement and lived within the European
town, the Africans, with no experience of urban living, required
something different. At first this was little more than a series of
squatters' camps but the illicit diamond trade, which cost the miners
dearly, resulted in the demand for greater control over the African
labour force, and the result was the development of compounds —
quarters for single male migrant labourers — where the mine companies housed, fed and clothed their workers under supervision.
Under the circumstances, the system proved to be efficient, and was
subsequently copied by mining concerns elsewhere, particularly on
the Witwatersrand.

Kimberley lost many of its commercial and service attractions
when gold was discovered in the Transvaal, and the centre of wealth
shifted. Even the South African School of Mines was transferred to
Johannesburg in 1904. Furthermore, diamonds were subject to
great price fluctuations, and only the rigid control of production and
marketing by Kimberley enabled the industry to progress.

Diamonds were also discovered in the Orange Free State and the
Transvaal. In the Orange Free State mining began in 1875, but
production remained negligible, compared with that in the Cape.
Nevertheless, in 1890 the Jagersfontein mine, with a total population of 3,655, was larger than the capital, Bloemfontein, and even in
1911 it was the second largest centre in the Province. In the Transvaal, mining at the Premier Mine began in 1902, and was rewarded
three years later with the discovery of the 'Cullinan' diamond, at
that stage the largest found in the world. The Premier Mine in 1911
possessed a total population the size of Potchefstroom's (12,600).

In 1913, the last full year of production before World War 1,

Fig 55 Kimberly Town, 1873. The mining camp grew into a makeshift town of corrugated iron structures. Unlike most other southern African towns, little planning was evident in its layout, and equally little effort was apparent in its maintenance.

South Africa produced diamonds worth £11.4 million, of which
£7.0 million came from the Cape and £2.7 million from the Transvaal. Although the major mines played a dominant role in the
industry, in the decade before World War 1 the alluvial workings
produced approximately 10 per cent of output and engaged a third
of the work force in the mining industry.[16]

Gold and the Development of the Transvaal

Gold was often assumed to exist in southern Africa, as the fabled
Land of Orphir was thought to be somewhere in the subcontinent,
but gold in payable quantities proved to be difficult to find. It was
discovered in the Transvaal in 1852, but little notice was taken of
the discovery.[17] Later, gold was discovered at Tati in Bechuanaland
in 1869, and more significantly in the eastern Transvaal.

In 1873 the first major rush took place at Pilgrims Rest, and
1,500 diggers arrived to work the alluvial deposits along the
streams.[18] They worked individually and experienced many difficulties owing to the rugged nature of the terrain, which complicated the
direction of the water courses. Once the bed rock was reached and
the alluvial deposit was exhausted, they moved to another site. No
attempt at crushing rock was made at first, as the diggers lacked the
capital to mine the lodes. In the four years, 1873–7, an estimated
£1.5 million worth of gold was mined at Pilgrims Rest.[19] The town
developed, with one main street and the usual selection of saloons
and hotels engaged in making the diggers' gold circulate freely, but
at the end of the boom it was virtually abandoned, with only 127
Europeans remaining in 1878, a mere five years after the initial
rush.[20]

A second rush took place in the Transvaal in 1882, when gold was
discovered close to the Swaziland border. Eureka City became
another gold-boom town, while Barberton became the centre of a
thriving small-scale mining area. Many claims proved to be remarkably valuable, but most were quickly worked out. In the period
1884–6 Barberton boasted two stock exchanges, imposing government offices, five churches, a masonic lodge, a club and a number of
hotels. Unlike Kimberley and Pilgrims Rest, the town was surveyed
by the government and plots were laid out as regularly as possible
(Fig 52). Some 2,106 standard 50 by 50-foot plots were surveyed,
several without a road frontage.[21] The field was not rich and the
crash, when it came, brought ruin for many, but it also resulted in the
concentration of a large number of experienced miners not far from

the Witwatersrand, when the discoveries were made there.

The discovery of gold in payable quantities on the Witwatersrand in 1886 prompted the major gold rush, which was to transform the Transvaal completely. The magnitude may be gauged from the fact that in the period 1 May–27 July 1886 only 133 prospecting licences were issued, whereas in the period 28 July–7 September, 1,207 licences were issued. On 20 September 1886 the first public diggings were proclaimed, resulting in the mushrooming of miners' camps amongst the workings on private lands and state ground, as at Kimberley, and by the end of September 1886 approximately 2,500 miners had arrived.[22]

It was soon apparent that a major discovery had been made, and the government proceeded to lay out a township on a portion of state ground in the centre of the diggings, while six other towns were founded along the line of the main gold-bearing reef. Unfortunately the government still imagined that Johannesburg and the other Witwatersrand towns would never be any larger than Barberton or Pilgrims Rest, and so it rejected the idea of broad streets and large plots. Plots of 50 by 50 feet were laid out, instead of the then standard government town plot of 60 by 120 feet (Fig 56b). Small blocks were thought to be advantageous, as higher prices were paid for corner sites by proprietors of saloons, hotels and other places of entertainment. As Shorten said of Johannesburg, 'the future City's central area was planned as a temporary expedient and one whereby the Government would gain the maximum revenue in the shortest possible time.'[23] Sites were provided for a market square, two public spaces and a cemetery, but the gridiron of narrow streets and cramped city blocks created a traffic problem which is still unsolved. In December 1886 the first 986 stands were auctioned for £13,000. In 1954 the municipal valuation of the same area was £80 million.[24]

Speculation and prospecting proceeded swiftly along the line of the main gold reefs. Farms which had been traded at low prices before the discovery suddenly became valuable almost overnight. Thus John Robinson spent £31,500 in ten months, securing many of the best pieces of land. Part of Doornfontein was offered for £250; two years later it was valued at £3 million.[25] Mining syndicates and companies were formed, for the opening of the Witwatersrand mines was to be of a different order from that at Pilgrims Rest and Barberton. Mines had to be sunk to depths of up to 100 feet, and this was beyond the resources of individual diggers. Thus the Witwatersrand goldfield rapidly became the scene of what were, in

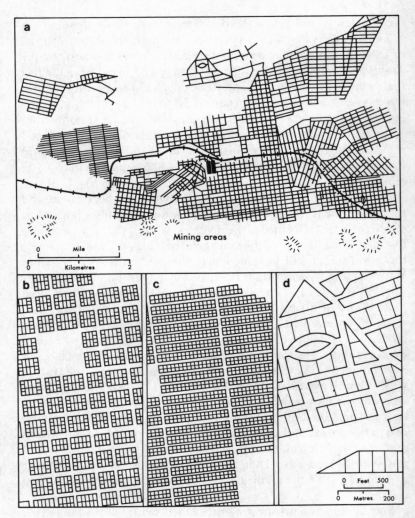

Fig. 56 Plan of Johannesburg, 1895, with enlargements of parts of (a) City centre, (b) Vrededorp, and (c) Park Town

contemporary terms, large-scale workings, in which the individual European digger was reduced to a paid employee of the large mining syndicates.

Johannesburg, with its hastily surveyed additions, soon became insanitary. The streams were contaminated with filth, and every dam and well became a menace to health. Stagnant water collected and typhoid was rife, remaining endemic for twenty years. The European death-rate was four times higher than the average for the previous fifty years in South Africa. From the first, supplies of fresh water presented a problem. Originally, the supplies came from local springs and streams, supplemented by the sinking of bore-holes, but they proved to be inadequate to meet the demands of the mines and the inhabitants. Later supplies, in the 1890s, came from dolomite formations approximately ten miles south of the cities, although once more exhaustive pumping rapidly cut the output. In 1903 the Rand Water Board was established to co-ordinate the plans of the various towns for procuring water. By 1911 it was apparent that local supplies would have to be augmented by others from the Vaal River thirty miles to the south, and plans were taken in hand for the construction of a major barrage.

The degree of expansion and the feeling of permanence were engendered by the richness of the strike. In 1885 gold production in the Transvaal had been worth only £6,010, but this rose to £1.5 million in 1889, and in 1898, the last full year before the Anglo-Boer War, it was worth £16.2 million. After being interrupted by the war, production again rose rapidly, reaching £37.4 million in 1913. The sudden wealth which came to the Transvaal created new towns and industries, but also considerable political instability so long as the goldfields lay, before 1900, in what was essentially a rurally orientated republic.

Permanence was demonstrated by the speed with which a modern city replaced the mining camp. Substantial two- and three-storeyed buildings of stone and brick were erected within a few years of the proclamation of a township (Figs 57, 58). Other more modest structures of iron, wood, stone and brick replaced the tent towns equally rapidly. By 1896 Johannesburg possessed over 14,000 buildings, nearly half of brick and stone, the remainder of wood and iron. The nature of the town was surprising when compared with the towns associated with many gold rushes, as J.W. Sauer, the Cape cabinet minister, remarked in January 1888:[26]

> When I came here I was fairly taken aback. In mostly every mining community where a town is just established, you see a town of tents; but it is different here. You come here and see a substantially built town filled with many large buildings, properly laid out squares and regular streets, and the spaces between filled with different houses. If you compare this with many other mining centres in the world the difference is in favour of Johannesburg.

Growth was reflected in the differentiation of the towns. The initial grids of 1886 were soon inadequate and new extensions were laid out. Although most of the extensions varied little from the original

Fig 57   Commissioner Street, Johannesburg, 1893. Johannesburg achieved a greater degree of grandeur than Kimberley. The wealth of the gold-fields was reflected in a townscape which in parts matched that of late-Victorian England.

Fig 58 Commissioner Street, Johannesburg, 1958. Johannesburg, southern Africa's first 'million'city' became the subcontinent's financial and commercial centre, achieving a measure of vertical growth rare in other southern African cities before 1960.

plans, two marked variants appeared. There were the Indian locations, laid out in small plots (Fig 56c), with the 'Poor White'
location at Vrededorp established on a similar pattern; there were
the wealthier suburbs established to separate rich from poor. Park
Town (1892) was the first of a series of exclusive districts, planned
with the idea of contemporary European garden or semi-rural
suburbs in mind. Large plots of an acre or more were laid out, with
an irregular road pattern (Fig 56d), and on the plots, distinctive
houses with imposing characteristics were built in an attempt to
reproduce 'Home' — England.[27]

Growth was rapid and, in spite of war and other fluctuations,
almost continuous between 1886 and 1914. Four years after the
discovery of gold, there were 13,114 Europeans on the Witwatersrand. In 1896 the population of Johannesburg alone had reached
61,292, including 39,454 Europeans. In 1911 the Witwatersrand
towns, from Krugersdorp in the west to Springs in the east, contained 465,320 persons. Johannesburg, the largest and now the
premier town of southern Africa, had 237,104 inhabitants, an
increase of 80 per cent in seven years. Johannesburg, furthermore,
had attained a municipal valuation of £33 million in 1914, compared with £29 million for Cape Town. In addition it was growing
faster than any other southern African city. Thus in the years
1911–14 the value of building plans approved in Johannesburg was
some £5.7 million, compared with £1.1 million in its nearest rival,
Durban.[28]

Such sustained development was not maintained without difficulty. Undoubtedly one of the most severe problems was the supply of
African workers.[29] The demand for labour was such that numbers
increased from 14,000 in 1890 to 99,000 in 1899, and the war led to
grave difficulties in the recruitment of labour, particularly within
the Transvaal. Agencies were established, with networks of stations
across southern Africa, in order to attract men to the gold-mines.
As a temporary expedient Chinese workers were introduced in
1904, but they proved to be politically unpopular. After reaching
53,000 in 1907, they were repatriated to China, and the search for
labour continued, particularly in Mocambique. Thus in the period
1910–13 the average number of African labourers was approximately 188,000, with a further 24,000 European mine workers.
Significantly, most of the African labourers were housed by the
mining companies in compounds, and not in the vast sprawling
suburbs typical of European habitation.

The government of the South African Republic and its successors benefited greatly from the gold discoveries. Annual public revenue, which had averaged £144,000 in the period 1881–5 was boosted to £2.6 million for the period 1891–5. As a result, government departments which had been close to bankruptcy were able to function effectively. In 1891 the Surveyor-General's Office, for example, was able to undertake a general survey of the country, a task beyond its capabilities ten years before.[30] Pretoria, as the capital, was able to embark upon a number of major projects, including the construction of several new government buildings in the 1890s. This process was continued under the colonial and Union governments, when Pretoria became the administrative, though not the legislative, capital of a united South Africa, and all government departments were located in the city. The city's European population reached 5,055 in 1890 and 21,000 fourteen years later, and by 1911, with a total population of 57,674, including 36,000 Europeans, Pretoria was the fourth largest city in southern Africa.

The Railway Network and Political Patterns

Transportation of men, animals and goods has been a major problem in the subcontinent's development, as the road improvements of the first half of the nineteenth century were insufficient to meet the needs of an expanding economy. The problems and inconveniences of ox-wagon transport were increasingly felt as the European population expanded, and particularly as the interior was opened up (Fig 59). The high costs of transportation were noted: rates varied, but in the 1860s cartage rates of approximately 1s (5p) per ton-mile governed the long-distance interior routes.[31] By the 1860s, the volume of traffic was not inconsiderable. In 1862 some 7,762 wagons left Durban for the interior, carrying an estimated 12,500 tons of merchandise. The journey to Pietermaritzburg (50 miles) took four days under favourable circumstances, and an estimated 88 wagons were on the road at any one time. Counts undertaken for the year 1870–1 revealed that some 7,348 wagons used the Pietermaritzburg–Durban road, with 4,052 passing the toll north of the Natal capital, bound for the interior.[32] In the same year 11,764 wagons carrying an estimated 15,868 tons crossed the Umgeni River, bound for the Natal North Coast and Zululand.[33] Enquiries in other parts of the subcontinent hinted at similar volumes of trade.

The lack of adequate transport facilities inhibited the development of resources. Thus the copper deposits in the Transkei, discovered in the 1860s, were never exploited, because the three-day

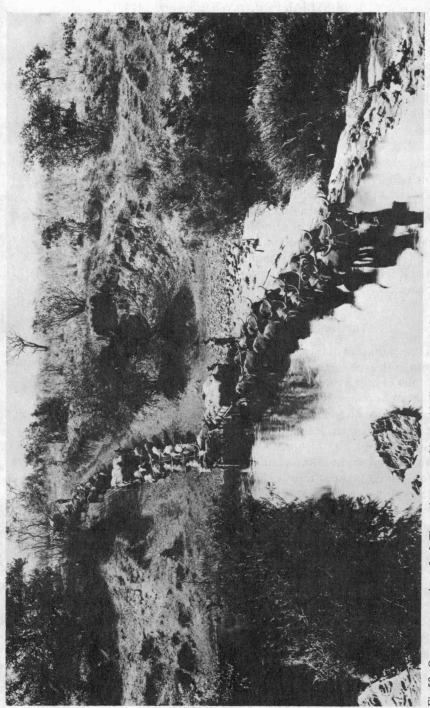

Fig 59 Ox-wagons crossing a ford. The main means of internal bulk transport, before the coming of the railways, was the ox-wagon. In an era when

ox-wagon journey to the sea would immediately make their working uneconomic. Similarly, many of the problems presented by the
first major ore deposits known to exist in the Cape Colony — the
copper of Namaqualand — were the result of inaccessibility, for
only a tramway constructed to export the ore could make exploitation profitable. Even the Natal coal deposits had to await the
railway before exploitation could begin. Consequently, through
much of the period until 1870, it was only gold which excited
attention, as other minerals and stones were regarded as
uneconomic propositions, owing to their high transportation costs.

The solutions for many of these problems of cost, inaccessibility
and loss of time were found in the development of the railway
system. The first suggestion that a railway should be built in southern Africa dated from 1845, but real impetus was given once
self-government had been achieved in the Cape Colony in 1853.
Proposals for lines from Cape Town, Port Elizabeth and Durban
were made, but it was not until 1860 that the first steam-train line
was opened. Ten years later less than 100 miles of track had been
laid. (Table 11).

Table 11 RAILWAY CONSTRUCTION IN SOUTHERN AFRICA 1860–1915

Period	Cape of Good Hope	Natal	Orange Free State	Transvaal	Rhodesia*	Total
	Mileage Completed in Period					
1860–5	57	2	—	—	—	59
1866–70	—	3	—	—	—	3
1871–5	91	—	—	—	—	91
1876–80	765	95	—	—	—	860
1881–5	697	77	—	—	—	774
1886–90	170	123	121	41	—	455
1891–5	123	72	262	524	96	1,077
1896–1900	198	145	59	309	653	1,364
1901–5	895	249	241	193	798	2,376
1906–10	341	176	307	639	55	1,518
1911–15	760	231	278	775	146	2,190
Total to 1915	4,097	1,173	1,268	2,481	1,748	10,767

*Including line through Bechuanaland and the Cape Colony, North of Vryburg
Sources: South Africa, *Annual Report of South African Railways and Harbours*, 1910 and 1960
 Southern Rhodesia, *Annual Report of Rhodesia Railways*, 1954

The first railways were short link-lines on the coast (Fig 60). At
Durban (1860) a line was laid between the Point (the port) and the
town of Durban, a distance of 2 miles; this was extended by a further

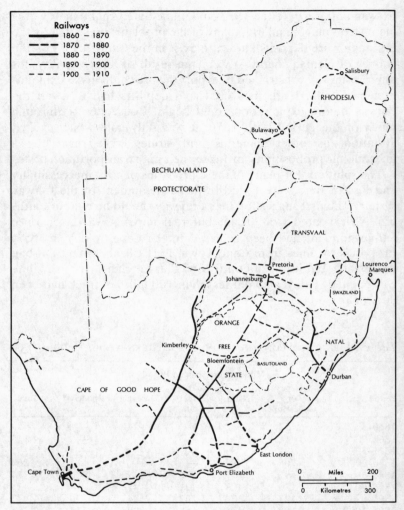

Fig 60   Development of the railway network of southern Africa, 1860–1910

3 miles in 1867. In the Cape Colony in the period 1860–4 some 57 miles of track were laid, linking Cape Town with Stellenbosch, Wynberg and Wellington, thus serving only the closely-settled agricultural regions. In the Cape the main towns of the west were linked, but further extension was uneconomic, as was the idea of the line in the Eastern Province. Since only the governments were in a position to raise the capital required for large-scale railway construction, the railways were purchased by the government of the

Cape (1873) and Natal (1877), and, in order to facilitate construction, the gauge was narrowed from 4ft 8½ins to 3ft 6ins, so that the mountain passes could be negotiated more economically.

The development of the Kimberley mines changed the financial position of southern Africa, in that capital brought into the economy provided the stimulus for railway construction. Transport to the diamond fields initially meant a 600-mile journey by ox-wagon from Port Elizabeth, taking approximately three months. Clearly the transport-riding business benefited substantially from the increased prosperity, as the diamond fields relied heavily upon imported goods, ranging from mining machinery to whisky. Major programmes of construction were undertaken to link the fields to Cape Town, Port Elizabeth and East London. The Cape Town line, which only reached Kimberley in 1885, had to traverse long stretches of comparatively unproductive Karroo land, where not even the most optimistic could suggest that close agricultural settlement was feasible, and the railways could expect little revenue from farming activities in such regions.

The railways affected the areas through which they passed in several ways. First, they lowered transport costs and thereby stimulated agricultural and pastoral activities, thus playing a part similar to that of railways in other parts of the world; secondly, they stimulated the development of new railway-orientated centres. De Aar at the junction of the Cape Town and Port Elizabeth lines, for example, established in 1884, possessed 1,201 inhabitants seven years later. Other junctions and railway yards appeared as small towns sprang up, entirely dependent upon the railway, and divorced from the surrounding rural communities. On a smaller scale, watering places became halts, sometimes developing other facilities, like Matjiesfontein where catering amenities were provided in the days before the dining-car. On a yet smaller scale platelayers' cottages were spaced every five miles, to facilitate regular inspection of the line.[34] Thirdly, the railways stimulated urban growth, where existing towns were by-passed, and new centres were established as subsidiary points on the railway, for transhipment of produce bound for the town. Thus Fraserburg Road grew as an out-station for Fraserburg, Montagu Road (Touws River) as an out-station for Montagu; and so forth. In most cases inertia of an existing town was sufficient to enable it to survive competition, but towns which did succeed in attracting the railway had a distinct advantage over their neighbours, particularly once rural decline set in.

In contrast to the leisurely pace of railway development prior to

1886, that following the discovery of the Witwatersrand goldfields was rapid. They provided a source of revenue and trade which the railway companies of the Cape Colony and Natal immediately sought to exploit. In addition, the Transvaal government wished to have a line to Lourenco Marques in Mocambique, independent of British control.[35] Involved negotiations on railway tariffs followed, and the whole economic fabric of southern Africa was considered.[36] The result was the construction of lines from the Cape and Natal ports and Lourenco Marques, in the period 1887–95, and the first train from Cape Town entered Johannesburg in 1892. Even the Orange Free State benefited from the desire of the Cape Government Railways to reach Johannesburg. In 1881 a Commission had recommended the construction of a line from Colesberg to Bloemfontein, but the sum involved (£716,000) was equivalent to the entire revenue of the state for the six previous years, and the scheme had to be dropped.[37] Eight years later the Cape government undertook its construction.

The railway boom continued with the penetration of areas still further north. The concept of the Cape to Cairo Railway seized the imagination of empire builders in the 1890s. The British South Africa Company built lines north from Kimberley to Bulawayo (completed in 1897), and from Beira, on the coast of Mocambique, to Salisbury (completed in 1899). Links between Bulawayo and Salisbury and Victoria Falls were started immediately and completed in 1902 and 1904 respectively (Fig 61). The Congo border was reached in 1909. Where possible, lines were constructed to link mining areas: thus the line between Salisbury and Bulawayo was built not along the watershed, but through the main mining centres of the period. Other lines were specially built to exploit mineral deposits, such as the line which ran from Pretoria to the northern Transvaal, for the copper deposits (1899). Indeed, the first line on the Witwatersrand had similarly been constructed to transport coal from Boksburg to the mines. It was known as the Rand Steam Tram, owing to parliamentary opposition to trains as such![38]

The end of the Anglo-Boer War (1902) led to a further boom in railway construction, which lasted, with fluctuations, until World War 1. In the years 1901–15 an average of over 400 miles of line was opened each year, more than doubling the total length of track in the subcontinent. In this period a major programme of branch-line construction was undertaken to link mines, towns, irrigation schemes and developing agricultural regions to the main-line system, while in much of the area south of the Witwatersrand, lines were

Fig 61   Train crossing the Victoria Falls Bridge. The railways helped to break down the isolation of large parts of the interior of the subcontinent, by providing cheap, rapid transport of men and materials.

built to link up established agricultural zones. To the north a programme of construction to facilitate development was embarked
upon. To reduce costs, 2ft-gauge lines were introduced for some of
the minor branch lines in the Cape and Natal.[39]

The Coal-Mining Industry

The rapid industrial development of southern Africa in the second
half of the nineteenth century led to a demand for coal on a vastly
increased scale. Imports from England were not the solution to the
problem of power, nor was the increased use of timber as a fuel.
Coal had been discovered in Natal in 1840, and in the north-eastern
Cape Colony in 1859. Collieries were started near Molteno (eastern
Cape) in 1864, but the coal was of poor quality and the area was
relatively inaccessible to the diamond fields. Production was largely, but not exclusively, for local consumption; the railways and
Kimberley used part of the output. Even in the period 1885–94
production was only 35,000 tons per annum. A peak was achieved
between 1899 and 1903, with an average of 200,000 tons per
annum, but thereafter decline set in and in 1913 only 67,481 tons
were produced, largely as a result of high costs.[40]

In Natal, exploitation in the 1880s led to the establishment of the
coalfield in the north of the Colony, and with the arrival of the
railway in 1890 it was possible to exploit the markets first of the
port, and then of the Witwatersrand. Production increased rapidly,
exceeding 1 million tons in 1895, and 5 million tons in 1913. Owing
to the low cost of production, Natal was able to develop an export
market, both as bunkers and cargo.[41] In 1913 this amounted to 2.3
million tons.

The production of coal in the Transvaal and Orange Free State
depended upon the Witwatersrand, and its discovery close to the
Witwatersrand undoubtedly assisted the development of the
gold-mines. Production in this area and along the line of the
Pretoria-Lourenco Marques Railway increased rapidly, reaching
1.9 million tons in 1898 on the eve of the Anglo-Boer War, and 5.2
million tons in 1913. Orange Free State production, in the neigh-
bourhood of the Vaal River, reached 610,000 tons in 1913.

New towns sprang up as colliery centres. In the main they tended
to be specialized, one-industry centres revolving around the mine,
with miners brought in by the companies, largely from Wales and
Scotland. Molteno, with Cyfergat, was the first coal-mining town,
established in 1874. It was planned on South African lines with a

grid of 500 plots, each 300 square feet — small by South African standards (Fig 52). Nevertheless, traditional approaches remained, for each plot owner was entitled to graze his livestock on the commonage.[42] In Natal several new towns were planned around Dundee, on the coalfield. Some, like Glencoe and Dannhauser, developed other functions and became administrative centres, but most remained mine settlements. In general, control over town layouts in Natal was minimal, with irregular mining-camp ground-plans appearing. In the Transvaal greater control was exercised by the imposition of the usual grid pattern, often with the minimal 50 by 50 foot plots.

The Opening of Rhodesia

The colonization of Rhodesia was essentially looked upon as a commercial venture, with the aim of finding the second Rand and the fabled land of Orphir.[43] It was gold rather than farming which attracted the pioneers. Thus it was the towns which were the centre of attraction, and mineral production was for a long time the yardstick by which the entire Rhodesian adventure was measured. Pioneer disappointment, first with Mashonaland, and then with Matabeleland, retarded development until 1907, when the agricultural potential began to be exploited.

The fabled Land of Orphir had attracted much attention in South Africa in the nineteenth century. Henry Hartley found gold on a hunting trip in the 1860s, while Frederick Selous discovered recently abandoned workings. [44] Conjecture was rife, particularly after Carl Mauch's descriptions of Great Zimbabwe were disseminated.[45] King Solomon's Mines were thought to have been in the land north of the Limpopo, and the myth was perpetuated by popular writing.[46] The British South Africa Company's offer of fifteen mining claims to pioneers was a powerful influence in attracting settlers to the new country. Thus in Matabeleland in 1895 the 3,637 Europeans were widely distributed — 1,537 in Bulawayo, 50 in Gwelo Township, 1,800 prospectors dispersed across almost 100,000 square miles, and only 250 on farms.

It was soon noted that the 'Ancients' had exhausted much of the workings, for no major reef was discovered, and deposits were widely scattered. Some 95,000 ounces had been produced by 1900, a far cry from the 7 million ounces dug from the Witwatersrand in its first ten years of existence. However, by the years 1906–13 production was averaging 600,000 ounces, thus making the major con-

tribution to the country's economy (1910 — £2.6 million). Other
minerals were also discovered. Coal at Wankie was of particular
value for the railway system, ending the need for bringing coal from
the south or collecting timber at strategic points along the route.
Although discovered in 1895, full-scale exploitation only began in
1903. In 1913 some 243,000 tons were raised. Minerals such as
asbestos, chrome and copper were also discovered but, although
exploitation began before 1914, production was small. Only
chrome from Selukwe (1913 — 63,000 tons) achieved any scale,
giving rise to a mining settlement of over 1,000 persons in 1911.

The planning of the Rhodesian towns owed a great deal to southern African experience and practice (Fig 62). Although the British
South Africa Company was intent on the rapid development of its
territories, an attempt was made to return to the more generous
planning of the first part of the century, rather than to that of the
meaner mining towns of the latter half. Major roads were constructed, 100–150 feet wide: indeed, roads took up nearly half the
area of most of the main Rhodesian towns, for road-width was
designed to allow two span of oxen to turn in the street at the same
time.[47]

The two main towns were large by the standards of new non-
mining foundations. In the plans of 1896, Salisbury contained 2,548
plots and Bulawayo 1,441. The other towns were smaller, ranging
from Umtali (1,179 plots) to Gwanda (317 plots).[48] The standard
grid pattern of streets was employed, but it was modified in the case
of Salisbury, where the line of the Kopje hill was taken for the
layout of streets in the commercial area. The administrative sector
of the town was laid out in another grid, which intersected the first at
an angle of 16°, giving rise to one of the most awkward town plans in
southern Africa (Fig 62). Bulawayo was split into two halves (business and residential sectors) by a stream, but the grid pattern of the
two linked up across the town gardens. The other towns adhered
more consistently to the regular grid. Plot sizes varied from the
standard 1/8-acre in the commercial areas to a special ½-acre in the
residential quarter of Salisbury and 1½ acres in Bulawayo (Fig 62).
In addition, substantial reserves were set aside for market places,
gardens, schools, hospitals, and government buildings. The scale of
the reserves was unparalleled in southern Africa: in Salisbury
approximately 100 acres were reserved, and in Bulawayo approximately 250 acres, mostly for parks and gardens.

Substantial townlands were assigned to the Rhodesian towns.
The first five foundations received an average of 21,000 acres

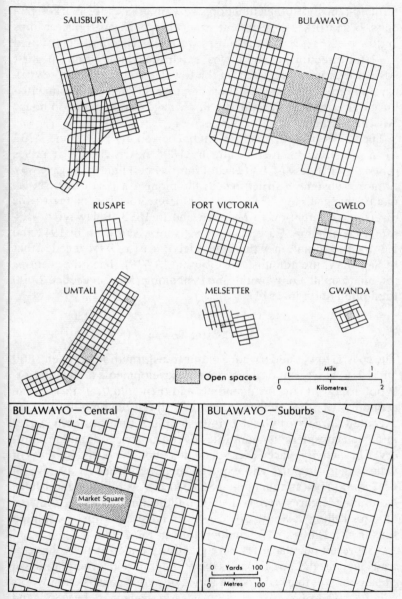

Fig 62   Rhodesian town plans, 1892–1898

apiece, Bulawayo being the largest with 29,000 acres. The townlands not only provided grazing for the citizens' animals but also

fulfilled a host of other functions, serving as sites for market gardens, brickworks, government experimental farms, police camps and race courses.[49] All these uses were extensive and determined the later directions of the towns' expansion. In addition, the first African locations were sited on the townlands, to house those Africans not accommodated by their employers. Thus Harare in Salisbury was established on the site of a village of that name, to house African workers.

The towns grew rapidly in the initial period. By 1894 some 1,733 town plots had been sold, and by 1896 nearly 5,000, at prices generally in excess of £30 each. Primitive buildings soon gave way to more substantial structures, as the pioneer aspect of the settlements changed (Fig 63). Two years later, however, owing to the diversion of attention to Matabeleland in 1893, Bulawayo possessed twice as many Europeans as Salisbury, and even in 1911 the European population of this industrial centre (5,199) exceeded that of Salisbury, the administrative capital (3,479). The other centres remained small. Only Umtali and Penhalonga Mine exceeded 2,000 total population in 1911.

The Coastal Towns

The coastal towns underwent a major transformation between 1860 and 1910, as a result of the economic developments in the interior. Wool, followed later by diamonds and then gold, transformed the economy of the subcontinent. All three commodities were exported, largely to Great Britain, and in return southern Africa imported considerable quantitites of consumer goods and machinery. This activity placed great demands upon the ports. In terms of value, trade (imports and exports) increased from an average of £5.2 million per annum in the 1860s, to £69.9 million in the 1900s. No tonnage figures were collected, but the annual average tonnage of ships calling at South African ports increased from 0.4 million tons in the 1860s to 12.1 million tons in the 1900s.

As a result port facilities were greatly extended as the volume of trade increased. Cape Town, as the premier port in terms of tonnage of shipping, embarked upon a series of major construction works (Fig 64). The open roadstead was clearly inadequate by 1860, and work began on the breakwater and the Alfred Basin, completed in 1870. In 1879 the major outer Victoria Basin, with an area of 67 acres and 2 miles of quay and jetty space, was completed. Vessels with draughts up to 35 feet were now able to enter harbour. Proces-

Fig 63   Pioneer Street, Salisbury, 1892. Pioneer towns in southern Africa often borrowed the building methods and styles of the indigenous in-habitants, until more substantial structures were erected.

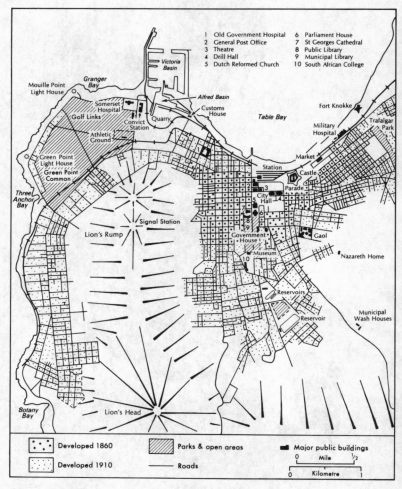

Fig 64   The growth of Cape Town, 1860–1910

sing and storeage plants were added, coal bunkering being the first and most important, owing to the development of steam ships. At first coal was imported from Wales, but, later, local supplies were railed to the coast. An oil-storage farm and chilling chambers for the meat export trade were also established just before 1914.

Equally spectacular developments occurred at Durban. The port suffered from the presence of a bar across the entrance to the Bay of Natal, which often had a depth of less than 6 feet, precluding the entrance of most ocean-going vessels.[50] Programmes designed to improve the situation began in the 1850s.[51] The construction of piers and the use of dredgers had, by the end of the century, reduced the bar problem and established a channel with a 25-foot clearance, but it was only in 1892 that the first ocean-going liner (2,820 tons) entered the Bay. Wharves were constructed along the edge of the Bay; by 1914 they had reached a total length of 2¾ miles.

Problems at the other ports were similarly overcome. Harbour works at Mossel Bay, Port Elizabeth, and East London resulted in considerably greater trade for all three. Intervening ports and prospective sites were bypassed, and places such as Port Beaufort ceased to exist, while others such as Knysna had only limited trade for a few years. The many fishing ports around the western Cape peninsula continued their trade, but Cape Town assumed the dominant role in the fishing industry.

These advances were made possible through the provision of new services. Water presented the towns with the greatest problems, and new supplies were vitally important. In 1860 Cape Town possessed two small reservoirs. New sources of water from Table Mountain were tapped, and major advances were made in 1881 with the construction of new, larger reservoirs above the city. New dams, constructed in the 1890s and 1900s on the top of Table Mountain, effectively ensured the city's supplies. It is worth noting that the first (1897) had a capacity of 225 million gallons, fifteen times that available to the city in 1860. In the 1880s the other coastal towns of Port Elizabeth (1880), Durban (1884) and East London (1885) undertook major water-supply schemes, and thereafter supply and demand were kept reasonably in step although increased domestic use rapidly increased the demand for water.

Urban expansion was assisted by the introduction of mass transport systems. In 1861 Cape Town introduced the first horse-trams on the subcontinent, and with them there began a new era of urban growth.[52] Trams were introduced in 1881 to Durban and Port Elizabeth. Electrification in the 1890s improved the service and made large-scale commuting possible. In addition, the construction of local railway lines and stations enabled urban workers to live further from the centre of town, and a string of new railway villages appeared in the period 1861–1914. Trams and trains also made possible a more spacious style of living in the countryside near the main centres, while the demand for villas on large plots increased with the growing prosperity of the ports and the rising affluence of the middle-class European. Thus the sprawl of the suburbs accelerated.

Growing prosperity also influenced the coastal towns through the emergence of the seaside holiday trade modelled on that of England. It was only in the 1890s that interest in beach holidays was aroused, but the completion of the subcontinent's railway system, together with increased affluence and leisure, resulted in the emergence of the first resorts. The development of distinct beachfront areas, with swimming-pools, hotels and entertainments was encouraged by traders. The pre-World War 1 boom was dramatic: by 1910 some 12,000 persons visited East London by train in the gala season.[53] An increasing number of winter holiday-makers visited Durban, while some 75,000 visited Muizenberg, near Cape Town, in the 1910–11 season.[54]

7

Rural and Urban
Adjustments 1914–1960

THE PERIOD BETWEEN World War 1 and 1960 was one of profound
change in the economy of southern Africa. Whereas before 1914
South Africa was still dependent upon primary industries, particularly agriculture and mining, for nearly half its national income, by
1960 manufacturing was almost as important as the two combined
(Table 12).[1] Mining remained the single most important sector of
the economy until 1943, when it was overtaken for the first time by
manufacturing. World War II had stimulated local production to
the extent of transforming the economy into that of a modern
industrial state. A similar but less significant trend was discernible
in the Rhodesian economy. In 1960, however, agriculture still
accounted for 20.7 per cent of national income, which was approximately an eighth of that of South Africa.

Table 12 SOUTH AFRICA: CONTRIBUTION TO
NATIONAL INCOME, 1911–1960

	Total £ million	Agriculture £ million (%)	Mining £ million (%)	Manufacturing £ million (%)	Commerce £ million (%)
1911	132.9	23.1 (17.4)	36.0 (27.1)	8.9 (6.7)	18.0 (13.5)
1920	243.5	50.0 (20.9)	51.9 (21.3)	26.0 (10.7)	40.9 (16.8)
1930	253.2	35.2 (13.9)	43.8 (17.3)	39.1 (15.4)	36.7 (14.5)
1940	431.3	50.7 (11.8)	98.3 (22.8)	75.6 (17.5)	61.8 (14.3)
1950	1,017.9	133.8 (13.1)	138.3 (13.6)	225.3 (22.1)	153.6 (15.1)
1960	2,255.0	248.0 (11.0)	315.0 (14.0)	525.5 (23.3)	287.5 (12.7)

N.B. Government sources excluded from tabulation, but not total-column

Allied to the substantial development of manufacturing industry
and the host of activities grouped as services was the enormous
growth of the cities. It is significant that there were comparatively
few new cities, as the developing industries were located in existing
centres and tended to reinforce the industrial pattern which had
emerged in the previous decades.[2] In contrast to the fluctuations in
the urban hierarchy in the previous sixty years, the period 1911–60
witnessed little change.[3] The four largest centres remained in the
same relative positions, increasing their share of total population
from 7.4 to 13.7 per cent of that of the subcontinent. In 1960
Johannesburg became southern Africa's first 'million city'.

The drift to the towns assumed substantial dimensions. The
number and proportions of the total living in the urban areas
increased from 1.5 million (20.7 per cent) by 1911 to 8.2 million
(38.8 per cent) in 1960. Whereas the number of urban Europeans
increased from 0.7 million to 2.8 million in the same period, urban
African numbers increased from 0.5 to 4 million in one of the major
migrations in the subcontinent. However, in 1960, whereas four-
fifths of the Europeans were urban-based, less than a third of the
Africans lived in towns. Strenuous efforts were made not only to
provide employment but also to stem the flow of Africans to the
towns, particularly after 1950.

The growth-rate of the European population declined in the
twentieth century. Throughout the nineteenth century the annual
rate of increase between censuses and estimates was between 3 and
5 per cent; after 1904, the rate hovered around 2 per cent. The
decline was due mainly to a slackening of immigration and a lowering of birth-rates associated with urbanization. Significantly, in the
pioneer society of Rhodesia, twentieth-century rates varied from
3.3 to 10.5 per cent per annum, as a result of massive immigration.

A major redistribution of the European population occurred
both between provinces and colonies, and between town and country. Most noticeable was the relative growth of the Transvaal and
the resultant decline of the Cape of Good Hope (Table 13, Fig 65).
Equally significant were the decline of the Orange Free State, which
experienced absolute decline in the 1930s, and the settlement of
Rhodesia. The movement from country to town was substantial. In
1911 some 51.6 per cent of the European population of the subcontinent lived in towns; by 1960, 83.3 per cent did so. In absolute
terms, the number of rural dwellers continued to rise until 1931, but
thereafter it declined, with a loss of 23.9 per cent between 1931 and
1960.

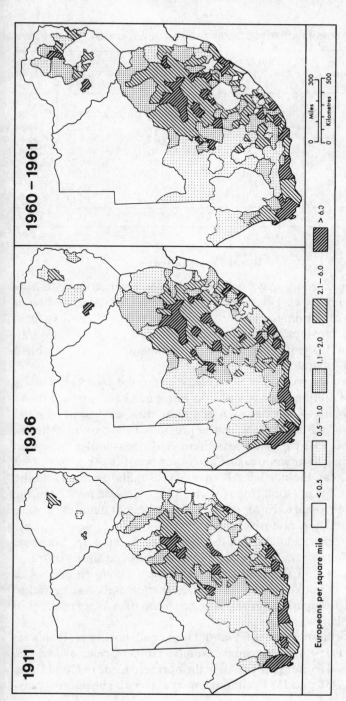

Fig 65   Distribution of European population in southern Africa, 1911–1960

Table 13 EUROPEAN POPULATION OF SOUTHERN AFRICA, 1911–1960

Province, Colony or Protectorate	1911 Total 000 (%)		1936 Total 000 (%)		1960 Total 000 (%)		Increase 1911–60 (%)
Cape of Good Hope	582	(44.7)	791	(38.3)	1,003	(30.2)	77.3
Natal	98	(7.5)	191	(9.2)	340	(10.2)	246.8
Orange Free State	175	(13.4)	201	(9.7)	277	(8.3)	58.0
Transvaal	421	(32.3)	821	(39.8)	1,468	(44.2)	249.2
Rhodesia	24	(1.8)	55	(2.7)	222	(6.7)	838.3
Bechuanaland	2	(0.1)	2	(0.1)	3	(0.1)	87.5
Swaziland	1	(0.1)	3	(0.1)	6	(0.2)	446.5
Basutoland	1	(0.1)	2	(0.1)	2	(0.1)	38.0
TOTAL	1,304 (100.0)		2,066 (100.0)		3,321 (100.0)		154.7

Rural Development

Three major trends may be discerned in the rural economy during the period between 1910 and 1960. They are first, an extension of the area of farming activity; second, an intensification of land useage in previously settled areas; and third, rural decline: this, because of its significance for the development of the subcontinent is treated separately.

The farming frontier was virtually exhausted by 1911. Only a further 44 million acres passed into European hands in the following fifty years — an expansion of a mere fifth, compared with the doubling which took place in the previous half century. Thus in 1960 some 46.2 per cent of southern Africa was under European ownership. The main areas of expansion were in Rhodesia (15.2 million acres), the northern Transvaal (8.7 million acres), and the northern Cape of Good Hope (18.4 million acres). In most cases the areas apportioned to European farms were of poor quality and were mainly used for extensive cattle ranching and, in general, only technical innovation allowed the land to be opened up. Borehole construction, tsetse fly eradication, and improved forms of transport — all aided the final advance of the farming frontier. The frontier was unlike that in Australia, for the desert was barred to European occupation, through the provision of African reserves in Bechuanaland.

The northern Cape of Good Hope and northern Transvaal became cattle-ranching regions. Numbers of European-owned cattle increased fivefold (621,000) in the northern Cape of Good Hope between 1930 and 1960, although increases in the northern Transvaal were less spectacular (304,000). None of these areas, however, was as fully occupied as had been the older parts of the Cape of Good Hope or Orange Free State. Farming areas were discontinuous, separated by African reserves to which European farmers had to adjust, rather than vice versa, as had been the case in the previous century. In Rhodesia much of the new area was similarly opened up for cattle ranching, mainly by large British-financed corporations based on extensive ranches.

Only three areas were planned first and foremost as crop-farming areas — Zululand, the Rhodesian lowveld, and the Karoi District of Rhodesia.[4] The first two were opened to produce sugar, and the third to extend the Rhodesian tobacco area. All three were carefully planned by the governments concerned, with provision for railways and, most important, an efficient agricultural extension service giving advice to the new pioneers. Gone were the days of leaving settlers to their own devices, to fend for themselves as best they might. Agricultural credit facilities were provided by the colonial governments after 1907, and the establishment of the Land and Agricultural Bank of South Africa and the Rhodesian Land Bank in 1912 made substantial amounts of capital, at low interest rates, available for agricultural improvement. In South Africa and Rhodesia agricultural credit rose from £3 million in 1912 to approximately £150 million in 1960. Agricultural schools and experimental farms were first established in the Cape Colony in 1898, and by 1914 there were four experimental stations in South Africa and three in Rhodesia, together with five agricultural schools in South Africa. Three Company central farms in Rhodesia fulfilled a similar function north of the Limpopo. Agricultural extension services to help farmers with their difficulties were also initiated. Co-operatives were authorized in South Africa in 1922, and a series of control boards was established in both Rhodesia and South Africa to regulate production and marketing.[5] Thus by 1960 State intervention in European agriculture in the two countries was considerable, but few of the facilities offered were available to African agriculturalists, or to Swaziland and Bechuanaland, whose European farms remained essentially grazing grounds for farmers living elsewhere.

Experiments before 1910 had demonstrated that intensification of land use was the most important means of increasing production. Indeed the physical volume of agricultural production in South Africa increased by 296 per cent between 1911 and 1960: field crops increased by 379 per cent, and livestock products by 224 per cent. The increase in field crops in terms of value amounted to an increase from £12.7 million in 1911 to £205.2 million in 1960, while livestock products suffered a relative, but not absolute, decline from £16.3 million in 1911 to £188.0 million in 1960. All this was achieved in South Africa on an agricultural area which increased by only a tenth. The value of crop production in South Africa overtook that of livestock production, after the dramatic stock losses of the 1930s and a rapid increase in cultivated area from 6.9 million acres in 1911 to 23.6 million acres in 1960, when it amounted to 10.4 per cent of the European farm area of South Africa (Fig 66).

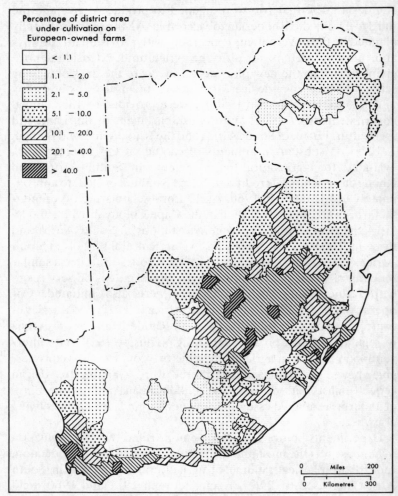

Fig 66   Cultivated areas on European farms, 1960

Maize remained the major crop grown throughout the period of Union, accounting for 33 per cent of the acreage in 1911, and 44.2 per cent in 1960. The maize areas, or 'Maize Triangle', of the southern Transvaal and northern and eastern Orange Free State had emerged as a marked feature by the 1930s. Locally, high proportions of land have been ploughed and planted during the present century, and the transformation is well illustrated in Figure 42. The maize acreage increased from 2.3 million acres in 1911 to 6.4 million acres in 1930, and 10.5 million acres in 1960, but yields remained fairly constant at 0.3–0.4 tons per acre, so that the Triangle was an area of extensive rather than intensive agriculture. The climatic and soil conditions which prevailed in this area of the High Veld allowed for the emergence of the nearest approach to a cereal-growing region. New railway spurs were constructed in the 1910s and 1920s to provide improved access to markets, while the marketing organizations assisted in the development of new strains of maize to be grown in more marginal areas, and to raise yields in those which already existed.

The area under sugar, the staple crop of the Natal coastal belt, was extended but, more particularly, existing areas were used more intensively. The acreage was thus increased from 200,000 acres in the early 1920s to 550,000 acres in 1960, and in terms of production, yields improved so that average productions rose from 163,000 tons in 1920–4 to 995,000 tons in 1956–60. The main concentration remained on the Natal north coast where 41.3 per cent of sugar acreage was to be found in 1960, compared with 36.8 per cent in 1930. Zululand failed to maintain the early expansion of production of the years between 1905 and 1930, with the result that its proportion declined slightly from 38.2 per cent to 34.5 per cent between 1930 and 1960. As a result of large-scale bush clearance the 'Sugar Belt' emerged, and the Natal north coast had 58.2 per cent of its entire area under sugar cane by 1960, the economy being geared to this industry through centralized milling and refining facilities.

The provision of irrigation works resulted in a rapid increase in the production of fruit and wine. The area under fruit trees and vines increased from 114,000 acres in 1911 to 514,000 acres in 1960 (Fig 67). In the same period the value of fresh-fruit production increased by almost fifty times. By 1930 some 865,000 acres of European land were under irrigation, and by 1960 this had been expanded to 1,941,000 acres. Of this a quarter was supplied by major irrigation-board schemes and government water works, the

Fig 67 Mazoe Citrus Estates, Rhodesia, 1960. Large irrigation works enabled new crops to be produced for export. The large citrus estates developed by the British South Africa Company produced a landscape of intensive centralized farming.

twentieth-century irrigation schemes being the successors to the
closer-settlement movement of the pre-Union period. In general
the schemes envisaged were in the interior of the country on the
Transvaal rivers and on the margins of the Cape mountain belt,
where they had been undertaken in the previous century. Small
irrigation farms were particularly popular in the 1930s when they
were seen as a means of overcoming rural and urban poverty in a
'back to the land' movement.

The largest of these schemes was undertaken near Warrenton, in
the northern Cape, where some 90,000 acres were placed under
irrigation and mainly divided into plots of 40–60 acres (Fig 68). At

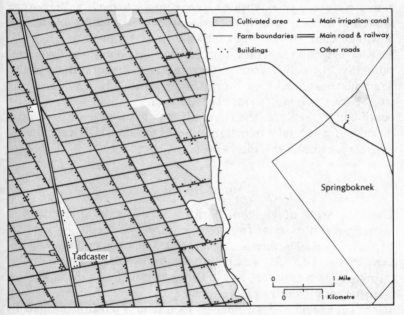

Fig 68   Part of the Vaal-Harts irrigation scheme

first, between 1934 and 1945, most of the settlers were in the 'Poor
White' class, but after World War II ex-servicemen received prefer-
ence. By the mid-1950s some 1,200 settlers and their families had
been placed, and the scheme was complete. Owing to problems of
water supply, soil drainage, and fertility, a rotation system based on
groundnuts, potatoes, peas, and wheat had to be evolved, and took
the place of the planned intensive system based on horticulture and
irrigated pastures for livestock. Hence holdings became larger than
was originally planned. The first major government scheme in the

Transvaal (1918–45) was the Hartebeespoort Dam, which irrigated 38,000 acres, and was planned to accommodate 1,400 settler families on plots of 18–30 acres. This was, however, of only limited success, owing to the small size of the plots. The next scheme, at Loskop on the Oliphants River, although irrigating the same area, sought to solve the problem by accommodating only 500 settler families on plot of 40–60 acres. On both schemes tobacco and wheat were the main objectives, although the development of horticulture and intensive dairying took place later, as the urban markets grew.

Elsewhere few major schemes were undertaken. Most irrigation works were either extensions to existing schemes or they were limited to improving existing farms rather than creating an entirely new landscape, as had been the case in areas north of the Vaal. Smaller irrigation schemes in the northern and eastern Transvaal primarily provided for fruit and vegetable production.[6] By 1960 the Transvaal possessed 7.7 million of South Africa's 12.3 million citrus trees. Nevertheless, in terms of production, the south-western Cape continued to dominate the fruit industry. Thus three districts produced a fifth of total production value, as the vineyards were almost entirely located in the south-western Cape.

Rural Decline

The rural areas of southern Africa were adversely affected by a number of factors in the twentieth century. The decline, which had begun in the 1890s, intensified, and affected much of the subcontinent by the 1930s; it was mainly caused by the inability of the farming system to absorb all the Europeans living on the land. The open-farming frontier of the nineteenth century had provided a safety valve against land hunger: its effective closure resulted in rural poverty.[7]

The Roman-Dutch laws of inheritance, whereby a man's property was divided amongst his heirs, remained the practice after their legal force was withdrawn. Subdivision and joint ownership became ever more common as alternative lands were unobtainable, while increased population pressure led to the emergence of the 'Poor White' problem, which was of major concern to the Union government, and to a lesser extent to that of Rhodesia. In 1932 the Carnegie Commission reported that there were in South Africa 300,000 'poor whites' who were unable to adjust to changing circumstances. Even the odd-shaped farms, the multiple ownership, and the poverty failed to warn the rural community that drastic remedies were needed. The Commission found one elderly man in the Marico District who intended dividing his 52 acres amongst his ten children so that 'each of them will have his own spot to settle on'.[8]

Allied to the poor proprietors were the *trekboers,* who moved about the country with small flocks of sheep or herds of cattle, resting where they might as squatters on other people's farms, their rent a share of the crops or of the livestock increase. Intensification of land use, particularly increased sheep populations, with attendant fencing and the breeding of improved strains, made the squatter and the migrant farmer unwanted, and improved management methods were necessitated by the overgrazing and reduced carrying capacities experienced in areas settled in the previous century.

It was drought, however, that dealt the final blow to a large section of the rural community. The period 1922–33 was particularly severe, although drought conditions became increasingly serious as grazing lands were denuded and water resources were used up. Depression resulted. The gross value of agricultural production in South Africa slumped from £64.7 million in 1928 to £37.4 million in 1933. Equally dramatically, the number of woolled sheep, the basis of the main agricultural export commodity, declined from 43.9 million in 1930 to 30.3 million in 1934, while land values fell by almost a third in the same period.[9] Depression in the pastoral industries continued until World War II.

European depopulation of the rural areas remained one of the dominant features of the period 1911–60. Although the European rural population of South Africa only fell by 15.2 per cent between the two dates, the decline was by no means uniform either in time or space. The highest rural total was reached in 1931, but decline in parts of the country had already set in by 1911. The small stock regions of the Cape and Orange Free State, in particular, suffered sustained and heavy losses of up to 83.6 per cent, and as the rural areas declined, so did the small country towns, usually with a time-lag of twenty years. Four-fifths of the towns of under 2,000 Europeans in 1951 declined in the following decade.

Rural decline in European numbers was not matched by a similar movement in the case of non-Europeans.[10] Between 1921 and 1960 the ratio of Europeans to non-Europeans declined from 1:2.96 to 1:8.54 in the European (ex-African reserve) areas of South Africa. In 1951 there were 600,000 Africans employed on European farms, yet a total of 2,400,000 Africans lived on the farms, often

with their own stock and cultivation areas. A survey in 1958 of part
(5,923 square miles) of the Orange Free State showed that only
75.9 per cent was occupied by Europeans. Proportions for the
north-east Orange Free State and northern Natal were 78.4 and
58.5 per cent respectively. Added to this, a police survey showed
that between 1945 and 1954 some 5,419 farms had been abandoned by Europeans, leaving European and African farms scattered and interspersed (Fig 69).

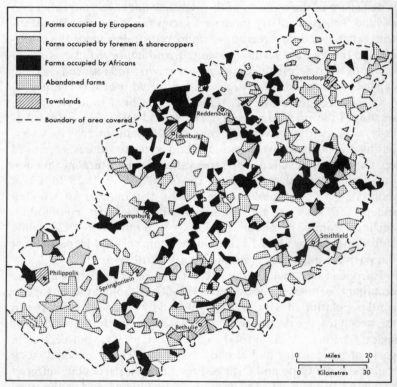

Fig 69   Farm occupation in part of the southern Orange Free State, 1958

Rural depopulation became a highly political issue, as land own-
ership was considered essential to the cultural development of the
White South African nation. Thus the official Commission of
Enquiry (1960) stated:[11]

> In fact, if the Christian civilisation of the White man is to survive in
> South Africa, an economically independent farming community of sterl-
> ing character and fully alive to its task, remains an essential ideal.

Alarm at the increasing 'blackness' of the rural areas, added to the desire to keep farmers on the land, undoubtedly led to substantial aid to the farming community in the form of subsidies, guaranteed prices, tax relief and so forth, but none of these measures was able to stem the flow to the towns.

The Expansion of Mining

Mining continued to play a vital role in the South African and Rhodesian economies in the period between 1910 and 1960, and in both countries gold-mining played the dominant role. Peak production was reached as increasingly difficult ores had to be mined. Gold production in South Africa increased from 7.5 million ounces in 1910 to 14.4 million ounces in 1941, and thereafter declined to 11.2 million ounces in 1947. An earlier decline occurred in Rhodesia, with production decreasing from 0.9 million ounces in 1916 to 0.5 million ounces in 1931. In both countries devaluation stimulated production in the early 1930s and early 1950s. In South Africa, however, a major new goldfield in the northern Orange Free State came into production in the 1950s (Fig 70). The result was a near-doubling of production between 1950 and 1960, reaching 21.4 million ounces in 1960. Gold therefore continued to provide some 80 per cent of mining production by value, and by the end of 1960 some 646 million ounces, worth £4,924 million, had been raised in South Africa.[12]

The Central Witwatersrand remained the principal area of production until 1923.[13] Some production occurred on the west Rand, but after 1910 the Far East Rand developed rapidly and overtook the declining Central Rand, becoming the principal area until the Orange Free State goldfield was fully exploited. In the 1940s the Far West Rand began production, and by the 1950s the Witwatersrand goldfield extended some 60 miles from east to west and 20 miles north to south.[14] The Klerksdorp goldfield, although discovered in 1887, and thereafter worked on a small scale, was only brought into operation in the 1950s. The Orange Free State field was discovered in 1938 and production started in 1952: as it was concealed, it has, unlike the other fields, been developed entirely by large concerns sinking a few major shafts. The shift to large mines tapping high-grade ores was illustrated by the fact that in 1960 five mines produced a quarter of southern African gold.

The goldfields gave rise to some of the most distinctive landscapes in southern Africa (Fig 71). The host of small workings had

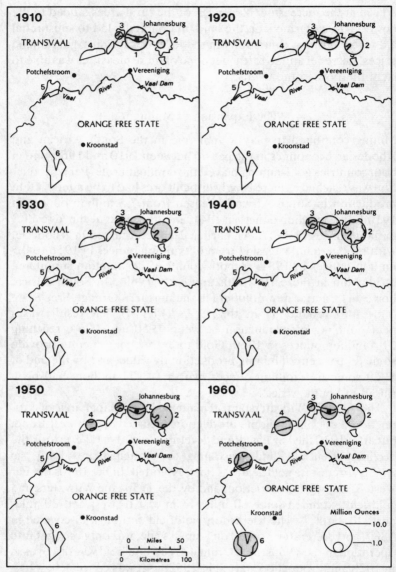

Fig 70　Areal distribution of gold production in South Africa, 1910–1960
1 – Central Witwatersrand, 2 – Far East Rand, 3 – West Rand, 4 – Far West Rand,
5 – Klerksdorp, 6 – Orange Free State

given way to large concerns by 1910, except in Rhodesia, where
small-scale workings were encouraged, and where as late as 1938
there were 1,548 gold producers. Small-scale workings with individual small shafts, or open-cast works, have scarred large stretches

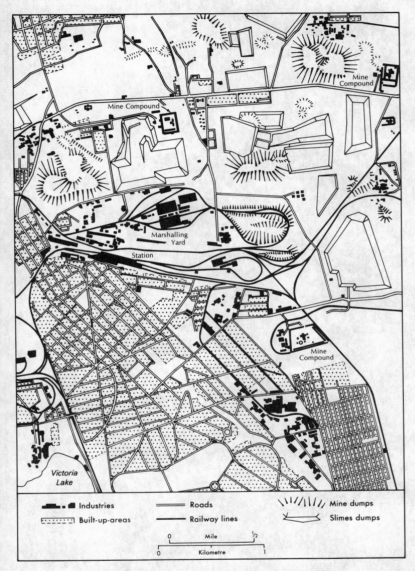

Fig 71   Mining landscape of Germiston, East Witwatersrand, c.1960

of the goldfield regions, particularly in Rhodesia, but it is the large-scale shaft mining, with its associated spoil heaps and slimes dumps, which has predominated (Fig 72). Through their sheer size, the mines influenced the development of a series of new towns and the Witwatersrand conurbation. The numbers employed in

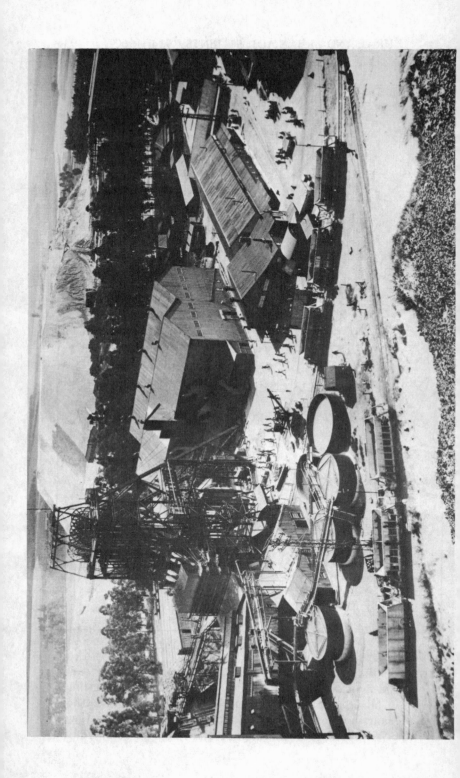

gold-mining remained at approximately 200,000 in the period
1910–30, but rose to nearly 400,000 in 1940. In the next twenty
years they fluctuated within wide margins, but did not again fall
below 300,000. The housing and provision of services for such large
numbers, particularly the migrant African majority, gave rise to
many problems.[15]

The mining companies built self-contained towns for their African and European staffs, with their own facilities, and thus prevented the emergence of the urban slums associated with the permanent drift to the towns. The majority of the African unskilled
migrant labourers were housed in hostels, which formed vast compounds, and in some of the later mines, particularly on the Orange
Free State fields, family accommodation for Africans was provided
to induce the more skilled African workers to remain at the mines.
The newer, larger mines were more spaciously laid out, with the
result that the Orange Free State and Far West Rand gold-mining
regions contrast in mining and urban landscapes with the older
areas. Thus Welkom, in the Orange Free State fields, was planned
and built according to the town-planning concepts of the late 1940s
(Fig 73).[16]

Coal-mining developed rapidly, as a result of the opening of new
fields and increased exploitation of existing fields.[17] Production
increased more than sixfold between 1910 and 1960 (Table 14).
Unlike the gold-mining centres, few of the coal towns gave rise to
any substantial settlement, as coal was exported to other parts of the
subcontinent. The presence of large reserves of easily exploitable
coal undoubtedly assisted in the industrial development of both
South Africa and Rhodesia.

Table 14 COAL PRODUCTION IN SOUTHERN AFRICA 1910–1960

Year	Transvaal	Natal	Orange Free State	Cape	Rhodesia	Total
			(millions of tons)			
1910	4.0	2.6	0.5	0.1	0.2	7.3
1920	7.2	3.3	1.0	—	0.6	12.1
1930	7.0	3.5	1.1	—	1.0	12.6
1940	13.1	4.4	1.5	—	1.4	20.3
1950	20.9	5.5	3.7	—	2.3	32.3
1960	26.2	6.2	9.2	—	3.9	45.4

In addition to gold, coal and diamonds, other metals and minerals

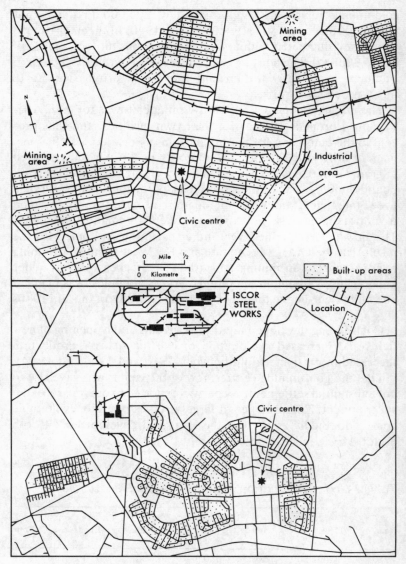

Fig 73 Town plans of Welkom and Vanderbijlpark, c.1960

were exploited throughout southern Africa, but they contributed, at most, only 15 per cent to the value of mining output between 1914 and 1960. Locally, asbestos, chrome and iron ore were of considerable significance — as for example in Swaziland, where in 1960 asbestos accounted for approximately half the value of the country's exports.

Manufacturing Industry

The development of manufacturing industry in southern Africa received considerable stimulus during World War I, as a result of the need to find import substitutes. After 1924 the South African coalition government attempted to improve the lot of the poor whites by providing industrial employment. In 1925 legislation extended protection to local industries, which thereafter enjoyed a high measure of assistance.[18] Owing to the restricted size of the market, the first new factories were largely concerned with producing consumer goods from imported raw materials and semi-finished products, rather than with processing local raw materials.

Despite economic fluctuations associated with the depression and the devaluation of the Pound, manufacturing industry expanded rapidly until World War II (Table 15).[19] The chief stimulus came with World War II, when import substitution and munitions production led to the establishment of major new branches of industry. During the war (1939–45), the net value of output increased in South Africa by 116 per cent. After the war, manufacturing industry made major advances, the contribution to the South African national income increasing from £140 million in 1946 to £529 million in 1960. In the same period Rhodesian production increased from £6.2 million to £50.6 million. Employment rose rapidly, almost doubling between 1945 and 1955.[20] Unfortunately the statistical basis of the industrial censuses in South Africa was changed in the years 1955–8, thereby ending comparability of figures.

Table 15 MANUFACTURING INDUSTRY IN SOUTH AFRICA 1924–1955

	1924-5	1938-9	1944-5	1954-5
Number of establishments	6,009	8,614	9,316	13,725
Number of workers 000 Total	115	236	361	653
(European)	(41)	(93)	(112)	(184)
(Non-European)	(74)	(143)	(249)	(469)
Net value of output (£million)	25	64	138	462
Value of metal products and machinery (£m)	4.1	16.5	27.9	172.0
Value of food beverages and tobacco (£m)	7.9	16.1	30.7	77.3
Value of textiles and clothing (£m)	2.0	7.2	20.2	61.4
Value of chemicals (£m)	3.0	6.1	12.4	47.0

The most important sector, in terms of growth, by the World War II period, was that of metal products and engineering. Sustained growth here was in part the result of direct government assistance and guidance which was made possible through substantial revenues obtained from the mining industry.[21]

Basic to the development of industrialization in southern Africa was the establishment of an iron and steel industry. Between 1911 and 1916, four blast furnaces were established in the Transvaal, three on the Witwatersrand and one at Vereeniging on the Vaal River.[22] All were dependent on the mining industry. In 1926 the industry was extended to Newcastle in Natal, based on the coal-fields, and the location for both internal and coastal markets. In an effort to reduce steel imports, the government, in 1928, established the South African Iron and Steel Corporation (ISCOR) works at Pretoria. The plant was based on coal from the eastern Transvaal, and high-grade iron ores from the north-western Transvaal. Undoubtedly this gave a substantial boost to Pretoria, which doubled its European population between 1931 and 1946.

Expansion in production was such that by World War II there was need for additional capacity, and a new site at Vanderbijlpark near Vereeniging was selected in 1942, as providing room for considerable expansion and unlimited water supply, both of which were lacking in the capital. A new town was laid out and by 1960 contained over 41,000 inhabitants (Fig 73).

In Southern Rhodesia an iron and steel works was begun in 1948, to supply both the Rhodesias. As in the case of the interior works of South Africa, isolation from the ports benefited the establishment and expansion of the industry. A railway rating policy, discouraging imports destined for the interior and encouraging trade between internal centres, helped to overcome the relatively high cost of the southern African product.[23]

Agricultural food-processing industries were the earliest to appear, and in 1924 this group accounted for no less than 32.2 per cent of the value of the net output of all manufacturing industries, and employed some 32,400 persons. Output continued to rise rapidly until 1960, but at a slower rate than that of other branches of manufacturing industry. Thus by the latter year, production amounted to £102.5 million (19.4 per cent of the total) with 117,000 employed.

The textile industry provided one of the earliest stages in industrialization. The market is large, and the work involved is relatively simple, and again expansion was rapid, with production increasing in

net value from £2.0 million to £73.0 million in the period 1925–60, and employment from 12,800 to 114,400. However, the industry remained in its infancy, and South African production accounted for only a little over one-third of internal consumption.

The chemical industry also gave a major area of expansion, arising out of the initial need for explosives in the mining industry. Production increased from £3.0 million in 1925 to £62.5 million in 1960. Developments in explosives, agricultural fertilizers, industrial chemicals and petroleum were substantial. It is of particular interest that the period after World War II witnessed the development of a major oil-from-coal plant by the South African Coal, Oil and Gas Corporation (SASOL) at Sasolburg, where coal was mined and processed into a wide range of chemical products, of which petrol is the most important. A new town was laid out, and by 1960 it had 11,890 inhabitants. In 1960, Sasolburg alone of the twenty-six largest manufacturing centres could be regarded as a 'one-industry town' with six-sevenths of manufacturing employment in petroleum products.[24]

Apart from industries tied to their sources of materials, industrial location in South Africa was highly concentrated into four major metropolitan regions. The southern Transvaal represented the largest concentration of population and basic industry in southern Africa, and therefore the most desirable location for many industries in the subcontinent.[25] The other three regions were the traditional port locations. The tendency throughout the period was for the inland location to expand at the expense of the coastal sites, and the relative decline of the western Cape was particularly striking in this respect (Table 16).[26]

Concentration on the southern Transvaal contributed to the rapid growth of population in the Witwatersrand area, as this was regarded as the most likely region for employment, and new industrial estates were laid out on the margins of most major cities to attract industries. The deliberate planning of separate industrial areas was a new phenomenon, and it was not achieved on any scale until the early 1940s.[27] Thus the older industrial areas, like those in Europe, exhibit a mixture of factories, houses and shops, while the newer industrial estates, such as Isando near Johannesburg, introduced a fresh concept in the separation of work and residence which, as planning legislation developed, was increasingly applied to older industrial areas.

The fortunes of other areas were more varied. While Durban maintained its relative position, the western Cape, which was

Table 16 OUTPUT AND EMPLOYMENT OF INDUSTRIAL REGIONS
AS PERCENTAGE OF THE SOUTH AFRICAN TOTAL, 1916/17–1960/61

	1916–17		1928–9		1938–9		1949–50		1960–61	
	Net output	Employment	Net output	Employment	Net output	Employment	Net output	Employment	Net output	Employment
S. Transvaal	37.4	28.2	34.7	34.1	44.0	43.9	45.6	44.1	46.8	45.3
Western Cape	22.1	20.9	22.4	19.6	18.6	16.5	17.1	15.8	16.8	16.2
Durban	11.7	11.1	11.6	11.5	12.2	10.9	12.3	11.1	11.7	11.5
Port Elizabeth	3.1	3.4	5.8	5.0	5.7	4.6	7.6	5.8	8.4	6.6
Remainder	25.7	36.4	25.6	30.0	19.5	24.7	17.4	23.2	16.3	20.4
TOTAL	100.0	100.0	100.1	100.2	100.0	100.1	100.0	100.0	100.0	100.0

1960–1 figures estimated based on published statistics, with allowance for motor car industry.

peripheral in the space economy of southern Africa, experienced rapid decline. Port Elizabeth, through the location of car-assembly plants in the 1920s, experienced the most spectacular rise of all. Between 1920 and 1960, the industry stimulated a higher rate of employment growth in the region than elsewhere in the country — 5.4 per cent per annum, compared with 5 per cent per annum in the southern Transvaal.[28]

In Rhodesia, too, manufacturing industry was, by 1960, highly localized in Salisbury (49 per cent of output) and Bulawayo (28.5 per cent). However, the small size of the Rhodesian market restricted the range of products in the pre-U.D.I. period. Thus food, beverages and clothing amounted to 40 per cent of all manufacturing output and 45.6 per cent of employment. In this respect Rhodesian industry reflected that of smaller South African centres, where employment in these products remained relatively more important.[29]

Urban Growth

Urban growth between 1911 and 1960 was very rapid, and comparatively uncontrolled. The numbers of persons living in the urban areas increased at an ever-accelerating pace, and in time the small nineteenth-century town gave way to the sprawling twentieth-century agglomeration, based on mass transportation and cheap land. In southern Africa an added factor was the urbanization of the African and Coloured populations, with the result that the urban areas of the subcontinent accommodated over five times as many people in 1960 as they had in 1911.

Town planners hesitated to develop a coherent policy towards the influx of large numbers of Africans and Coloureds into the urban areas. The scale of movement was not realized, neither was its permanence. Thus, although areas were set aside for 'locations' where Africans could live, no consistent policy was pursued; only reactions to successive crises of epidemics and crime. Urban slums appeared with the mining settlements, but they were generally small and restricted. Some municipal and private housing was provided for urban workers to prevent the situation becoming unmanageable.

Housing construction ceased in 1939 for the duration of the war, but the drift to the towns assumed record proportions as a result of the massive development of manufacturing industry under the impetus of wartime conditions. Thus in the period 1936–46, an

additional 1¼ million people, half of them Africans, were housed in
the cities. Little provision was made for the new urban dwellers,
either during or immediately after the war. Towns became over-
crowded, and new slum shanties appeared on the edge of the cities
(Fig 74). The magnitude of the problem may be gauged from the
fact that in 1951 there was a shortage of 167,000 housing units for
urban Africans, who by then numbered twice the total of fifteen
years previously.[30]

The slum settlements remained a noticeable feature of the cities
until the 1960s, but instead of increasing in size, as they had in the
1940s, resolute government action led to their gradual clearance. In
the ten-year period 1950–60, some 123,000 new houses for Africans were built by the government, and approximately another
50,000 by local authorities (Fig 75). Government expenditure on
housing and the provision of new services, particularly transport,
was estimated at £100 million in this period.[31] Clearly a scheme of
this magnitude, resulting in the creation of new cities, had a remarkable impact upon the urban landscape of South Africa (Fig 76).

The largest creation was the establishment of Soweto in the
Johannesburg district. The initial chaotic conditions and growth of
the African locations ceased in 1904, when bubonic plague led to
the clearance of the old locations and the construction of a new one
some 12 miles from the city centre. However, municipal housing
was slow in construction and usually the bare sites were provided,
often resulting in the erection of housing estates of a very insanitary
nature. By 1921 only 227 municipal houses and 1,688 single-quarter
barracks had been built. The Witwatersrand cities relied upon the
mines to house their own workers and upon house servants being
accommodated on their employers' properties. Housing schemes
for others who came in search of work were totally inadequate. A
policy of *laissez-faire* resulted in appalling conditions. Thus in
Sophiatown as many as 300 people were accommodated in sixty
back-to-back rooms, on a ⅛-acre plot. In 1948 it was estimated that
there were 50,000 African families living in shanty conditions in
Johannesburg and its surroundings. Municipal housing schemes,
which in 1946 had reached 9,691 houses and 9,141 hostel places,
were rapidly expanded to 51,714 houses and 24,310 hostel places
by 1960. The total cost was of the order of £20 million.[32]

Similar programmes were undertaken in other major South African cities. Shanty towns with as many as fifty houses to the acre were
replaced by new towns to house the African urban population.[33]
The main effort resulted in vastly extended townships with schools,

Fig 74 Maroka Township, Transvaal, c.1950. The rapid urbanization of the African population resulted in the erection of shanty townships, as the government, both national and local, was unprepared for the influx of so many people.

Fig 75 Jabavu Township, Transvaal, c.1960. Massive government housing schemes for Africans led to the creation of new cities throughout South Africa in the 1950's The results were monotonous (middle), but a vast improvement over the shanties (foreground).

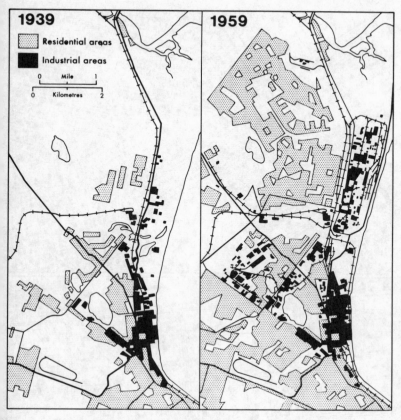

Fig 76   Port Elizabeth, northward expansion, 1939–1959

churches, open spaces and other amenities, but a general lack of local shopping facilities and independent employment: they were essentially satellite towns. Densities of approximately fifteen houses per acre were general, and may be compared with those of British new towns. However, comparison was usually made with European suburbs, built on more generous proportions of less than eight houses per acre. The result in the African towns was generally a monotonous landscape, with little variation (Fig 77).

The rehousing of the African population was part of the South African government's over-all policy of segregation under the Group Areas Act.[34] Implementation of residential segregation in urban areas was the aim of the government, and it was vigorously pursued.[35] Oddly, the results looked little different from those in the other countries of southern Africa, where class was the criterion of

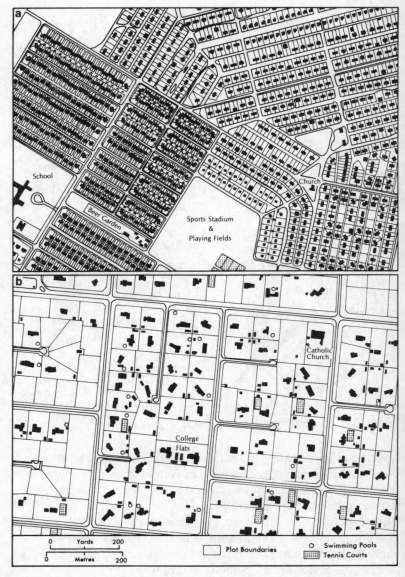

Fig 77   Contrasting town layouts in Salisbury, a. Harare, b. Mount Pleasant

township layout. Rehousing of Africans in South Africa, neccessi-
tated by prevailing slum conditions, enabled segregation to be
achieved more rapidly than was the case with Coloured and Asian

communities who were better housed and residentially more integrated with the Europeans. The magnitude of the shift in population may be shown by Fair and Shaffer's 'index of dislocation', which indicated that there were 512,000 'displacements' between 1951 and 1960, as a result of the operation of the Group Areas Act.[36] Of these 383,000 were Africans. Cape Town and Johannesburg were the scenes of the greatest changes. Allied to this major reorganization was an attempt to stem the flow of Africans to the urban areas by placing restrictions on the movements of those without jobs to go to.

The Rural-Urban Fringe

If the main movement was from the rural areas to the towns, there was a significant return flow, leading to large-scale small-holding development. The marked difference between rural and urban land values in southern Africa encouraged the wholesale division of land around the main cities into small-holdings of under 60 acres in extent. By 1955 there were some 87,200 such holdings in South Africa, of which nearly two-thirds were to be found in the Transvaal.[37] In addition there were some 2,700 small-holdings in the Cape Province classed as townships, so that in all it was estimated that there were probably 90,000 small-holdings in South Africa, covering a million acres.[38]

Small-holding development was essentially a phenomenon of the motor-transport age following World War I, although its origins were earlier. In the Transvaal the republican government had provided small rural plots for citizens, to stem the drift to the towns after the rinderpest outbreak of 1896 and the idea of planned agricultural holdings continued thereafter. By 1955 there were 34,437 holdings on 416 schemes in the Transvaal. Half the holdings were less than 5 acres, and half the schemes contained less than fifty holdings.

The major area of small-holdings (including agricultural holdings) in South Africa was the Pretoria-Witwatersrand area. There were three main periods of subdivision, closely associated with the economic development of the subcontinent. The first, after World War I, reached a peak in 1922, when 1,845 holdings were approved in one year; the second was immediately before World War II, with a peak in 1936, when 2,016 holdings were established; the third was from 1945 to 1954, when over 1,000 holdings were established each year.[39] The rate at which land was being subdivided, not only in the

Transvaal but also in Natal, led to action on the subject, for few of the purchasers of small-holdings were farmers: the majority were town-dwellers who preferred rural living conditions, with pleasanter surroundings, lower rates and a healthier environment, than those in the cities. Many small-holdings outside the Orange Free State were purchased as speculative investments and left undeveloped.

Controls on the rate of subdivision were minimal until the 1950s. Transvaal legislation, indeed, assisted subdivision, by reducing survey costs. Only the Orange Free State limited the numbers established, and control there was extended to such an extent that no small-holdings were allowed on the goldfields.[40] In the other provinces, control came later, in the period 1949–54. Subdivisions, however, could be established if justified on agricultural grounds, but nevertheless the substantial oversupply of small-holdings effectively left a ring of unused or partially used land around most cities.

Small-holdings represent the first stage of urban development (Fig 78). Further subdivision occurred where circumstances permitted, and many small-holdings adjacent to expanding cities were converted into regular suburbs when the townlands had been exhausted. Salisbury, for example, possessed comparatively small townlands for a large city (20,400 acres), and this resulted in the first rural township being laid out in 1898.[41] In 1910 some 2,700 acres had been divided into holdings of less than 50 acres; by 1940 this figure had increased to 14,500 acres. The boom years following World War II, and the establishment of the Federation, led to rapid expansion, with the result that by 1960 there were some 65,700 acres subdivided into plots of less than 50 acres around the capital, and a further 19,200 acres divided into units of 50–125 acres.

In a comparatively short space of time, some areas went through several stages of development in the period from 1910 to 1960, as settlement became closer. Large farms were divided into medium-sized holdings, and the latter, on a piecemeal basis, into townships of various densities. The general small-holding landscape of trees and farm buildings, where the owners could keep animals, and where the lack of services was compensated for by the rural environment, was distinctive. The degree of farming use was generally substantial on those holdings which were occupied. A sample survey in 1955–6 showed that on average at least 3 acres per small-holding were cultivated; this was proportionately higher than in the surrounding farming areas. Small-holdings were temporary, as the pressure to subdivide was strong and, once begun, it undermined

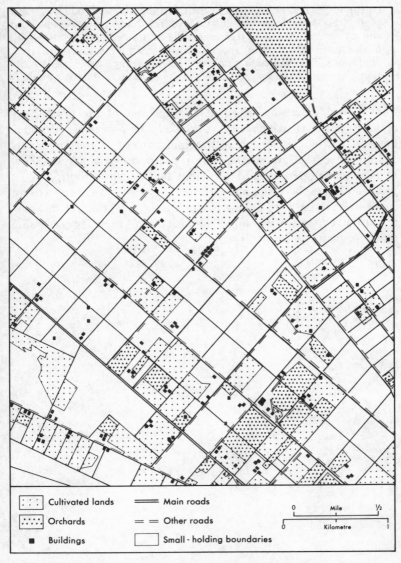

Cultivated lands   Main roads

Orchards   Other roads

Buildings   Small-holding boundaries

0   Mile   ½

0   Kilometre   1

Fig 78   Small-holding landscape, south of Johannesburg, c.1960

the whole concept of rural living. In 1949 the dilemma was expressed by a local association in the Transvaal concerning its members' 20 to 30-acre plots:[42]

It is not large enough to be farmed as an independent source of livelihood, but ideal for persons in other employment who wish to live in rural surroundings and to supplement their earnings by the produce of their plot. If this land were cut up into units of from 5 to 6 acres, persons who cannot maintain the same standards will be attracted to the locality with a consequent lowering of land values and development of semi-urban conditions. The Association does not desire to emphasise class distinctions, but attaches importance to the maintainance of existing conditions.

The gradual extension of small-holdings and of the urban area created patterns which often showed their origins. Private-enterprise urban expansion, as the final stage of urbanization, was usually piecemeal, and was so in most southern African towns. Few housing developers owned sufficient land to plan thousands of plots, and they therefore adapted to the layout of the pre-existing small-holding pattern. Owing to the lack of any effective machinery, urban expansion was more chaotic than in countries possessing effective planning legislation.

8

African and European
Contact to 1960

EUROPEAN SETTLEMENT in southern Africa differed from most contemporary settlements in having to adjust to the presence of a large
body of indigenous peoples; this, in turn, determined much of the
nature of the European colony. The indigenous Africans soon
provided a labour force, upon which, as time went by, the Europeans came increasingly to rely. Attitudes to physical labour
ensured that southern Africa would never become a major colony
of settlement, since the European labouring classes were not
required and were, indeed, discouraged from coming to South
Africa. After 1700, only men of capital were sought from Europe,
and moves to introduce poor European labour, either convicts or
free men, were resisted. In the nineteenth century, even on such
enterprises as the surface diamond and gold workings, which in
other parts of the world were the work of individual diggers, the
Africans soon provided the motive power. Indeed, the presence of a
large labour supply was often given as an attraction to potential
settlers, whether in the nineteenth-century agricultural or the
twentieth-century industrial context.

The Africans, together with the other groups whom the Europeans encountered, played a vital role in the development of southern Africa, although after their initial conquest, they often
remained as shadowy figures for the Europeans. That the reaction
to subordination was not passivity has been well demonstrated in
both Rhodesia and South Africa.[1] Until recently, though, investigations have tended to concentrate on the anthropological aspect of
African life.[2] Tribal customs, dress and economy excited most
attention, while African adaptations to European society have also
been extensively studied.

What does remain essentially vague is the geography of the African past, both pre- and post-conquest. Basic information, such as the numbers and geographical distribution of the African population, is sketchy.[3] Many figures can be regarded as little more than vague estimates, often based on the supposed carrying capacity of the land or, later, on the number of huts estimated in each area. Two examples may serve to illustrate this point. First, the African population of the Transvaal in the late-nineteenth century illustrates the unreliability of statistics. Before 1878 no estimate of any kind may be regarded as approaching reality, but between 1878 and 1891 five figures were produced, which may be compared with the 1904 census return (Table 17).

Table 17 AFRICAN POPULATION OF THE TRANSVAAL 1878–1904

Year	Number	Source
1878	569,304	Transvaal *Blue Book* 1878
1879	774,930	Transvaal *Blue Book* 1879
1880	773,700	Report of the Commission on the settlement of the Transvaal Territory, 1881, P.R.O. CO 291.18.1
1886	299,848	*Jeppe's Almanac*, 1889
1891	649,560	*South African State Almanac for 1893*
1904	1,057,275	Transvaal *Census of the Transvaal and Swaziland*, 1904

Secondly, even when figures were reasonably well known as a result of properly conducted censuses, classification presented problems. Thus in the Cape of Good Hope the number of Hottentots returned at the five censuses of 1865, 1875, 1891, 1904, and 1911 were, rounded to the nearest thousand, 82, 99, 43, 86 and 27 respectively.[4] Nor is the lack of accuracy restricted to the nineteenth century and before. Problems of enumeration persist today. As late as 1961 Rhodesia published its African population figures to the nearest ten, and after that there was some hesitancy, as each successive census discovered substantially more people than had been expected. Thus statistical accounts of the general distribution of population are open to considerable error.

Error persists when the African economy is considered. Until recently, statistics on production and trade are either intelligent guesswork on the part of the statisticians, or they are absent altogether. Livestock numbers are notoriously difficult to estimate, and are liable to violent fluctuation according to disease, drought and war. The prosperity of many African societies prior to the arrival of European settlers, based as it usually was on livestock and crop raising, cannot be statistically examined, and as yet little indirect investigation has taken place.

In establishing what the Africans accomplished and what impact they made upon the landscape before documentation, there is the utmost dispute. Rhodesia contains a large number of stone ruins and elaborate hill terracing, including the large ruins of Great Zimbabwe. The stone-builders appear to have been active until the early nineteenth century in the Wankie area of Rhodesia and the northern Transvaal, although the main constructions are several centuries older.[5] However, no completely satisfactory explanation of either the origin or the purpose of the ruins has been put forward, and proponents of indigenous origin have vied with those seeking an external influence.[6] Furthermore, the vast gold-workings undertaken by the 'Ancients', including shaft mining, suggest not only considerable technical knowledge, but also substantial trade. Such activity had ceased by the time the Europeans reached the areas concerned, although legend of it survived, and drove many men on to the fabled goldfields.

In the light of statistical inaccuracies and lack of certainty during the historical period, even on such important elements as the Zimbabwe culture, historical geography of the pre-European era and for the African areas has, until the present century, been largely neglected. Undoubtedly through archeological investigation and a study of the oral traditions of the African people, many of the gaps in our knowledge may be filled in. What follows must be regarded as highly tentative, orientated towards the partition of the subcontinent between the European settlers and its indigenous inhabitants.

The First European Contacts

The first indigenous peoples whom the early voyagers and settlers encountered were the Hottentots and the Bushmen, who were nomadic pastoralists. They occupied the coastal belt from South West Africa to the eastern Cape, and the interior as far as the Kalahari Desert. The population was sparse and grouped into small clans, who built temporary quarters and moved on as the seasons proceeded.

Hottentot contact with the Europeans in the south-western Cape effectively changed the local economy when traditional seasonal grazing lands were appropriated by the Dutch. Disease, particularly the smallpox epidemics of 1713, 1735, and 1767, decimated the approximately 200,000 Hottentots thought to have been living in the Cape Colony in 1652.[7] The majority of those remaining were gradually displaced by frontier farmers; their cattle were seized or killed by Europeans, Africans and Bushmen, until they were finally reduced to working for the European farmers. Remarkably, there was little resistance to European encroachments. By contrast, the Bushmen resisted the Europeans, who interfered with the free range of game animals, but they were slowly driven back to the Kalahari Desert and ceased to constitute a danger to settlement, after the widespread use of firearms by both Africans and Europeans in the nineteenth century.

The Hottentot population gradually merged with the Coloured peoples, descended from mixed marriages, freed slaves, and other non-Europeans settling in the Cape Colony. The majority were content to work for the European farmer, but two other options were open, and these influenced the settlement of the subcontinent. The first was to seek refuge at a mission station. In the first half of the nineteenth century, many of the mission stations for Hottentots and Coloureds were extended.[8] A number was established near the colonial frontier, and experienced a more chequered career than those such as Genadendal in the more settled West. The largest settlement was established in 1829 by the London Missionary Society on the Kat River on the eastern frontier.[9] Some 150,000 acres of land, including irrigable valley bottoms, were set aside for Coloureds and Hottentots. Growth was rapid, and by 1830 there were 900 inhabitants in the settlement, 2,114 in 1835, and 6,000 in 1849. Unfortunately a large number joined the Xhosa in the Frontier War of 1851 and were dispossessed, their lands being thrown open to European settlement. Other missionary refuges had similar problems. For example at Carnarvon some 200,000 acres were set aside for Hottentots in 1839, before European settlement was of any significance in the area.[10] However, the granting of individual title to the Hottentots in 1882 proved to be disastrous, as in the following fifty years they sold the land to Europeans.

The second alternative to working for European farmers was to retreat before them. Such an alternative was limited, however, by the presence of sedentary Africans to the east of the Colony, and by the desert to the north. One of the scattered Hottentot clans was nevertheless able to leave a major mark upon the development of southern Africa — the Griquas. The Griquas, who had various origins, established a series of states north of the Orange River at the beginning of the nineteenth century. They survived both the destruction of the African tribal wars and the intitial thrust of the European colonists in the 1820s and 1830s respectively, and in the lands adjacent to the Orange River they established the rudiments of ordered government, pursuing an economy little different from that of the European frontiersmen — cattle-herding on a semi-subsistence basis. Under the influence of the missionary societies the first towns north of the Orange River were established at Griquatown in 1804 and Philippolis in 1825. In the latter year there were approximately 5,000 Griquas in the area.[11]

The arrival of the Europeans in ever-increasing numbers disturbed the political economy of the Griquas, for they granted leases to European farmers and thereby alienated large tracts of land in the Philippolis area. As a result of political changes in the area north of the Orange River in the period 1854–9, the Griquas lost much of their land and finally in 1861–2, half the Griqua nation moved to Griqualand East on the Cape Colony-Natal border, where Kokstad was founded. The other half remained in Griqualand West, but after the diamond rush of 1870 they were effectively brought under British control. In both Griqualands, the Griquas sold their lands piecemeal to Europeans, until their status differed little from those who had stayed in the Cape Colony.

The Africans

If European contact was overwhelming to the Hottentots and Bushmen, the meeting of the Europeans and sedentary Africans was on a more equal footing. Beyond the area occupied by the Hottentots and Bushmen, more settled and organized Bantu-speaking Africans formed a barrier to European colonization. The Africans were not homogeneous, but included several major groupings, of which the Nguni, Sotho and Shona were the most important.[12]

The Nguni peoples, whom the Europeans met first, inhabited the coastal belt from the Fish River to the southern Transvaal, with outliers in the northern Transvaal and Rhodesia. Two of their dialects, Xhosa and Zulu, have been stabilized, although Swazi and Ndebele show variants of Zulu. In 1960 there were approximately 7.2 million Nguni-speakers in southern Africa. Initial European observation suggests that they were densely settled, and well organized into villages and permanent settlements of up to 2,000 inhabitants (Fig 79). They were, furthermore, cultivators, as well as herdsmen and hunters. Although far more than the Hottentots,

Fig 79 Matabele Kraal, c.1895. Distinctive African rural settlement patterns persisted in the early stages of European penetration. The Matabele kraal was centred on the cattle enclosure, which was surrounded by the dwellings and storage huts, with the cultivated fields in the background.

they were capable of rapid movement, particularly under Shaka Zulu during the period of warfare, when whole tribes moved on a subcontinental scale. Nevertheless, movement in general was slow, as outward colonization of new lands proceeded.

The Sotho peoples inhabited the interior plateaux between the Orange and Limpopo Rivers. Their economy was also based on cultivation and herding, but with the accent strongly on herding for economic purposes. Their distribution was therefore closely related to the absence of the tsetse fly, which attacked their cattle, thereby denying them access to the Limpopo valley and the Transvaal lowveld. The Sotho lived in larger settlements than the Nguni, with as many as 10,000 or even 20,000 persons in the major villages. Except in Botswana, this organization was shattered in the 1820s, as a result of large-scale warfare, which reduced the economy to ruins. In Lesotho, recovery took place on the basis of cultivation in smaller villages.

The Shona-Venda peoples of the northern Transvaal and Rhodesia had an economy based on cultivation and hunting, but without the large herds which characterized the Nguni and Sotho economies. They were engaged in mining and smelting, as apparently were some of the northern Sotho, and they also built extensively in stone, with far greater elaboration and permanence than elsewhere in the subcontinent. Structures such as Great Zimbabwe and others testify to a high degree of organization and agricultural development in the centuries before the arrival of the Europeans.

The comparatively settled pattern of eighteenth-century southern Africa was badly disturbed by the rise of the Zulu kingdom in the early nineteenth century. A standing army was instituted by Dingiswayo (c.1808 − 18). During the reign of Shaka Zulu (1818−28) armies embarked upon a series of campaigns which affected a fifth of the African continent. Whole areas were devastated, people were killed, cattle and grain were removed. The Zulu armies attacked their fellow Nguni, the Xhosa and the Swazi, while a rebel Zulu army under Mzilikazi invaded the core of the Sotho lands, and was not displaced until the *trekkers* arrived in 1837. He then invaded Rhodesia, which his Matabele ruled until 1890–3. By the time the *trekkers* had defeated the Zulu in 1838, there remained only scattered remnants of the tribes over much of southern Africa. Thus in large tracts of open country in central Natal, the Transvaal, and northern Orange Free State, the *trekkers* entered areas which appeared to be empty and uninhabited. The time of the forced migrations (the Difaquane) had a profound effect upon the population of southern Africa: traditional economies were destroyed, and a large proportion of the population was killed or reduced to destitution. Even cannibalism appeared.[13] It was, however, in the breaking of resistance to European attack that the greatest significance lay, and the resultant weakness was exploited to the full by the later European settlers in dividing the land of southern Africa between European and African. On the positive side, the growth of national cohesion and the birth of new nations during the Difaquane had a powerful effect on the development of African nationalism in the twentieth century.[14]

The Eastern Frontier of the Cape

Initial contact between black Africans and European settlers first took place on the eastern frontier of the Cape Colony. Traders and missionaries had penetrated deeply into Africa during the seventeenth and eighteenth centuries, and as early as 1702 a group of traders clashed with the Xhosa; by 1770 regular trade, with a wagon road, reached the Fish River. Transport by ox-wagon was common, and south of the Vaal there was no tsetse fly to prevent it. Trade with Cape Town was profitable, even over a distance of 700 miles.

As the colonists moved eastwards, so the Xhosa moved westwards over the Fish River. Both sought grazing and hunting grounds. Raiding began, and continued until the middle of the nineteenth century, with the Europeans raiding as far as the Buffalo River in 1793, and the Xhosa as far as Knysna in 1799. The Dutch East India Company tried to limit contact between the two groups, and the boundary of the Colony was drawn west of the Xhosa settlement, but in the 1770s settlers moved eastwards, until in 1781 the Xhosa were driven across the Fish River. Despite government attempts to limit it, contact grew, for trade was profitable. Cattle and ivory were exchanged for metal, beads, horses and muskets. Farmers required herdsmen, as they were constantly short of servants on the frontier, and service gave the Africans the means to acquire the horses they desired. From 1799 onwards, missionaries attempted to establish mission stations and convert the Xhosa to Christianity.[15] The London Missionary Society founded several stations, such as Bethelsdorp near Port Elizabeth and Theopolis in Albany. Between 1823 and 1845, a chain of Methodist mission stations was established throughout the Xhosa lands, and the pattern was to be repeated in other parts of the subcontinent (Fig 80). The constant raids and wars in the period from 1779 onwards

Fig 80 Pandamenka Mission, Bechuanaland, c.1880. Mission stations were established throughout southern Africa in the nineteenth Century. Outside the western and southern Cape, building styles were mostly similar to those of the indigenous population.

kept the frontier unsettled. Successive governments vacillated between establishing a neutral territory between the colonists and the
Xhosa, and direct annexation of the Xhosa lands; this finally took
place between 1848 and 1894. It was in the Ciskei, the area between
the Fish and Kei Rivers, that the greatest contradictions of policy
occurred, until finally the area was divided between African
reserves and European close-settlement areas. Earlier attempts at
settling Coloureds and Hottentots on the frontier had failed, as they
had usually joined the Xhosa in the course of the frontier wars, and
the Xhosa, unlike the Hottentots, did not disintegrate before the
Europeans. The continuous European expansion eastwards was
thus clearly blocked by the presence of a settled African population,
which could not be moved *in toto*, without disastrous repercussions
elsewhere in southern Africa.

The territorial implications of this vacillating policy are to be seen
in changes between the 'one large reserve' policy, which placed the
boundary between the Cape Colony and the Xhosa lands successively on the Fish River and the Keiskamma River, and the 'multiple small reserve' policy. The latter policy of partition, as applied to
the Ciskei (British Kaffraria), proved to be the ultimate solution,
with the Africans living on a large number of blocks of land, interspersed with European farms. East of the Kei, little land was given to
European settlers, and the Africans remained comparatively undis-
turbed, with a measure of self-government unique in South Africa.

The Rural Reserve Policy

The Great Trek introduced an important new element into the
territorial relations between Europeans and Africans. The basis of
these relations was the statement that there should be no equality
between the two in political affairs. The *trekkers* treated the tribes
they met as separate entities, either on the basis of treaty relations,
or, later, as overlords demanding tribute from them. Thus in Natal,
in the period 1839–42, the *trekkers* gained as tribute more than
sufficient cattle to recompense them for their losses on the trek.

Significantly, the *trekkers* occupied areas which appeared to be
deserted, so that they might have as little contact with the tribes as
possible. However, in Natal large numbers of Africans appeared,
both as refugees from Zululand and from hiding in Natal itself, to
present a major problem for the *trekkers*. A policy of exclusion
failed, and the Republican government decided upon the establishment of one large reserve in 1841, to be situated in the south of

the country for so 'long as their behaviour remained satisfactory'.[16] The tribal system was to be maintained in the reserve, under Republican suzerainty. It should be noted that not all the Africans were to be placed in the reserve; some were to remain on the European farms as a labour force, and the government limited the number to five families per farm. The numbers of Africans continued to grow, and the one-reserve policy was abandoned in favour of a multiple small-reserve policy, with a reserve in each subdistrict. This decision was to prove of vital importance for the present day.[17]

The *trekkers'* reserve policy in Natal was formalized by the British administration.[18] The Natal Locations Commission recommended the establishment of ten medium-sized reserves, approximately 350 square miles each, supporting 10,000 people apiece. Within the reserves the Africans were free to continue their tribal system, where civilizing influences could gradually transform the traditional society. All told, some 2.1 million acres — a fifth of the Colony — were set aside. The *trekkers'* policy of separation and the creation of special African areas was one which was to be applied increasingly in southern Africa as the Europeans penetrated African-occupied areas. The Natal government introduced a modification by creating a series of mission reserves, where Africans could be brought up as Christians, free of the tribal system. The missionary societies, principally the American Board of Missions, had been active in the area since 1835 and had obtained some 175,000 acres for the purpose.

The reserve policy was not applied with such determination in the interior republics. Areas were assigned to tribes which had assisted the *trekkers*, although promises of land were often tardy in implementation: in the Transvaal, promises made in the 1830s were not fulfilled until the 1880s.[19] The Transvaal government, furthermore, was not in effective control of all its territory, and as late as 1867 the Venda forced the withdrawal of settlement from the Zoutpansberg, which was only re-occupied in 1879 after the British annexation. Final subjugation of the African tribes was only achieved in 1898. Under such unsettled conditions the emergence of a reserve policy was slow. Thus in 1904 only 1.3 million acres had been set aside as reserves, although a further 0.5 million acres were held in trust for Africans, and some 2.6 million acres of private land and 0.6 million acres of Crown Land were occupied by them. Even when the African areas were consolidated at 2.3 million acres, only 3.2 per cent of the area of the Transvaal was set aside for African use.

The Orange Free State similarly began with a mixture of small reserves and one large reserve, Basutoland. Moshoeshoe I of Basutoland managed to resist the inroads of the *trekkers*, although increasing pressure upon him resulted in the loss of the most fertile parts of his kingdom in 1866. The separate existence of Basutoland was preserved through British annexation.[20] Elsewhere, the Africans of Thaba Nchu maintained tributary status until 1884 when, as a result of internal strife, they were incorporated into the Orange Free State. In 1885 some 254,000 acres at Thaba Nchu were assigned to Africans on the basis of individual property, but by 1902 only 200,000 acres remained in their hands.[21] Once more individual African ownership proved disastrous to long-term African interests in a competitive world. By 1911 only 160,000 acres of reserve existed in the Orange Free State.

Elsewhere, British annexation in the second half of the nineteenth century resulted in the establishment of reserves to protect African interests. The Transkeian territories were largely left in African hands, although several substantial blocks were assigned to European control, or, in the case of East Griqualand, to the Griquas, only later (1879) transferred to Europeans. North of the Orange, the Imperial government established reserves in both Griqualand West and British Bechuanaland. It was, however, in Zululand that the largest changes occurred. In 1904 Zululand was divided into two sections, 3.9 million acres as African reserves, and 2.6 million acres as Crown Land open for European settlement.[22] As in Natal proper, the reserve boundaries were highly complex, with blocks of the two sections intermixed. This was the result of an attempt to disturb the existing settlement patterns as little as possible.

The rural reserve policy was generally applied in the second half of the nineteenth century. It was essentially static and it assumed a stable rural economy. Such an assumption proved to be false.

The African Reserves of South Africa

The Union of 1910 presented the new government with the problem of reconciling divergent ideas on land ownership by Africans. No restriction on African land purchases existed except in the Orange Free State, but the reserves where traditional land ownership prevailed, with the exception of certain areas in the Cape Province and Natal, were small, and clearly some modification of the nineteenth-century inheritance was needed. The 1913 Natives

Land Act attempted to produce an interim settlement, pending the report of a commission of enquiry. Under the Act, some 36.8 million acres (8.2 per cent of the area of the Union) were guaranteed as African reserves. The provision reflected the previous reserve policies, with 25.9 per cent of Natal, but only 1.8 per cent of the Orange Free State, declared Scheduled Reserves. At the same time, approximately 10.7 million acres of Crown and alienated land were occupied by Africans, mostly in the Transvaal. The Act also prevented further African land purchases in Natal and the Transvaal.

World War I and the political problems which followed led to the shelving of any further action on the African land question until 1936, when the Native Trust and Land Act attempted to divide the country once and for all between the Europeans and the Africans (Fig 81). [23] Some 15.4 million acres were released for legal African occupation, but they included those already occupied, and only 4 million acres of European-occupied land were to be released. Furthermore, in order to prevent territorial integration, the African

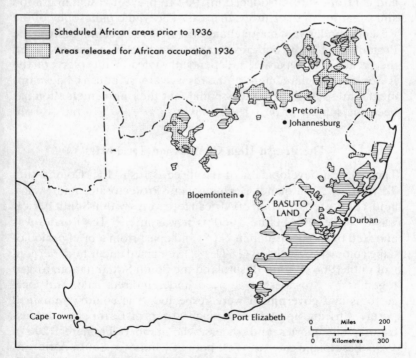

Fig 81   The African areas of South Africa, 1960

right to purchase land in the Cape was abolished, and the government undertook to purchase African-owned farms in European districts ('black spots').

Although the Act did little more than recognize the existing state of affairs, progress on its implementation was slow. No doubt this was due to the cost, which in 1936 was estimated at £10–£15 million, but twenty-five years after the Act had been passed, only 10.0 million acres had been acquired, and only 11 per cent of the 0.4 million acres of 'black spots' had been expropriated. The main changes had occurred in the Transvaal, where provision of reserves in 1913 had been noticeably inadequate.

A declining proportion of the African population lived within the African areas. In 1936 the figure stood at 45.5 per cent, but by 1960 this had declined to 37.5 per cent. However, in numerical terms, the numbers in the Reserves increased from 3.0 million in 1936 to 4.1 million in 1960. African emigration, both temporary and permanent, was substantial. In 1936 some 447,000 were temporarily absent in the European areas; by 1951 this had risen to 569,000, and controls were introduced in 1952 to prevent casual migration and squatting in the European areas. The whole philosophy of the Reserves underwent major changes in the 1950s, culminating in the Promotion of Bantu Self-government Act of 1959, which envisaged the creation of separate, independent states in the place of the Reserves.[24] Englargement of the reserve areas, industrial development, and so forth became essential, but their implementation has been the subject of post-1960 activity.

The British High Commission Territories

The political development of the three British High Commission Territories, Basutoland, Bechuanaland Protectorate, and Swaziland, contrasted with that of African territories within South Africa, was as noticeable before 1960 as it was after.[25] Basutoland was annexed by Great Britian in 1868, and apart from a brief period of Cape colonial government (1871–84), remained under Imperial control until 1966. Within Basutoland the South Sotho nation, forged together by Moshoeshoe I, lived under indirect rule, and local customs and government were respected. The country remained purely African, apart from a small group of European administrators, missionaries, and traders, who numbered a mere 1,296 in 1956. Basutoland acted as a vast pool of labour for South Africa: in 1892 some 30,000 men worked on the diamond fields and railways.

In 1956 a fifth (154,782) of the total population was temporarily absent. In addition, permanent migration to South Africa provided another escape from local poverty, and in 1951 there were 219,000 Basutos living there permanently. Rates of permanent and temporary migration were highest from the crowded lowlands, where densities of 300 persons per square mile had been reached by 1960.

Bechuanaland Protectorate came under British protection in 1885 as a move to forestall the Transvaal and German governments. It provided an essential link with the interior of the continent, and hence its acquisition was vital to British interests. Comparatively little land within the Protectorate was settled by Europeans, and this was mainly in blocks adjacent to the Transvaal. Reserves for the various African tribes were demarcated, but the remaining Crown Land was not regarded as suitable for European settlement, and remained unoccupied. The European presence amounted in 1956 to a mere 1 per cent (3,173) of the total population.

Swaziland, owing to its proximity to the Transvaal, had a far more chequered career. Transvaal interest in Swaziland became of major importance after 1875, when European participation in Swazi internal disputes began in earnest. The Swazi kings made land concessions to Europeans over much of the eastern Transvaal, and granted monopolies, including that of collecting revenues within the remainder of the Swazi kingdom. The influx of European fortune seekers led to the establishment of a Transvaal protectorate in 1895. Swaziland was, therefore, annexed by Great Britian in 1900 as a part of the Transvaal, and subsequently separated from it in 1906. In 1907 the areas conceded by the Swazi kings were reduced, but even then only half the total area remained in Swazi hands. Thus European influence was strong in Swaziland, where 9,200 Europeans resided in 1960, out of a total population of 270,000.

South African attempts to incorporate the three territories, as envisaged in the 1909 South Africa Act, establishing the Union, failed as a result of the increasing divergence of the British and South African governments on African policy.[26] However, as late as 1955 official Union programmes assumed eventual incorporation. Nearly half the area of 'Greater South Africa' would therefore be African land.[27]

Land Apportionment in Rhodesia

Rhodesian policy with regard to African land varied considerably

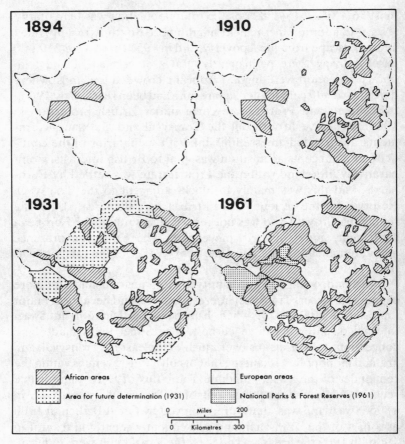

Fig 82   Land apportionment in Rhodesia, 1894–1961

between 1890 and 1960 (Table 18). The initial pioneers made no
provision for African reserves, and so European farms were located
throughout the country in the period 1890–6, without regard to the
previous inhabitants. In 1894 the Imperial government, which possessed supervisory powers over the country, appointed a commission which established the first two reserves in Matabeleland, covering approximately 4.3 per cent of Rhodesia (Fig 82).[28] The African
rebellions of 1896 led to a reappraisal of the situation; this resulted
in a substantial increase in the African areas, amounting to 26 per
cent of the country by 1910. Each District Commissioner established African Reserves, where tribal customs could be maintained,
according to the assessed needs of the African population in his

district. The Reserves thus varied substantially in size, and were highly fragmented. The Rhodesia Native Reserves Commission in 1917 believed that a final allocation of land between Africans and Europeans was essential, together with the realization on the part of the Africans that 'it cannot be assumed that every unborn Native is to enjoy an indefensible right to live on the soil under tribal conditions, and by the primitive and wasteful methods of cultivation practised by their forefathers'.[29]

Table 18 DIVISION OF LAND IN RHODESIA 1894–1960

Year	Percentage European	Percentage African	Percentage unassigned	Percentage National	Total
1894	15.0	4.3	80.7	—	100.0
1910	23.4	26.0	50.6	—	100.0
1925	32.8	22.0	45.2	—	100.0
1931	50.8	30.1	18.5	0.6	100.0
1960	53.2	43.5	—	3.3	100.0

At the end of Company rule a further Land Commission found that there was general agreement on the desirability of establishing separate areas, within which the rights of each race would be protected from the encroachment of the other.[30] African land purchases outside the Reserves at this date (1926) were small, a mere 45,000 acres. In 1931 the Land Apportionment Act provided for the division of the country into a European area, where Africans would not be allowed to purchase land; the African Reserves; a Native Purchase Area, where Africans alone could purchase land; and an area for future determination. The areas for future determination were mostly inferior, in the south-eastern lowlands, the Zambezi Valley, and on the Bechuanaland border. Gradually the undetermined area was allocated to various purposes, mostly additional African Reserves, until in 1958 it had ceased to exist. By 1960 the African area had grown from the 30.1 per cent assigned in 1931 to 43.5 per cent of Rhodesia. Within the European area some 7.2 million acres of national and game parks had been included.

In the period 1931–60, the African areas had largely been designated into districts where the Africans lived in tribal conditions. Between 1936 and 1959 some 113,000 Africans had been moved from the European to the African area, but this action became increasingly unpopular, and finally ceased. The government sought to create a middle group of land-owning Africans, through the provision of the Native Purchase Area, within which individual tenure and European agricultural extension services attempted, in some cases successfully, to develop African agriculture. Progress was slow, but by 1960 some 8.1 million acres were assigned to this category.

The pattern of the African areas, with extreme fragmentation, is remarkable in the southern African context.[31] The rapid changes in policy within the span of seventy years resulted in the redrawing of the map of Rhodesia more than once. The comparative permanence of the pattern in South Africa is in marked contrast. Even more remarkable was the assignment in 1960 by Rhodesia of some 43.1 million acres for its African population of 3.3 million, compared with 37.0 million acres for the African population of 10.9 million in South Africa.

Economic Relations Between Black and White

Contact between Europeans and the indigenous population was continuous from the start of the Cape settlement, and attempts at restricting it were thwarted as a profitable two-way trade was built up. The Dutch and later administrations lacked the degree of control necessary to prevent interaction and indeed indigenous labour became indispensable to the running of European agriculture. By the nineteenth century the African population was looked upon as a source of labour, and the establishment of the rural reserves as a reason for the shortage of labour.[32] African agriculture was resented by European farmers, not because it competed with their own efforts, but because it gave the Africans a livelihood independent of that earned by labouring for the Europeans. Thus as Trollope observed in 1878: 'It never seems to occur to a Natal farmer that if a Zulu has enough to live on without working, he should be as free to enjoy himself in idleness as an English lord.'[33]

The breakdown of the traditional African social structure led to increased contact between Europeans and Africans, as the latter demanded goods, skills and education. In British Kaffraria the intermixing of European and African areas was aimed at bringing civilizing influences to bear upon the Africans with a view to their integration into European society.[34] The growth of trade was such that, for example, 60,000 woollen blankets were being sold each year in King William's Town by 1875.[35] Other products also found their way into the African market: the trade in guns, north of the

Orange River, throughout the nineteenth century was one particularly notorious example.

Nevertheless, before the mineral discoveries, comparatively little change had occurred north of the Orange River, as the *trekkers* had little material civilization to offer the Africans.[36] Economically, the latter became fixed to the land they occupied, in a semi-feudal relationship with the *trekkers*, with marked duties and rights on both sides.[37] The problem of farm labourers — of whom there were either too many or too few — elicited much comment in the nineteenth century. All states attempted to limit the number of Africans on private farms, but without success. Some industrialists, in the period after 1870, even purchased farms in order to secure a labour pool, which could pay rentals in the form of labour on the mines. Other attempts to obtain labour involved payment in cattle, which led to inflation of the cattle currency and consequent overstocking in the second half of the nineteenth century.[38]

Initial African contact with Europeans was not necessarily detrimental. It has been shown in Rhodesia that, although European pioneers carved out large estates for themselves, the African inhabitants were at first little disturbed.[39] They were in fact regarded as an asset by the Europeans, who in turn gave them technical and military aid. European agriculture usually started at little more than subsistance level and was generally inefficient, so that it was easier for the pioneer to buy provisions from the Africans on the farms than to grow them himself. In Rhodesia, in particular, there was a marked African resistance to working for the Europeans as labourers. Payment of hut taxes was therefore made from increased African agricultural production, rather than from migrant labour. Thus in 1903 Rhodesian African sales of grain and livestock amounted to £350,000, while in the 1903–4 season European holdings accounted for only 5 per cent of the total marketed crop.[40] Under such conditions of mutual dependence no attempt was made to move Africans from 'European' land.

In Rhodesia, as elsewhere, conflict in the rural areas only came as the European owners began to develop their holdings, and hence to displace the African inhabitants. It was, however, the recession of 1921–3 which, together with political developments, hurt African interests most and reduced the Africans to dependence upon the Europeans. In 1920 Rhodesian Africans sold 19,800 tons of maize at £5 per ton; in 1921 they sold 4,360 tons at 50s (£2.50) per ton — a drop in earnings from about £100,000 to under £10,000. Similarly, in 1919 they sold some 20,000 head of cattle at £7–£8 each, while in 1922 they sold practically none.[41] The collapse of commercial African agriculture forced an increasing number out of the Reserves and on to the European labour markets. It has been forcefully postulated that, whereas Rhodesian government intervention assisted European farmers in time of crises, no such aid was offered to African farmers.[42] Indeed, the assistance offered to European farmers was largely carried out at the expense of African interests, leading to the economic stagnation of the African areas, which by 1960 accounted for only 30 per cent of total Rhodesian agricultural production.[43]

The escape route from rural poverty was found in the migratory labour system. It was the mineral discoveries which most profoundly transformed the economic relationships between Africans and Europeans. Africans worked on the diamond fields, for money which would purchase cattle, food and a host of new items and in the 1870s labourers came from as far afield as Barotseland, north of the Zambezi River. There were approximately 10,000–12,000 at Kimberley, and the number remained reasonably constant until 1914. Other diamond mines in the Orange Free State and Transvaal employed rather more than 20,000 in 1914.[44]

The opening of the gold-mines vastly increased the scale of labour demand. In the 1890s there were on average 50,000 Africans working on the Witwatersrand mines, and by the 1910s this had risen to 185,000. By the 1950s the average number was 323,000, over half of whom came from outside South Africa. The numbers required to work the mines, once African labour was an accepted part of mining, exceeded purely casual arrivals, and active recruitment was needed to attract sufficient labour.[45] In the period 1901–12 competition for labour gave way to an organized system whereby two agencies, the Witwatersrand Native Labour Association and the Native Recruiting Corporation, established stations throughout southern Africa to organize recruitment. Contracts for six to eighteen months resulted in the system of migratory labour on a vast scale, affecting the entire subcontinent, and the return to the African areas was substantial, amounting in 1954 to some £4.9 million, of which some £1.5 million went to the Reserves of South Africa, £0.5 apiece to Basutoland and Bechuanaland, and £0.2 million to Swaziland.[46] In this manner the gold-mines helped to maintain the African areas, without any major structural change within them, while the mining industry through its health and education services also acted as a powerful influence in breaking down traditional tribal isolation.

The presence of such a large, yet unstable, labour force profoundly affected the organization of the gold-mining industry. The labour turn-over in African employment (over 100 per cent per annum in gold-mining), compared with the semi-permanent employment in many manufacturing industries influenced the appearance of the towns. Vast compounds for single labourers, first developed at Kimberley, spread to the Witwatersrand, thereby preventing the emergence of the extensive housing estates of the European industrial cities of the nineteenth century. Permanent migration to the towns, with the attendant housing problems, only came in the twentieth century, with the rise of permanent African employment. The gold-mines also proved to be the area where the industrial colour bar was most intensively applied.[47] Consequently the retardation of the emergence of an urban African middle class had marked effects upon the type of African urban area which developed.

The decline of commercial African agriculture and the rise of mining employment effectively prevented the economic separation of Africans and Europeans. Employment was even considered desirable as a means of civilizing the Africans. Lord Grey in 1849 expressed the opinion that Africans should 'be placed in circumstances in which they should find regular industry necessary for their subsistence'.[48] This aim was achieved through the build-up of population pressure in the Reserves and the need for their inhabitants to earn a living. By 1873 it was estimated that possibly half the able-bodied African males in Natal were in employment in some capacity, and by 1882 less than half the African population of the Colony was in the African areas.[49] The Reserves of Natal ceased to be self-sufficient in food by the end of the nineteenth century, when signs of famine were prevalent.[50] In such circumstances Africans were forced on to the labour market as cheap, if highly inefficient, labourers, who were considered preferable to imported European labourers or convicts. In view of the wages paid to the Africans, this was scarcely surprising, as the price of agricultural labour, in the mid-nineteenth century, might range from £6–£12 per annum plus food, compared with approximately £36 per annum for English agricultural labourers. European labour in the colonies was traditionally more expensive than in England: in 1908 it was shown that European wages were approximately three times those obtaining in England. Thus the solution to the labour shortage was seen to be African labour.[51]

The more impoverished parts of the subcontinent were most

susceptible to economic pressures, and consequently became integrated into the industrial labour system of the subcontinent faster than the more prosperous African areas. Basutoland was one of the first and most significant exporters of labour in southern Africa. At the time of the 1911 Census some 5.8 per cent of the population was absent, and by 1956 this had risen to 19.5 per cent.[52] By 1936, over half the African male population of South Africa, between the ages of fifteen and fifty-four, was absent from the Reserves, ranging from 69 per cent absent in the northern Transvaal to 41.6 per cent in Zululand.[53] In many cases the income earned by labour on the mines was in excess of income from the land.[54] The situation was such that 'few native households in the Reserves depend solely on agriculture for their livelihood. Yields from crops and animals are so low that supplementary income must be obtained from elsewhere.'[55] Maybe the most telling illustration of the nature of the labour supply was the observation that the flow of labour was governed by the size of the maize crop in the Reserves, and not by the requirements of industry.[56]

The African Landscape

The African landscape in southern Africa is highly varied, but is characterized by higher population densities in terms of farm size, field area, method of farming, and finally distinctive building styles. All these characteristics have been transplanted on to European-owned lands where either the European farmer allowed his workers areas of their own, or where the land was abandoned by its owner. Thus 'African' landscapes may be seen in areas which are technically 'European'.

The higher densities of population are most characteristic. In 1960 the African areas of South Africa possessed a density of 71 persons per square mile, compared with 29 persons per square mile in the remainder of the country. In 1962 in Rhodesia the density of rural population in the African areas was 32 persons per square mile, compared with 15 persons per square mile in the European areas. By 1960 high rural densities exceeding 100 persons per square mile were recorded in Basutoland and the African areas of both South Africa and Rhodesia.

The relatively small size of land holdings is another feature of the African rural areas, associated with the high rural densities and systems of land tenure.[57] Thus in Rhodesia in 1961 there were 398,000 African cultivators with an average of 8.7 acres of arable land apiece, and communal grazing. In South Africa in 1955 the average area of arable land per African farmer varied from 3.2 acres on irrigation schemes to 8.9 acres on the Bechuanaland border.[58] In established individual-tenure areas in Rhodesia, the average size of African holdings was only 216 acres. Even on special irrigation schemes the distinction between European and African was maintained. Thus in Natal in the period 1904–11 the average size of a European government irrigation plot was 60 acres, while that for an African was 1 acre, excluding grazing lands.

Architectural styles also added to the distinction between European and African areas. Traditional African styles of architecture varied greatly, depending upon the availability of materials, and ranged from the grass-mat huts of Namaqualand to the stone houses of the Sotho areas. In the main they were individually small. The royal palaces of the Zulu kings were a series of grass huts, not one large edifice. Although initially many European settlers lived in houses little better or larger than the local Africans, they soon built grander structures, according to the patterns they brought from Europe or elsewhere in southern Africa. Gradually African construction was influenced by European building methods and, although the results did not generally compare favourably with contemporary European architecture and layout, the traditional building styles — the reed houses and the various circular rondavels — gradually gave way in many areas to rectangular houses with corrugated iron roofs. Their decoration and propinquity proclaimed their African origin.

Outside the designated African areas of southern Africa, African land characteristics have remained. Large tracts of 'European' land were occupied solely by Africans, and upon them African landscapes were created, giving a patchwork appearance to many agricultural regions. Thus by 1960 in South Africa some 3.0 million acres (1.3 per cent) of European farm land were officially set aside for African uses. In Natal 6.9 per cent was returned as so occupied. It must also be remembered that by 1960 the farm population of the European areas was 83.8 per cent African and Coloured. In the Orange Free State this proportion reached 97.5 per cent. Consequently the African cultural imprint upon the landscape was distinctive and sometimes dominant, and a seventh of the cattle on European farms were African owned in 1960, while a tenth of the maize acreage on European farms was planted by Africans.

The existence of two landscapes, often so closely interwoven as at times to appear one, is a distinctive feature of southern Africa, in

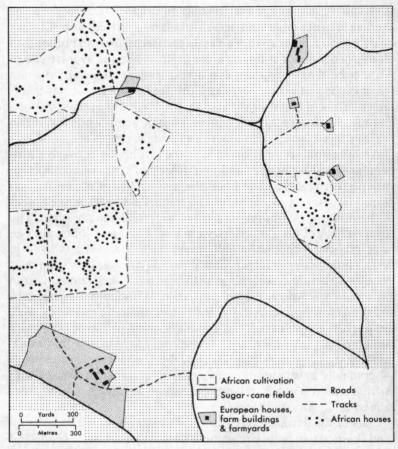

Fig 83　Intermixture of European and African landscapes in a 'European' farming area

contrast to most European settlements of the mid-latitudes (Fig 83). The evolution of the African sector of the landscape and its impact upon the European areas deserve further investigation.

9

Perspectives on the Historical Geography of Southern Africa

THE TRANSFORMATION of the landscape through the agency of European settlement has been the theme of this work. Southern Africa, as one of the 'new worlds' of eighteenth- and nineteenth-century colonization, was open to the influences of these worlds, as well as those of Europe. Colonization models from that of Turner onwards are therefore applicable, if in modified form. Southern Africa experienced a unique development, with several features which separated it from its contemporaries. Thus the classic-wave thesis was diverted into new channels. An investigation of the unfavourable perceptions, indigenous population, and internal political friction is basic to any understanding of the southern African experience, since each determined, to some extent, the course of colonization. Finally, there is the question of what remains in the landscape of the formative period of European endeavour. Relict landscapes open a field of investigation as yet little touched, but important for any re-creation of the past.

The Frontier Thesis

The frontier thesis postulated by Turner in 1894 with regard to the settlement of the United States can be applied as a model of colonization to many pre-World-War I areas of European expansion.[1] Geographical applications in the form of landscape evolution have inspired a number of important works dealing not only with the United States, but also with Canada, Australia and New Zealand.[2] In the United States, investigators have benefited from the wealth of census and other material, which has often been lacking in other territories, including southern Africa.[3] Nevertheless, American

writings have influenced the view of the frontier presented elsewhere in the English-speaking world, just as the flow of men, plants,
animals, machines and ideas within that world influenced the southern African frontier.

Spatial aspects of Turner's frontier thesis were evolved in an area
of unified political control. Such unification and compatibility of
information are absent within southern Africa, where, except for a
brief period from 1900 to 1910, political unity among the
European-controlled states was absent after the 1830s. The statistical backing for many ideas is thus lacking, and hypotheses must be
regarded more cautiously than is necessary in better documented
lands.

The distinct phases of settlement which Turner recognized in the
evolution of frontier society and, by implication, of the landscape,
are recognizable in southern Africa. The stages of the pathfinders
— the equivalent of the North American fur-traders — the cattle
men, the miners, the pioneer farmers, the commercial farmers and
the urban pioneers — all assisted in transforming southern Africa
from a wasteland into the developed landscape of today.

Within this process of transformation, land played a vital role,
and the availability of land was the subject of exhaustive debate.
The ease with which it could be obtained controlled the spread of
settlement and, effectively, the form of the frontier.[4] Initial settlement was usually associated with free land grants to attract settlers.
Later, land sales, at a high fixed or minimum price, were the official
policies of the United States of America and the British Empire.
Thereafter cheap or free land, in return for improvements and
occupation, became the dominant element in land policy. Most
settlements experienced all three phases. Certainly southern Africa
suffered from them all.

The frontier movement may best be illustrated by the spread of
the European population, although other indicators such as land
alienation, livestock densities, areas cultivated, and town foundation would provide amplification of the movement. First it must be
stressed that European population alone can be examined. Other
ethnic groups were poorly documented and, in the case of the
Africans, formed a separate entity or a buffer to European settlement. Owing to the small numbers involved in southern Africa, the
United States figure of 2–6 persons per square mile to represent the
frontier is clearly unrealistic if Europeans alone are considered
(Table 19). Outside the Cape peninsula no district achieved two
persons per square mile until 1837, or six persons per square mile

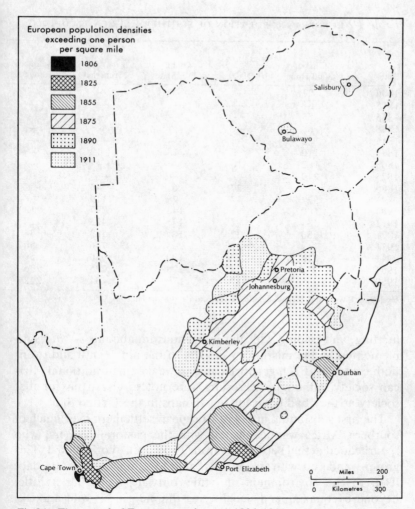

Fig 84   The spread of European settlement, 1806–1911

until 1855. Even in 1911 comparatively little of the subcontinent was by North American standards settled. In view of these limitations, a figure of one European per square mile is a more realistic basis for reviewing frontier movement (Fig 84).

The settlement frontier exhibits three distinct coastal points of origin – the western Cape, the eastern Cape, and Natal. From these three origins the interior was opened up fitfully, rather than continuously colonized across the subcontinent. Parallels with Turner's thesis do occur in this movement. The first stage of exploration —

Table 19 EUROPEAN POPULATION OF SOUTHERN AFRICA 1806–1960

	(000)				
Date	Cape of Good Hope	Natal	Orange Free State	Transvaal	Southern Rhodesia
1806	27	—	—	—	—
1815	37	—	—	—	—
1825	53	—	—	—	—
1835	68	—	1	—	—
1845	82	3	—	—	—
1855	110	7	13	12	—
1865	182	16	—	—	—
1875	249	—	—	—	—
1880	—	27	61	43	—
1890/1	377	47	78	119	—
1904	580	97	143	297	13
1911	584	98	175	423	24
1921	650	137	189	543	34
1931	749	177	205	706	50
1941	826	218	199	950	69
1951	935	274	228	1,205	136
1960	988	337	277	1,464	222

Excluding Basutoland, Bechuanaland Protectorate and Swaziland

hunting, and trading with the indigenous inhabitants — was supplemented by the missionary activity of the nineteenth and twentieth centuries. Each group assisted in weakening traditional African society, although the results were not so disastrous for that society as they had been for the Indians in the United States.

The first substantial influx of European settlement over much of southern Africa was associated with the pastoral farmers, who spearheaded actual settlement from 1700 until World War I. This group wandered with its animals, able to a high degree to adapt itself to the environment and thus outwardly altering it little, beyond overgrazing and slaughtering the indigenous wild animals. Owing to the generous land-disposal policies pursued by successive governments, population densities were initially low, and only after a generation or two were densities of even one European per square mile built up. The pastoral frontier was finally terminated by increasing aridity, African hostility, and the greater attractions of the cities. However, the pastoralists secured title to the land in a manner which was rare on other frontiers, and pastoralism showed a far greater resistance to change than it did on many contemporary settlement frontiers.

It was the advent of mining which transformed southern Africa from a series of relatively poor and backward states into a rapidly expanding and prosperous region. The discovery of diamonds, and later of gold, in the second half of the nineteenth century had revolutionary results, the more so as the discoveries occurred in areas on the outer limits of established European settlement. The Transvaal was thus transformed from a peripheral state into the hub of the southern African economy, and the success of its mining industry spurred on the plans to open Rhodesia, which was said to offer even greater rewards. Thus the mining frontier, through the introduction of men and capital, led to a new direction in the political economy of the subcontinent.

The arable farmer producing cash crops appeared early in southern Africa, in the western Cape. However, transport costs severely limited the areas where his activities could profitably be pursued, and it was only as a result of large-scale railway construction, associated with mining development, that commercial crop production in the interior could be economically pursued. Large-scale arable agriculture is generally a product of the present century, aided by substantial government grants in the form of capital works and technical assistance. Thus the elements of land clearance and ploughing, so important on other frontiers, were only locally of significance. Crop farming, which formed the basis of a dense rural population in the United States, did not play the same role in southern Africa. This is a marked deviation from the Turner thesis.

Towns played a vital role in the colonization process, although the early dominance of Cape Town was not maintained, as new areas were opened up at considerable distances from the initial settlement. By 1904 over half the European population of the subcontinent lived in towns. Urban centres as places of trade, commerce and industry, together with care for physical and moral welfare, played an important role in maintaining a cohesive society, and the success of the urban areas was closely watched by British administrators.[5]

The process of settlement included many of the features of the North American model, but it had distinctively southern African traits. As the prime indicator, European population densities provide only part of the total picture. The elements of landscape transformation, such as livestock grazed, arable areas tilled, land alienat and, finally, towns built, also need to be examined. Stateme livestock densities must be viewed with caution, owing to t curacies of data collection, but a major period of expansio 1846 and 1914 appears to outweigh all previous and ments. Within this period, most of the major de livestock raising took place, and sales of wool, ostrich feathers, mohair, beef, hides and skins boosted the southern African economy. Nevertheless, environmental limits were placed on the expansion, and by World War I these had generally been reached. In contrast, the major advance of cultivation took place after the grazing industry had realized its limitations, and it was predominantly a twentieth-century phenomenon. As to land alienation, the nineteenth century witnessed the major part of this process. Although estimates are liable to substantial inaccuracies, approximately 11 million acres had been alienated by 1806. By 1860 this had risen to approximately 100 million acres, and to 227 million acres by 1911. Such mass alienation of half the subcontinent was mostly for pastoral farming, in the form of grazing licences and later perpetual quit-rent grants. In contrast, comparatively little land was sold on freehold tenure. Some 600,000 acres had been alienated in fee simple by 1860, when the distinctions between tenures were blurred. Land sales in freehold were intended for plots reserved for arable agriculture, but owing to the security afforded to pastoral perpetual quit-rent tenure, the official breaking up of pastoral holdings, which occurred in Australia or the United States, had little place in southern African development.[6] Thus land tenure acted as a major brake on the operation of the complete spatial aspects of the Turner thesis in the subcontinent.

Plural Societies

Ever since their arrival, the Europeans in southern Africa have been faced with the problems of living with a substantial indigenous population. As time has gone by, the situation has become more complex, as other immigrant groups arrived, and it was appreciated that there was a wide range of African peoples present in the

The basic question was whether to practise integra-

Dutch colony neither was effectively

rred, and the various races lived in

, but the Europeans remained in a

ir technical and administrative skill.

was, however, reasonably even, and

r cent of the population of the Cape

ing attitudes of the Cape Colony were

he slight non-European majority constituted no threat to European dominance in all fields. Contact with the major African tribes, and the incorporation of vast areas with substantial African populations, effectively changed these attitudes.[7] Thus in Natal in 1852, Europeans constituted only 6.3 per cent of the population, while in the Transvaal, as late as 1880, they formed only 5.3 per cent of the population. Furthermore, the African tribes which the Europeans met beyond the northern and eastern boundaries of the Cape Colony were more cohesive and resistant to European penetration than were those in the Cape Colony west of the Great Fish River.

The idea of segregation and separation occurred at an early stage, when European pioneers met the Xhosa tribes in the eastern Cape, and the Great Fish River was fixed as the boundary separating Europeans and Africans. Expedients such as neutral zones were introduced in an attempt to separate the two rival forces. Certainly the idea of segregation into separate areas had to be accepted by the *Voortrekkers* on the Great Trek, in order to maintain their control, and more particularly to protect their herds from theft. Thus the first rural Reserves came into being in 1840 as places where 'surplus' rural Africans could live without interfering with the European population. The idea was applied to other parts of southern Africa, often in attempts to provide some security for the Africans to live unmolested by European land-seekers. Thus in the second half of the nineteenth and much of the first half of the twentieth century, rural Reserves were viewed as places necessary for both European and African security.

Separation was not to be economic. Europeans demanded African labour on their farms, and later on in the mines and factories. The rural Reserves, with their steadily rising populations, provided a pool of cheap labour. High turnover and inefficiency were not considered important. The presence of cheap Black labour led to colonial resistance to the introduction of poor or convict White labour, with far-reaching implications for the Black–White numerical balance in the subcontinent.[8]

Within the European areas, Africans and other groups lived in close proximity to the Europeans. In the rural areas they often farmed part of the Europeans' land on their own account, while in towns and villages they frequently lived in huts and houses at the rear of the owners' houses, on a master-servant basis. Segregation appeared as a result of rising prosperity on the part of Coloureds and Asians, who were able to build their own residential areas, such as the Malay Quarter in Cape Town. To a large extent this reflected

economic class, rather than race, as most such areas remained
mixed to some extent. But it was only in the Cape Colony that
mixing progressed very far. Elsewhere segregation in urban areas
was the result of design, through the establishment of African
locations and Indian bazaars. Such locations ranged from areas set
aside for African occupation to fully constructed housing estates,
and they were largely the product of the present century, as the
influx of Africans into the towns assumed substantial proportions.
In 1904 there were under 0.4 million Africans in the urban areas of
South Africa and Rhodesia, but by 1960 there were 4.0 million.

The enforcement of segregation in urban areas in South Africa,
together with effective segregation through economic status elsewhere, resulted in the emergence of separate suburbs for the various racial groups. They were often laid out to different standards,
with smaller plots and a general lack of service facilities in the
non-European areas. The 1950 Group Areas Act of South Africa
aimed at complete urban segregation, and this was virtually accomplished in the following twenty-five years, with the resultant
replanning of substantial tracts of the major cities.[9] The emergent
pattern shows the more affluent (Europeans) remaining in the
centre, and the less affluent (Non-Europeans) living on the
periphery, and it has produced cities which, socially, have affinities
with the pre-industrial structure.[10]

The Political Element
in Southern African Development

The influence of political theory upon the development of southern
Africa has been profound. European governments; local, colonial,
and republican governments; and the various elements of southern-
African European society, have been far from harmonious in their
dealings with one another. Discord, dispute and war have been the
lot of southern Africa since the eighteenth century. Dissension has
varied from administrators attempting to govern dissident colonists
to the clash of the British Empire with the South African republics
in 1899. Such dissension has been reflected in the evolution of the
subcontinent, and in turn in its landscape.

The first and most persistent controversy was between government and governed over the capabilities of the southern African
environment. Governments, particularly those in Amsterdam and,
later, London, possessed only vague ideas of a land very different
from their own. Thus official planning in Europe for close settle-

ment, African policy, and a host of other matters, differed from the attitudes of the settlers. Under the Dutch, the administration was weak, and settlers were able to impress their own ideas on society and the landscape, from ever larger areas for farms to virtual independence from government interference. The freedom accorded eighteeenth-century settlers was at variance with British attempts, in the nineteenth, to regulate the course of events and settlement more closely. Dissent over the nature of society, from slavery to the size of farms, led to one of the major breaks in southern African political development, the Great Trek. Thus north of the Orange River, settler government for the settlers became a reality on the frontier, far greater than that established in the United States. Settler concepts of land ownership maintained pressure on the frontier until the end of the nineteenth century, while the colonial governments pursued their own ideas. In terms of landscape development, few greater contrasts could be realized than that between the settler concept of vast cattle farms and the Imperial concept of close settlement (Fig 85).

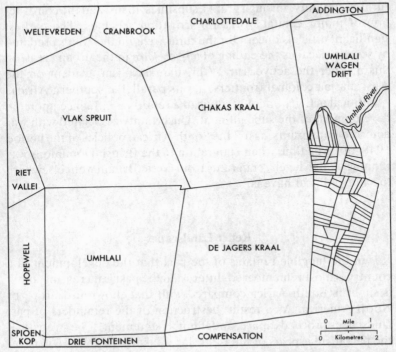

Fig 85 The imprint of two perceptions of farming upon the landscape Natal North Coast

Once established, the separate settler republics remained a source of potential trouble for the British Imperial government, through instability and, later, international power balances. Containment of the republics and republicanism was the aim of successive governments, both Imperial and Colonial. The railway pattern, in particular, reflects the political realities of the late-nineteenth century onwards, when economically the Transvaal had become the key to the southern African economy. Rhodesia's access to the sea clearly reflects these changes. In 1897 a line from the Cape Colony was constructed through Bechuanaland, instead of through the more potentially profitable area of the northern Transvaal. In 1956 a line was built to Lourenco Marques to avoid South Africa. Only in 1974 was the first direct Rhodesia-South Africa railway constructed as a sign of changing political alignments.

Rural-urban divisions, usually reinforced by the Dutch (Afrikaans)-English dualism have also played their part, as elsewhere, in determining development. Although profits were made from mining and, later, manufacturing, on a scale undreamt of from agriculture alone, part of these profits was diverted to assist the rural community, through grants, subsidies, loans, and the construction of major capital works for irrigation schemes. The earliest significant official concern for the rural areas, in the 1890s predated by several decades the ending of *laissez-faire* in the urban areas. In this manner the active, rural Christian socialism, evident on the Australasian colonial frontiers, has its parallel in southern Africa.

Political activity undoubtedly had a retarding influence upon the development of the subcontinent. Uncertainty associated with war deterred immigrants, as did the South African policies of the period 1948–60. At a time when emigration to the British Dominions was running at high levels, emigrants from Great Britain went elsewhere to safer political havens.

Relict Landscapes

It is in the tangible remains of the past that the development of a country is most remembered. Interest in the past is increasing, but it is slight in South Africa compared with that shown in Europe or North America. As a result, destruction of the reminders of past landscapes proceeds apace, and Plumb's statement, 'The strength of the past in all aspects of life is far, far weaker than it was a generation ago; indeed few societies have ever had a past in such a galloping dissolution as this',[11] might have been written specifically about southern Africa.

However, much remains, particularly in the rural areas. The farmers' general tendency to build new structures next to the old, rather than on the sites of the old, has resulted in several generations of buildings surviving on many farms. In the south-western Cape, farmsteads of the eighteenth and nineteenth centuries remain in some numbers, and careful restoration works on this distinctively southern African style have preserved several of them. The agricultural system of the south-western Cape has undergone continuous intensification, yet the basic outlines of vineyards and orchards have remained remarkably similar for over 150 years. In the extensive pastoral districts, where the land has been too poor for any extensive arable cultivation, the landscape has also remained comparatively unchanged since early European settlement, and changes have been limited to the construction and destruction of farmhouses, and the large-scale introduction of barbed-wire fencing and windmills in the present century. It is in the areas where cultivation has been possible that the major rural changes have occurred. The emergence of the 'Sugar Belt', the 'Timber Belt' and the 'Maize Triangle' has profoundly altered the pre-existing landscape, so that its predecessor of the nineteenth century is unrecognizable.

Thus, in the rural areas, the landscapes of 1960 are still (1975) generally recognizable, except where irrigation schemes have been undertaken, or the area has been re-zoned for African occupation. Even then the farmhouse may stand as a reminder of past occupation.[12] The rural landscapes of 1910 are less recognizable, as major changes in agricultural methods and production have transformed much of the wetter, eastern portion of the subcontinent. The landscape of 1860 is more or less restricted to the Cape Province and parts of the interior provinces, where sheep-raising remains the major enterprise, although the ubiquitous windmill and barbed-wire fence seem to indicate major changes. In attempting to discern the landscape of 1806, few points of reference remain: even the property-boundary lines which are so marked a feature of the present rural landscape had not been surveyed except in the south-western Cape. A few houses survive, but little else. Any attempt at the reconstruction of an era prior to 1806 must rely almost entirely upon documentary evidence.

The pace of change in the urban areas has been much more rapid. In most towns building booms since 1960 have removed much of the landscape, just as previous ones changed Victorian townscapes to those of the mid-twentieth century (compare Figs 35 & 36). Since 1960 the major non-administrative cities such as Durban and Johannesburg have probably witnessed the redevelopment of at least half the buildings in their central areas, while vast new housing estates have added to urban sprawl, and even the main centres of government such as Cape Town, Pretoria and Salisbury have been redeveloped to the extent of approximately one-third. Townscapes have been further transformed by the construction of skyscrapers, which, except in Johannesburg, were rare before 1960. There has been no attempt to control skylines, as there has been in Washington and Leningrad, and even historic core areas such as Church Square, Pretoria, and the Gardens, Cape Town, have been intruded upon by high-rise buildings.

Most smaller urban centres have not shared to the same extent in the post-1960 wave of prosperity, and hence of rebuilding. As a result, in non-metropolitan towns much of the townscape of 1960 remains, and indeed much of 1910 can still be seen in the towns based on the rural areas which have experienced comparatively little growth in this century. Most have acquired accretions in the form of African and/or Coloured townships, but the centres of the towns themselves have been little affected. Owing to the major developments of the late-nineteenth century, however, few smaller towns can be traced back further. Even Stellenbosch has been the scene of vast internal changes in the last hundred years.[13]

A major exception to the large-scale destruction has been the survival of government buildings. In general most towns have retained these even if they are used for purposes other than those for which they were originally intended. Owing to the care and attention lavished upon them, they have been subject to preservation campaigns, when other structures around them have been demolished. Thus in Cape Town the virtual sole survivors of the Dutch settlement are the public buildings, which give a rather misleading impression of the architectural styles of their period.

Preservation of historic landscapes is nevertheless becoming of increasing concern in southern Africa, where a greater interest in the past is now evident. This has been reflected in the proclamation of national monuments within wide fields, including the domestic architecture of the nineteenth century and the restoration of individual structures, and in increasing attention to the preservation of precincts. In reconstructions such as the Mine Museum at Kimberley, representative buildings in the town have been re-erected on a new site, to re-create the townscape of early Kimberley. More often it has involved the restoration of as much of the town as possible. Stellenbosch and Graaff-Reinet are examples of this approach. Finally, in the smaller centres, whole villages may be capable of restoration if the original, usually Victorian, structures remain and the financial resources are available, as at Pilgrims Rest and Matjiesfontein.

Industrial archaeology is as yet little developed. Interest in factories, mines and railways is limited. However, an important work on mills appears likely to raise interest, as southern Africa possesses a considerable range of industrial relicts.[14] Mining landscapes in particular, often little changed, represent each stage of the development of southern Africa's industry; Victorian and later factory landscapes also survive, but owing to the rapid pace of industrialization in southern Africa, most early industrial sites have been redeveloped several times. In some fields such as railway construction, southern Africa offers considerable scope for the industrial archaeologist, because of the policy of maintaining a viable system and the retention of steam as a means of locomotion.

Any reconstruction of the past must rely heavily upon the materials available, and these include the pictorial records.[15] Artists such as Thomas Baines and Thomas Bowler have left a vast store of prints, paintings and sketches of southern Africa, from the late eighteenth century to the advent of photography. Not only can the changes in urban and rural society be seen, but some artists, particularly Baines, explored widely and left a record of parts of the subcontinent as yet little touched by European occupation.[16] Photographic records of the later nineteenth and early twentieth century are comprehensive, but a gap in the records exists between 1914 and about 1950, which will undoubtedly present a problem in future.[17] Certain photographers, particularly Arthur Elliott, have left the most complete and valuable records of their time.[18] In recent years photographic accounts of various towns such as Cape Town, Johannesburg and Grahamstown have shed renewed light upon them, and reflect increasing general interest in the past.[19]

Conclusion

SOUTHERN AFRICA has experienced over 300 years of European endeavour and colonization, as a part of the global migration to the new lands of promise. In that time European settlement followed the pattern set in several other countries such as Australia, New Zealand, Canada and the United States, and so much of the cultural landscape of the subcontinent has affinities with those countries, rather than with other parts of Africa.

In the process of development, a number of significant features distinguished southern Africa from the other European settlement-areas of the eighteenth and nineteenth centuries. The first was the relative importance of the European pastoralist, as a result of government indifference and the poor natural resources of the subcontinent. The pastoral farmer dominated frontier development and, through his control of land, was able to resist the changes which occurred on other frontiers. The pastoral period, through continuity for over 200 years, influenced political development to an extent unparalleled elsewhere in contemporary colonization movements. The second distinguishing feature was the presence of a large African population which acted as a barrier to settlement to an extent that the indigenous population of North America and Australasia did not. The Africans also provided the labour force, to the detriment of European settlement: poor labourers from Europe were not required as they were elsewhere. The third feature was the poverty of the physical environment. Only occasionally, as a result of often fraudulent propaganda campaigns, could southern Africa have been described in terms comparable with those used of North America or even Australia. Intending European emigrants saw little to encourage them to settle in the subcontinent. It was only the discovery of minerals which was able to transform a basically backward pastoral region into a modern industrial state, and their late discovery is the key to an understanding of the historical geography of southern Africa.

Since 1960 rapid transformations have been under way, as new societies and economies have been brought into being. However, this has not been a revolutionary break with the past so much as a swift evolution, and the past is still of vital importance to any comprehension of southern Africa today.

Notes and References

Statistics

Statistical references and notes have been omitted where the figures were obtained from published Census Reports, Statistical Yearbooks or Colonial Blue Books. All such works to which reference was made appear in the Bibliography.

Units of measurement and currency

Dutch units of measurement were used in the period prior to 1806, after which Imperial measure was used throughout southern Africa until the early 1970s. The only Dutch unit which remained in use in parts of the subcontinent was that for land, based on the *morgen* (2.11654 acres). For purposes of continuity Imperial measure has been used throughout.

Dutch units of currency, the guilder and the rixdollar, were used until the 1820s when sterling was introduced. South Africa decimalized its currency in 1961 and Rhodesia in 1970. Sterling values have been retained throughout.

Preface

1   Dickson (1972), 187–206
2   Lucas (1898); Pollock & Agnew (1963)
3   In North America works such as Clark (1968); Meinig (1968) and (1971); and in Australia, Williams (1974); and Jeans (1972) provide insights into the range of possible approaches open to the historical geographer of the 'new lands' of the eighteenth and nineteenth centuries.
4   A preliminary study to present an African view of South African history is Were (1974). More detailed studies of African history such as Saunders & Derricourt (1974, reveal the range of material available. However, it will probably only be when oral traditions are analysed in detail that comprehensive histories of the African past will be possible.

Chapter 1 *Assessments of Southern Africa*

1   King (1963), 217-70
2   Raven-Hart (1967) 177
3   Kokot (1948), 22-3
4   Van der Stel (1932)
5   Forbes (1965)
6   Thunberg (1795), i, 163
7   Barrow (1801), i, 27, 35
8   Barrow (1801), ii, 327
9   Barrow (1801), ii, 371
10 Christopher (1973), 14-22
11 Hockley (1949), 15
12 Great Britain (1849), 512
13 Great Britain, Emigrants' Information Office (1888)
14 Great Britain, Emigration Commissioners (1870), 9
15 Methley (1849), 1
16 Burton (1850), 77-8
17 Currey (1968), 63
18 Powell (1970), 67, quoting *Age* (Melbourne) 6 March 1860
19 Hitchins (1931). Carrothers (1929) and relevant Annual Reports of
    the Colonial Land and Emigration Commissioners and the Board
    of Trade
20 Buchan (1902)
21 Burton (1902), 11
22 Southern Rhodesia (1924) i
23 Cole (1961), 159
24 London Public Record Office, C.O.291.18. 186-7
25 Botswana National Archives, File H.C. 66/58
26 Van Reenen (1923), 178-92
27 South Africa (1923), 3
28 Acocks (1953)
29 Tyson (1971), 711-20
30 Gevers (1948), 17-44
31 Kokot (1948), 135
32 Penrith & Jansen (1974), 21
33 Penrith & Jansen (1974), 21
34 Transvaal, *Census* (1904), ii
35 Ransford (1972)
36 Dicke (1932), 792-6
37 Great Britain (1901), 14
38 De Chavonnes & Van Imhoff (1918), 105
39 Great Britain Colonial Land and Emigration Commissioners(1849)
40 Mann (1859), 122-3: Natal Land and Colonization Company (1865),
41 South Africa (1911), v
42 Natal (1879), 3
43 Fox (1913), 6, 67

Chapter 2 *The Dutch Foundation*

1   Raven-Hart (1967), 177-8
2   Wilson & Thompson (1969), i, 187-9
3   Marshall (1944), 40

4	Leibrandt (1900), iii, 83-4
5	Leibrandt (1900), iii, 156
6	Picard (1968)
7	Lewcock (1963)
8	Pearse (1968)
9	Lewcock (1963), 6 , quoting Percival (1804)
10	Marshall (1944), 38, 53
11	Guelke (1974), 36-111
12	Deeds Office, Cape Town, grant volumes
13	Leibrandt (1900), iii, 81-2
14	Guelke (1974), 117 , translation of Van der Stel (1679)
15	Van Rensburg (1954), 1-96
16	Guelke (1974), 190, 259; Theal (1897), i, 296; ii, 187
17	De Chavonnes & Van Imhoff (1918)
18	Guelke (1974), 295
19	Pearse (1968)
20	Neumark (1957); Van der Merwe (1938)

21 Guelke (1974), 235-8
22 Botha (1923), 574-80
23 Botha (1919), 149–60; 225–33; De Smit (1970, Cape of Good
      Hope, (1876)
24 Barrow (1801), 135
25 Walton (1965)
26 Reyburn (1934), 41
27 Guelke (1974)
28 This increase may in part be the result of the more efficient
      collection of statistics by the British administration.
29 Barrow (1801), ii, 64-5
30 De Puyfontaine (1972)
31 Fransen & Cook (1965)
32 Van Zyl (1968), 167-290
33 Fisher (1969)

Chapter 3   *Agricultural and Pastoral Development 1806–1860*

1   Galbraith (1963)
2   Duly (1968)
3   Visagie (1970), 17-31
4   Duly (1968), 69
5   Duly (1968), 74-5
6   Great Britain (1827)
7   Duly (1968), 16
8   Cape Of Good Hope,
9   Surveyor-General's Office, Cape Town, diagram volumes
10 Edwards (1934); Hockley (1949)
11 Cory (1913), ii, 17
12 Makin (1971)
13 Dickason (1973)
14 Butler (1974)
15 Walker (1965)
16 Cape of Good Hope, *Blue Book* (1840)
17 Baumann (190?)

18   South African Republic (1884)
19   Hattersley (1950)
20   Natal Archives, Records of the Land Commission, 1843
21   Deeds Office, Pietermaritzburg, grant volumes
22   Surveyor-General's Office and Deeds Office,Bloemfontein, diagrams
23   Baumann & Bright (1940)
24   Deeds Office, Kimberley: Farm *Than* (Barkly West Quit Rent)
       Volume 1—8
25   Burroughs (1967)
26   Duly (1968); Robertson (1937), 367-411
27   Byrne (1848); Christopher (1850)
28   *Emigrants' Journal and Natal News,* 1 (1850)
29   Hattersley (1950)
30   Christopher (1969), 485-99
31   Surveyor-General's Office,Pietermaritzburg, diagram volumes
32   Clark (1972), 45, quoting John Moreland (1850)
33   Cape of Good Hope (1860); and *Appendix* (1861); Cape of Good
       Hope (1864)
34   Hockley (1949), 110
35   Walton (1965)
36   Orange Free State Archival Records (1854-7), ii 264-5
37   Walton (1965)
38   Surveyor-General's Office,Bloemfontein, survey diagrams
39   Transvaal, *Blue Book* (1879)
40   Williams (1956)
41   Deeds Office, Pietermaritzburg, grant volumes
42   Osborn (1964)
43   Osborn (1964), 55, quoting Adolph Coqui (March, 1856)
44   Kearney (1973), 23

Chapter 4   *Urban Expansion 1806—1860*

 1   Collins (1965), 179
 2   Albertyn (1959), 79
 3   Gordon (1970), 21
 4   Schumann (1938)
 5   Muller (1973), 19-30
 6   Davies (1963), 15-44
 7   Natal (1859)
 8   Kearney (1973)
 9   Lewcock (1963)
10   Reynolds & Reynolds (1974)
11   Surveyor-General's Offices and Deeds Offices, Pietermaritzburg,
       Bloemfontein and Pretoria; Archives, Bloemfontein, survey
       diagrams and town plans
12   Surveyor-General's Office, Pretoria
13   Kearney (1973), 8-10
14   Kearney (1973), 24, quoting C. Barter (1852)
15   Natal (1848)
16   Great Britian Colonial Land Emigration Commissioners (1852)
17   Kruger (1966)
18   Du Plessis (1965)

19   In 1855 some 77 Europeans and 5,751 Coloureds were enumerated in four listed stations. However, in 1865 there were 512 Europeans and 19,415 non-Europeans in thirty-one listed mission stations. The four listed in 1855 showed an accumulation loss of 200, suggesting that the 1855 figure might have exceeded 20,000

Chapter 5   *Closing the Agricultural and Pastoral Frontier 1860–1914*

1   Stigger (1971), 11-23
2   Cape of Good Hope (1854)
3   Cape of Good Hope, *Blue Books* (1856-1900)
4   Van der Merwe (1945); Van der Merwe (1947)
5   Van der Merwe (1962)
6   Public Record Office, London: C.O.291.18.101
7   Surveyor-General's Office, Pretoria, survey diagrams
8   Deeds Office, Pretoria, Inspection Reports
9   Brookes & Webb (1965)
10   Great Britian (1886)
11   Transvaal (1903)
12   Transvaal (1900-01)
13   Orange Free State (1892–98)
14   Orange River Colony Farm List (1902)
15   Orange River Colony (1902)
16   Christopher (1971), 560-75
17   Osborn (1964)
18   Christopher (1969)
19   Greyling & Davies (1970)
20   Osborn (1964)
21   Birkby (1951), 150-64
22   Natal (1904)
23   Natal Archives, Department of Lands lease volumes
24   Marais (1937); Deeds Offices, Bloemfontein and Kimberley, owners' registers
25   Cape Archives, Cape Town
26   Halford (1950?)
27   Great Britain (1886)
28   Cape Archives, Law Book of the Kalahari Desert State
29   Botswana National Archives, File H.C. 144
30   Department of Surveys and Lands, Gaberone, survey records
31   Botswana National Archives File S499/7– Farming statistics regarding European owned farms. In 1950 there were only 171 European males on the farms
32   Cary (1970)
33   Palmer (1968)
34   Olivier (1943)
35   Palmer (1968)
36   Fox (1913)
37   Fox (1913)
38   British South Africa Company (1907), (1909)
39   Odlum (1909)
40   Fox (1913), 41

41   Weinmann (1972)
42   Hodder-Williams (1971), 39-63
43   Weinmann (1972)
44   British South Africa Company, *Reports on the Administration of Rhodesia, 1898–1900* (1900)
45   Fox (1913)
46   Van der Merwe (1962)
47   Wilson & Thompson (1969), i, 424–46
48   Bley (1971)
49   Olivier (1943)
50   Sorrenson (1968)
51   Hyatt (1914)
52   Cape of Good Hope, (1899), (1904); South Africa Republic (1895); Transvaal (1901)
53   Cape of Good Hope (1909), 26
54   Natal (1876)
55   Natal (1879)
56   Billington (1960); Roberts (1924)
57   Deeds Office, Pietermaritzburg, Deed of Grant No 1848, Wilgefontein
58   Natal (1880)
59   Natal (1882)
60   Christopher (1970), 569–78
61   Natal Land and Colonization Company (1865)
62   Natal Land and Colonization Company, land registers, 1861–1910
63   Meiring (1959), 38
64   Els (1968), 115–26
65   South Africa (1918)
66   Wallace (1896), 223–4
67   South African Republic (1898)
68   Transvaal (1900–01)
69   Transvaal (1906); Transvaal (1907)
70   Transvaal (1901); 52
71   Transvaal (1904)
72   Streak (1970)
73   Botswana National Archives, File H.C. 144
74   Transvaal (1908), 8
75   Transvaal (1900–01);Deeds Office,Pretoria,ownership records
76   Tansvaal (1908). 66
77   Transvaal (1908), 189 Figure K
78   Rossouw No 1 (1951), 347–450; Cape of Good Hope (1898)
79   Transvaal (1908), 173
80   Transvaal (1908); Orange Free River Colony (1908)
81   Transvaal (1904)

Chapter 6   *Industrial Foundations 1860–1914*
1   Schumann (1938)
2   Paish (1911), 180
3   Arndt (1928)
4   Browett & Fair (1974), 111–20

5   Transvaal, Report on the Townlands of the Transvaal (1903). In the Transvaal between 1860 and 1900, thirty-four new towns received an average of only 9,000 acres of townlands, compared with over twice that area in the years 1838—60. The contrast is even more marked when it is remembered that the Church founded the town of Middlesburg in 1867 with over 32,000 acres of townlands, one of the largest endowments in southern Africa.

6   Transvaal, *Census* (1904)

7   Surveyor-Generals' Offices, Cape Town, Pietermaritzburg, Bloemfontein, and Pretoria

8   Davies & Rajah (1965), 45—58

9   Kearney (1973)

10   Allen (1971), 1

11   Picard (1969)

12   Smalberger (1975)

13   Robertson (1974)

14   McNish (1968); McNish (1969)

15   McNish (1970)

16   South Africa, *Year Book* (1918), 582—91

17   Shorten (1970), 49

18   Cartwright (1962); Herring (1948)

19   Shorten (1970), 52

20   Transvaal, *Blue Book* (1878)

21   Surveyor-General's Office, Pretoria

22   Shorten (1970), 68

23   Shorten (1970), 87—8

24   Leyds (1964), 6

25   Sauer (1937), 117—19

26   Shorten (1970), 133

27   Avon (1972)

28   South Africa, *Year Book* (1918)

29   Wilson (1972)

30   South African Republic (1884,1893—97)

31   Natal Central Railway Company (1864)

32   Natal (1871), 7, 11

33   Natal (1871), 9

34   The Railway System became a major employer. Thus in 1910 the African Railways system employed almost 50,000 of whom 26,000 were Europeans *(South African Railways and Harbours Report of the General Manager for the year ended 31st December, 1910 (1911)*

35   Coetzee (1940)

36   Van der Poel (1933)

37   Orange Free State (1881); De Burger (1898), 22. Revenue for five years 1874/5—1879/80 £705,800.

38   Shorten (1970), 153

39   South Africa (1918), 709—10. Cost of construction: 3ft 6in gauge — £7,864 per mile, 2ft 0ins — £2,817 per mile.

40   South Africa (1918), 599. Cape coal cost 11s 7d (58p) per ton to raise in 1911, that in the Transvaal only cost 4s 8d (23p) per ton.

266

41   South Africa (1918), 599. Pit-head price of coal per ton:
      1911   Natal   5s 5d (27p)   United Kingdom 8s 2d (41p)
      1912   5s 7d (28p)   9s 1d (45p)
      1913   6s 2d (31p)   10s 2d (51p)
42   Meintjes (1974), 26—7
43   Baines (1877)
44   Selous (1893), 337
45   Mauch (1969)
46   Haggard (1885)
47   Tanser (1965)
48   British South Africa Company (1896—7)
49   Tanser (1974)
50   Davies (1963), 15—44
51   Hart (1967), 95—103
52   Picard (1969)
53   South Africa (1911), 12. In 1909, only 9,000 had travelled.
54   South Africa (1911), Visitors to Durban 1907 — 4,061; 1910—
      7,855. Visitors to Muizenberg 1909/10—48,652; 1910/11—74,967.

Chapter 7   *Rural and Urban Adjustments, 1914—1960*
1   South Africa, *Union Statistics for Fifty Years, 1910—1960* (1960)
2   Cook (1972), 72—83
3   Davies (1967), 9—19
4   Kay (1970); Osborn (1964); Roder (1965)
5   Wilson & Thompson (1971), ii, 136—53; Dunlop (1971), 23—43
6   Cole (1956)
7   Carnegie Commission (1932); Southern Rhodesia (1934)
8   Carnegie Commission (1932), i, 121
9   South Africa (1944)
10   South Africa (1960)
11   South Africa (1960), 3
12   Transvaal (& Orange Free State), *Chamber of Mines, Annual
      Reports* (1910—60); Chamber of Mines of Rhodesia, *Annual
      Reports* (1939—60)
13   Scott (1951), 561—89
14   Cole (1957), 249—65
15   Wilson (1972)
16   Fleischer (1968)
17   Scott (1951), 53—68
18   South Africa (1958)
19   Houghton (1964)
20   Southern Rhodesia (1961)
21   Houghton (1964)
22   Scott (1951), 137—49
23   Southern Rhodesia (1936); Tow (1960)
24   Davies & Young (1970), 595—605; Davies & Young (1970), 699—713
25   Moolman (1961), 34—40
26   McCrystal (1969), 149—53
27   Floyd (1966)
28   Phillips & De Coning (1969)

29	Southern Rhodesia (1961)
30	South Africa (1964)
31	South Africa (1964)
32	Lewis (1966), 45–85
33	Calderwood (1955)
34	Van Reenen (1962)
35	Horrell (1966)
36	Fair & Shaffer (1964), 261–74
37	South Africa (1957), 3
38	South Africa (1957), 4–6
39	South Africa (1957), 7–8
40	South Africa (1957), 19
41	Christopher (1972), 207–12
42	Transvaal (1949), 13

Chapter 8 *African and European Contact to 1960*

1	Hunter (1961); Ranger (1970)
2	Holden (1855); Thompson (1827)
3	Daniel (1973), 23–31
4	South Africa, *Census* (1912), xxii
5	Desmond Clark (1959)
6	Garlake (1973); Gayre (1972)
7	Guelke (1974), 28
8	Kruger (1966)
9	Kirk (1974), 411–28
10	Steynsberg (1952)
11	Marais (1937)
12	Wilson & Thompson (1969), i
13	Wilson & Thompson (1969), i, 395
14	Were (1974), 80–2
15	Du Plessis (1965)
16	Agar–Hamilton (1928)
17	Best & Young (1972), 63–74
18	Brookes & Hurwitz (1957)
19	Transvaal (1904)
20	Sanders (1975)
21	Orange River Colony (1902)
22	Natal (1904)
23	Tatz (1962)
24	Biermann (1963), 58
25	Great Britain (1960)
26	Hyam (1972)
27	South Africa (1955), 46–7
28	Great Britain (1896)
29	Great Britain (1917), 9
30	Southern Rhodesia (1925)
31	Christopher (1971), 39–52
32	Robertson (1934), 413
33	Trollope (1878), i, 325
34	Wilson & Thompson (1969), i, 261–8

35   Robertson (1934), 434
36   Robertson (1935), 3–25, 5
37   Grasskopf (1933), 261–80
38   Robertson (1935), 7
39   Palmer (1973)
40   Arrighi (1970), 197–234
41   Palmer (1973), 19
42   Palmer (1973), 11–24
43   The African areas of South Africa produced under 10 per cent of
      total South African agricultural production by 1960.
44   Robertson (1935), 11
45   Wilson (1972)
46   South Africa (1955)
47   South Africa (1925)
48   Great Britain (1850), 198
49   De Kiewiet (1937), 201
50   Welsh (1971), 188–93
51   Transvaal (1908)
52   Basutoland, *Annual Report* (1964)
53   South Africa (1946), 45
54   South Africa (1946), 41–2
55   South Africa (1946), 41
56   South Africa (1946), 43
57   Kay (1970)
58   South Africa (1955), 85–6

Chapter 9   *Perpectives on the historical geography of southern Africa*

1   Billington (1961)
2   See Preface, note 3. The contrast in approaches in viewing the
      same area is well illustrated by comparing Meinig (1962), and
      Williams (1974).
3   A study such as Lemon (1972), would be impossible in southern
      Africa owing to the small size of the population and lack of
      information in the eighteenth century.
4   Pattison (1957); Thrower (1966)
5   Kosmin (1971), 25–37
6   Heathcote (1965)
7   Welsh (1971)
8   Walker (1957), 241–2; Reynolds (1969), 70–133
9   Davies (1971), 75
10   Davies, R.J. The form of the South African City, (a lecture
      delivered to the Society for Geography Conference, Rhodes
      University, Grahamstown) (1974).
11   Plumb (1969), 15
12   Siddle (1971), 570
13   Smuts (1974)
14   Walton (1974)
15   One of the most important collections was formed by William
      Fehr, and is now housed in the Castle and Rust-en-Vreugd, Cape
      Town.

16 Baines (1973 & 1975)
17 The main sources of photographs, of a more geographical nature, are the African Museum, Johannesburg; the Alexander McGregor Memorial Museum, Kimberley; the Cape Archives, Cape Town; and the National Archives of Rhodesia, Salisbury.
18 Elliott (1969). The collection of over 10,000 prints of the western and southern Cape was taken in the period 1900–30, and includes a number of earlier photographs, which Elliott copied. It is now housed in the Cape Archives.
19 Rosenthal (1974); Picard (1969), Appendix; Van der Riet (1974)

Bibliography

Unpublished Records

Extensive use was made of the records of several Archives, Museums and Land Offices:
Public Record Office, London
British Museum, London
Cape Archives, Cape Town
Surveyor-General's Office, Cape Town
Deeds Office, Cape Town
Natal Archives, Pietermaritzburg
Surveyor-General's Office, Pietermaritzburg
Deeds Office, Pietermaritzburg
Orange Free State Archives, Bloemfontein
Surveyor-General's Office, Bloemfontein
Deeds Office, Bloemfontein
National Museum, Bloemfontein
Transvaal Archives, Pretoria
Surveyor-General's Office, Pretoria
Deeds Office, Pretoria
Africana Museum, Johannesburg
Deeds Office, Kimberley
Alexander McGregor Memorial Museum, Kimberley
Local History Museum, Durban
Killie Campbell Museum, Durban
The Botswana National Archives, Gaborone
Department of Surveys and Lands, Gaborone
The National Archives of Rhodesia, Salisbury
The Department of the Surveyor-General, Salisbury

Deeds Office, Salisbury
The Department of the Surveyor-General, Bulawayo

Official Publications

Basutoland, *Annual Reports*, 1930–64

Bechuanaland Protectorate, *Statistical Blue Book*, 1904/05–1921/22

Bechuanaland Protectorate, *Annual Reports*, 1930–65

Bechuanaland Protectorate, *Census*, 1946

British South Africa Company, *Report on the Company's proceedings and the condition of the Territories within its sphere of operations*, 1889–92, 1892–4, 1894–5, 1896–7

British South Africa Company, *Reports on the Administration of Rhodesia*, 1897–8, 1898–1900, 1900–02

British South Africa Company, *Rhodesia Lands for Settlers*, 1907

British South Africa Company, *A Land of Sunshine, Southern Rhodesia*, 1909

British South Africa Company, *Central Farms for the Introduction of New Settlers*, 1909

Cape of Good Hope, *Blue Book of the Colony* 1821–85, thereafter *Statistical Register of the Colony*, 1886–1909

Cape of Good Hope, *Report from the Select Committee appointed to Inquire into the System of Selling Crown Lands*, 1854, A21/1854

Cape of Good Hope, *Abstract of Population Returns, 1855*, 1857, G.42-'57

Cape of Good Hope, *Return of the value of Landed Property in the several divisions of the Cape of Good Hope in the years 1858–9*, 1860, G.1-'60, plus *Appendix*, 1861, G.16-'61

Cape of Good Hope, *Return of Road Rates levied by Divisional Councils, 1858–63*, 1864, G.33-'64

Cape of Good Hope, *Census, 1865*, 1866, G.20-'66

Cape of Good Hope, *Report of the Surveyor-General for 1875*, 1876, G.30-'76

Cape of Good Hope, *Census, 1875*, 1876, G.42-'76

Cape of Good Hope, *Report of the Select Committee on Colonial Agriculture and Industries*, 1883, A1-'83

Cape of Good Hope, *Census, 1891*, 1892, G.6-'92

Cape of Good Hope, *Report of the Select Committee on Agricultural Distress*, 1898, A1-'98

Cape of Good Hope, *Report on the question of the joint utilisation of the waters of the Orange River*, 1899, G.69-'99

Cape of Good Hope, *Report by the Director of Irrigation on his tour through the north-western Districts*, 1904, G.94–'04

Cape of Good Hope, *Census, 1904*, 1905, G.19–'05

Cape of Good Hope, *Proceedings of the First South African Irrigation Congress*, 1909, G.39–'09

Great Britain, *Reports of the Commissioners of Inquiry upon the Government and Finances of the Cape of Good Hope*, 1826/27 (282) XXI

Great Britain, *Third Report of the Select Committee of the House of Lords on Colonization from Ireland*, 1849 (86) XI

Great Britain, *Correspondence relative to the establishment of the Settlement of Natal*, 1850 (104) XXXVI

Great Britain, *Report of the Commissioners . . . land settlement in British Bechuanaland*, 1886, C4889

Great Britain, *Matabeleland: Report of the Land Commission of 1894 and correspondence relating thereto*, 1896, C8130

Great Britain, *Report of the South Africa Land Settlement Commission*, 1901, Cd627

Great Britain, *Papers relating to the Southern Rhodesia Native Reserves Commission, 1915*, 1917, Cd8674

Great Britain, *Basutoland, Bechuanaland Protectorate and Swaziland: Report of an Economic Survey mission*, 1960

Great Britain, Colonial Land and Emigration Commissioners, *Annual Reports*, 1842–73

Great Britain, Emigration Commissioners, *Information for Emigrants to the British Colonies*, 1870

Great Britian, Emigrants' Information Office, *Handbook No 9 Cape of Good Hope*, 1888

Natal, *Blue Book of the Colony* 1850–92/3 (except 1851); thereafter *Statistical Yearbook* to 1909

Natal, *Report on the Division of Natal into separate Magistracies and selection of sites for Towns*, 1848

Natal, *Plan and Papers on the subject of a harbour at Port Natal, South Africa, by J. Vetch*, 1859

Natal, *Report on the construction of Railways in the Colony*, 1871

Natal, *Report on Crown Lands and European Immigration*, 1876

Natal, *Reports of the Land and Emigration Board*, 1879–92

Natal, *Census*, 1891

Natal, *Census*, 1904

Natal, *Report of the Zululand Lands Delimitation Commission*, 1904

Orange Free State, *Census*, 1880

Orange Free State, *Report of the Railways Commission*, 1881
Orange Free State, *Census*, 1890
Orange Free State, *Annual Reports of the Surveyor-General*, 1892–8
Orange River Colony, *Farm list by Districts*, 1902
Orange River Colony, *Report on leasing of Government Farms in the late Orange Free State*, 1902
Orange River Colony, *Census*, 1904
Orange River Colony, *Blue Book of the Colony*, 1905/06
Orange River Colony, *Report on Poor Whites*, 1908
Rhodesia and Nyasaland, *Report on the Agricultural and Pastoral Production of Southern Rhodesia, Northern Rhodesia and Nyasaland*, 1960
Rhodesia and Nyasaland, *Census of European Population*, 1961
Rhodesia and Nyasaland, *Census of Production in 1960 and 1961*, 1963
South Africa, *Official Yearbook of the Union of South Africa*, 1911–60 (with interruptions)
South Africa, *Report of the General Manager of Railways and Harbours for the year ended 31st December, 1910*, (1911) U.G. 39–1911
South Africa, *Report from the Select Committee on Closer Land Settlement* (1911), Senate S.C. 6–'10–'11
South Africa, *Census, 1911* (1912), U.G. 32–1912
South Africa, *Report of the Ostrich Feather Commission* (1918), U.G. 12–'18
South Africa, *Final Report of the Drought Investigation Committee* (1923), U.G. 49/1923
South Africa, *Report of the Mining Regulations Commission* (1925), U.G. 36/1925
South Africa, *Report of the Agricultural and Pastoral Production of the Union of South Africa, 1929–30* (1932), U.G. 12–'32
South Africa, *Report of the Agricultural and Pastoral Production of the Union of South Africa, 1933–4* (1935), U.G. 44–'35
South Africa, *Transfers of Rural Property, 1st April 1927 to 31st March 1944* (1944), U.G. 27–'44
South Africa, *The Native Reserves and their place in the Economy of the Union of South Africa* (1946), U.G. 32/1946
South Africa, *Summary of the Report of the Commission for the Socio-Economic Development of the Bantu Areas within the Union of South Africa* (1955), U.G. 61–'55
South Africa, *Report of the Commission on Smallholdings in the*

periurban areas of the Union of South Africa (1957), U.G. 37/1957

South Africa, *Report of the Commission of Enquiry into the Policy relating to the Protection of Industries* (1958), U.G. 36/1958

South Africa, *Annual Report of the General Manager, South African Railways and Harbours, 1959–1960* (1960), U.G. 62/1960

South Africa, *Report of the Commission of Inquiry into European Occupancy of the Rural Areas* (1960)

South Africa, *Union Statistics for Fifty Years, 1910–1960* (1960)

South Africa, *Industrial Census 1959–60,* Special Report 283 (1961)

South Africa, *Report on Agricultural and Pastoral Production, 1959–60* (1963–4), R.P. 10/1963, R.P. 18/1963, R.P. 10/1964, R.P. 16/1964

South Africa, *Report of the Department of Bantu Administration and Development 1960–62* (1964), R.P. 78/1964

South Africa, *Urban and Rural Population of South Africa, 1904 to 1960* (1968)

South African Republic, *Report of the Surveyor-General* (1884)

South African Republic, *Census,* 1890

South African Republic, *State Almanac for 1893* (1892)

South African Republic, *Annual Report of the Surveyor-General 1892–97* (1893–7)

South African Republic, *Improvement of the land through irrigation* (1895)

South African Republic, *Johannesburg Health Committee Census* (1896)

South African Republic, *Report on Mapoch's Ground* (1898)

Southern Rhodesia, *Official Yearbook of Southern Rhodesia* (1924, 1930, 1932, 1952)

Southern Rhodesia, *Census,* 1904

Southern Rhodesia, *Census,* 1911

Southern Rhodesia, *Census,* 1921

Southern Rhodesia, *Handbook for the use of prospective settlers on the land* (1924)

Southern Rhodesia, *Report of the Land Commission* (1925)

Southern Rhodesia, *Report on Unemployment and the relief of destitution in Southern Rhodesia* (1934)

Southern Rhodesia, *Census,* 1936

Southern Rhodesia, *Report of the Committee of Enquiry into the Protection of Secondary Industries in Southern Rhodesia,* 1946

Southern Rhodesia, *Census,* 1951

Southern Rhodesia, *Annual Report of Rhodesia Railways*, 1954

Southern Rhodesia, *Report on the Agricultural and Pastoral Production of European Farms, 1954–1955* (1955)

Southern Rhodesia, *Report on the Census of Industrial Production 1938–1953* (1955)

Southern Rhodesia, *Review of the Economy of Southern Rhodesia* (1961)

Southern Rhodesia, *Census of Africans in Southern Rhodesia, April/May 1962* (1964)

Swaziland, *Annual Reports*, 1930–60

Transvaal, *Blue Book of the Colony*, 1878, 1879, 1902/03–09

Transvaal, *Lists of farms and owners in the twenty districts and Mapoch's Ground*, 1900–01

Transvaal, *Report on Irrigation in South Africa, by W. Willcocks*, 1901

Transvaal, *Swaziland Concessions Report*, 1903

Transvaal, *Report on the Townlands of the Transvaal*, 1903

Transvaal, *Census of the Transvaal Colony and Swaziland*, 1904

Transvaal, *Report relative to the Acquisition and Tenure of Land by Natives in the Transvaal*, 1904

Transvaal, *Burgher Land Settlements, 1903–1904* (1904)

Transvaal, *Report of the Surveyor-General* (1904)

Transvaal, *Report on the Reconnaisance of the Basin of the Great Marico River*, 1906

Transvaal, *Report on the Reconnaisance of the Great Oliphants River Basin*, 1907

Transvaal, *Report of the Transvaal Indigency Commission* (1908), T.G. 13–'08

Transvaal, *Control of subdivision of farm land and agricultural holdings* (1949), T.P. 5/1949

Books

Acocks, J.P.H., *Veld Types of South Africa* (Pretoria, 1953)

Agar-Hamilton, J.A.I., *The Native Policy of the Voortrekkers, 1836–58* (Cape Town, 1928)

Albertyn, J.R., *Land en Stad: 'n sociologies-godienstige studie* (Cape Town, 1959)

Allen, V., *Kruger's Pretoria* (Cape Town, 1971)

Arndt, E.H., *Banking and Currency Developments in South Africa, 1652–1927* (Cape Town, 1928)

Avon, H., *Park Town 1892–1972, A Social and Pictorial History* (Johannesburg, 1972)

Baines, T., *The gold regions of South East Africa* (1877)

Baines, T., *The Victoria Falls, Zambezi River* (Salisbury, 1973)

Baines, T., *The Brenthurst Baines* (Cape Town, 1975)

Barrow, J., *An Account of Travels into the Interior of Southern Africa* (1801)

Baumann, G. & Bright, E., *The Lost Republic* (1940)

Biermann, H.H., *The Case for South Africa: Speeches by Mr E.H. Louw* (New York, 1963)

Billington, R.A., *Westward Expansion. A History of the American Frontier* (New York, 1960)

Billington, R.A., *Frontier and Section. Selected Essays of Frederick Jackson Turner* (Englewood Cliffs, 1961)

Bley, H., *South-West Africa under German Rule, 1894–1914* (1971)

Brookes, E.H. & Hurwitz, N., *The Native Reserves of Natal* (Cape Town, 1957)

Brookes, E.H. & Webb, C. deB., *History of Natal* (Pietermaritzburg, 1965)

Buchan, J., *The African Colony, Studies in the Reconstruction* (Edinburgh, 1903)

Burroughs, P., *Britain and Australia, 1831–1855; A study in Imperial relations and Crown Lands Administration* (Oxford, 1967)

Burton, A.R.E., *Handbook for Settlers* (Pretoria, 1902)

Burton, J.H., *The Emigrants' Manual, New Zealand, Cape of Good Hope, Port Natal* (Edinburgh, 1850)

Butler, G., *The 1820 Settlers, An Illustrated Commentary* (Cape Town, 1974)

Byrne, J.C., *Emigrants' Guide to Port Natal* (1848)

Calderwood, D.M., *Native Housing in South Africa* (Johannesburg, 1955)

Carnegie Commission, *The Poor White Problem in South Africa* (Stellenbosch, 1932)

Carrothers, W.A., *Emigration from the British Isles, with special reference to the development of the Overseas Dominions* (1929)

Cartwright, A.P., *The Gold Miners* (Johannesburg, 1962)

Cary, R., *Charter Royal* (Cape Town, 1970)

Chamber of Mines of Rhodesia, *Annual Reports* (Salisbury, 1939–60)

Christopher, J.S., *Natal, Cape of Good Hope* (1850)

Clark, A.H., *Arcadia: the geography of early Nova Scotia to 1760* (Madison, 1968)

Clark, J., *Natal Settler Agent. The career of John Moreland 1849–51* (Cape Town, 1972)

Coetzee, W.J., *Spoorwegontwikkeling in die Suid-Afrikaanse Republiek, 1872–1899* (Cape Town, 1940)

Cole, M.M., *Land Use Studies in the Transvaal Lowveld* (Bude, 1956)

Cole, M.M., *South Africa* (1961)

Collins, W.W., *Free Statia* (Cape Town, 1965)

Cory, G.E., *The Rise of South Africa* (1910–30)

Currey, R.N., *Letters and other writings of a Natal Sheriff: Thomas Phipson, 1815–76* (1968)

Davies, W.J., *Patterns of non-White population distribution in Port Elizabeth with special reference to the application of the Group Areas Act* (Port Elizabeth, 1971)

De Burger, *Almanac and Free State Yearbook. 1898* (Bloemfontein, 1897)

De Chavonnes, M.P. & van Imhoff, Baron, *The Reports of De Chavonnes and his Council and of Van Imhoff, on the Cape* (Cape Town, 1918)

De Kiewiet, C.W., *The Imperial Factor in South Africa: A Study in Politics and Economics* (Cambridge, 1937)

De Puyfontaine, H.R., *Louis Michel Thibault 1750–1815, His Official life at the Cape of Good Hope* (Cape Town, 1972)

Desmond Clark, J., *The Prehistory of Southern Africa* (1959)

Dickason, G.B., *Irish Settlers to South Africa. History of the Clanwilliam 1820 settlers from Cork Harbour* (Cape Town, 1973)

Du Plessis, J., *A History of Christian Missions in South Africa* (Cape Town, 1965)

Duly, L.C., *British land policy at the Cape 1795–1844: a study in administrative procedures in the Empire* (Durham, 1968)

Dunlop, H., *The Development of European Agriculture in Rhodesia 1945–1965* (Salisbury, 1971)

Edwards, I.E., *The 1820 Settlers in South Africa* (1934)

Elliott, A., *Architectural Beauty of the Old Cape* (Cape Town, 1969)

Fisher, J., *The Afrikaners* (1969)

Fleischer, M., *Welkom* (Johannesburg, 1968)

Floyd, T.B., *More about Town Planning in South Africa* (Pietermaritzburg, 1966)

Forbes, V.S., *Pioneer Travellers in South Africa* (Cape Town, 1965)

Fox, H.W., *Notes and Information concerning land policy* (1913)

Fransen, H. & Cook, M.A., *The Old Houses of the Cape* (Cape Town, 1965)

278

Galbraith, J.S., *Reluctant Empire: British Policy on the South African Frontier, 1834–1954* (Berkeley, 1963)

Garlake, P.S., *Great Zimbabwe* (1973)

Gayre, R., *The Origin of the Zimbabwean Civilization* (Salisbury, 1972)

Gordon, R.E., *Dear Louisa, History of a Pioneer Family in Natal, 1850–1888* (Cape Town, 1970)

Greyling, J.J.C. & Davies, R.J., *Indian Agricultural Holdings on the Natal North Coast – Land subdivision, land ownership, and land occupation* (Pietermaritzburg, 1970)

Haggard, H.R., *King Solomon's Mines* (1885)

Halford, S.J., *The Griquas of Griqualand* (Cape Town, 1950?)

Hattersley, A.F., *The British Settlement of Natal: A Study in Imperial Migration* (1950)

Heathcote, R.L., *Back of Bourke: A Study of Land Appraisal and Settlement in Semi-arid Australia* (Melbourne, 1965)

Hitchins, F.H., *The Colonial Land and Emigration Commissioners* (Philadelphia, 1931)

Hockley, H.E., *The Story of the British Settlers of 1820 in South Africa* (Cape Town, 1949)

Holden, W.C., *History of the Colony of Natal, South Africa* (1855)

Horrell, M., *Group Areas: The Emerging Pattern, with Illustrative Examples from the Transvaal* (Johannesburg, 1966)

Houghton, D.H., *The South African Economy* (Cape Town, 1964)

Hunter, M., *Reaction to Conquest* (1961)

Hurwitz, N., *Agriculture in Natal, 1860–1950* (Cape Town, 1957)

Hyam, R., *The Failure of South African Expansion, 1908–48* (1972)

Hyatt, S.P., *The Old Transport Road* (1914)

Jeans, D.N., *The Historical Geography of New South Wales to 1901* (Sydney, 1972)

Jeppe, F., *Jeppe's Almanac, 1889* (no imprint)

Kay, G., *Rhodesia: A Human Geography* (1970)

Kearney, B., *Architecture in Natal, 1824–93* (Cape Town, 1973)

King, L.C., *South African Scenery* (Edinburgh, 1963)

Kokot, D.F., *An Investigation into the evidence bearing on recent climatic changes over southern Africa* (Pretoria, 1948)

Kruger, B., *The Pear Tree Blossoms: A History of the Moravian Mission Stations in South Africa, 1737–1869* (Genadendal, 1966)

Leibrandt, H.C.V., *Précis of the Archives of the Cape of Good Hope: Letters Despatched from the Cape 1652–1662* (Cape Town, 1900)

Lemon, J.T., *The Best Poor Man's Country. A geographical study of early southeastern Pennsylvania* (Baltimore, 1972)

Lewcock, R., *Early nineteenth century architecture in South Africa. A study of Interaction of two cultures 1795–1837* (Cape Town, 1963)

Leyds, G.A., *A History of Johannesburg: The early years* (Cape Town, 1964)

Lucas, C.P., *Historical Geography of the British Colonies Vol. 4: South Africa* (Oxford, 1898–1903)

McCrystal, L.P., *City, Town or Country, The economics of concentration and dispersal, with particular reference to South Africa* (Cape Town, 1969)

McNish, J.T., *The Road to El Dorado* (Cape Town, 1968)

McNish, J.T., *Graves and Guineas* (Cape Town, 1969)

McNish, J.T., *The Glittering Road* (Cape Town, 1970)

Makin, A.E., *The 1820 Settlers of Salem, Hezekiah Sephton's Party* (Wynberg, 1971)

Mann, R.J., *The Colony of Natal, An Account of the characteristics and capabilities of this British Dependency* (1859)

Marais, J.S., *The Cape Coloured People 1652–1937* (1937)

Mauch, C., *The journals of Carl Mauch: his travels in the Transvaal and Rhodesia, 1869–72* (Salisbury, 1969)

Meinig, D.W., *On the Margins of the Good Earth: The South Australian Wheat Frontier, 1869–1884* (Chicago, 1962)

Meinig, D.W., *The Great Columbia Plain: a historical geography* (1968)

Meinig, D.W., *South-West: Three peoples in geographical change* (New York, 1971)

Meintjes, J., *Dorp van Drome, Die Geskiedenis van Molteno, 1874–1974* (Molteno, 1974)

Meiring, J.M., *Sundays River Valley* (Cape Town, 1959)

Methley, J.E., *The New Colony of Port Natal* (1849)

Natal Central Railway Company, *Report of Frederick Boileau Elliott* (1864)

Natal Land and Colonization Company, *Plan of Assisted Emigration and Land Settlement* (1865)

Neumark, S.D., *Economic Influences on the South African Frontier, 1652–1836* (Stanford, 1957)

Odlum, G.M., *Agricultural and Pastoral Rhodesia* (1909)

Olivier, S.P., *Die Pioniertrekke na Gazaland* (Cape Town, 1943)

Osborn, R.F., *Valiant Harvest, the Founding of the South African Sugar Industry, 1848–1926* (Durban, 1964)

Pattison, W.D., *Beginnings of the American Rectangular Land Survey System, 1784–1800* (Chicago, 1957)

Pearse, G.E., *Eighteenth century architecture in South Africa* (Cape Town, 1968)

Penrith, J. & Jansen, C., *The Great Karoo* (Cape Town, 1974)

Phillips, B. & De Coning, C., *Secondary industry in the Port Elizabeth/Uitenhage Region* (Port Elizabeth, 1969)

Picard, H.W.J., *Gentleman's Walk* (Cape Town, 1968)

Picard, H.W.J., *Grand Parade, The Birth of Greater Cape Town, 1850–1913* (Cape Town, 1969)

Plumb, J.H., *The Death of the Past* (1969)

Pollock, N.C. & Agnew, S., *Historical Geography of South Africa* (1963)

Powell, J.M., *The Public Lands of Australia Felix* (Melbourne, 1970)

Ranger, T.O., *The African Voice in Southern Rhodesia, 1898–1930* (1970)

Ransford, O., *The Great Trek* (1972)

Raven-Hart, R., *Before Van Riebeeck: Callers at South Africa from 1488 to 1652* (Cape Town, 1967)

Reynolds, R. & Reynolds, B., *Grahamstown from Cottage to Villa* (Claremont, 1974)

Roberts, S.H., *History of Australian Land Settlement, 1788–1920* (Melbourne, 1924)

Robertson, M., *Diamond Fever, 1866–69* (Cape Town, 1974)

Roder, W., *The Sabi Valley Irrigation Projects* (Chicago, 1965)

Rosenthal, E., *The Rand Rush, 1886–1911, Johannesburg's first 25 years in pictures* (Johannesburg, 1974)

Sanders, P., *Moshoeshoe, Chief of the Sotho* (1975)

Sauer, H., *Ex Africa* (1937)

Saunders, C. & Derricourt, R., *Beyond the Cape Frontier: studies in the history of the Transkei and the Ciskei* (Cape Town, 1974)

Schumann, C.G.W., *Structural Changes and Business Cycles in South Africa, 1806–1936* (1938)

Selous, F.C., *Travel and Adventure in South East Africa* (1893)

Shorten, J.R., *The Johannesburg Saga* (Johannesburg, 1970)

Smalberger, J.M., *A History of Copper Mining in Namaqualand* (Cape Town, 1975)

Smuts, F., *Stellenbosch – our oldest village* (Stellenbosch, 1974)

Sorrenson, M.P.K., *Origins of European Settlement in Kenya* (Nairobi, 1968)

Streak, M., *Lord Milner's immigration policy for the Transvaal, 1897–1905* (Johannesburg, 1970)

Tanser, G.H., *A Scantling of Time* (Salisbury, 1965)

Tanser, G.H., *A Sequence of Time* (Salisbury, 1974)

Tatz, C.M., *Shadow and Substance in South Africa: A Study in Land and Franchise Policies Affecting Africans, 1910–1960* (Pietermaritzburg, 1962)

Theal, G.McC., *Records of the Cape Colony* (Cape Town, 1897—1903)

Thompson, G., *Travels and Adventures in Southern Africa* (1827)

Thrower, N.J.W., *Original Survey and Land Subdivision. A Comparative Study of the Form and Effect of Contrasting Cadastral Surveys* (Chicago, 1966)

Thunberg, C.P., *Travels in Europe, Africa and Asia. . .between. . .1770 and 1779* (1795)

Transvaal (& Orange Free State) Chamber of Mines, *Annual Reports* (Johannesburg, 1940–1960)

Trollope, A., *South Africa* (1878)

Van der Merwe, P.J., *Die Trekboer in die Geskiedenis van die Kaap Kolonie* (Cape Town, 1938)

Van der Merwe, P.J., Trek, *Studies oor die Mobiliteit van die Pioniers bevolking aan die Kaap* (Cape Town, 1945)

Van der Merwe, P.J., *Pioniers van Dorsland* (Cape Town, 1947)

Van der Merwe, P.J., *Nog Verder Noord* (Cape Town, 1962)

Van der Poel, J., *Railway and Customs Policies in South Africa, 1885–1910* (1933)

Van der Riet, F., *Grahamstown in early photographs* (Claremont, 1974)

Van der Stel, S., *Simon van der Stel's journal of his expedition to Namaqualand, 1685–6* (1932)

Van Reenen, T.H., *Land: its ownership and occupation in South Africa* (Cape Town, 1962)

Walker, E.A., *A History of Southern Africa* (1957)

Walker, E.A., *The Great Trek* (1965)

Wallace, R., *Farming Industries of Cape Colony* (1896)

Walton, J., *Homesteads and Villages of South Africa* (Pretoria, 1965)

Walton, J., *Watermills, windmills and horsemills of South Africa* (Cape Town, 1974)

Weinmann, H., *Agricultural Research and Development in Rhodesia under the Rule of the British South Africa Company, 1890–1923* (Salisbury, 1972)

Welsh, D., *The Roots of Segregation; Native Policy in Colonial Natal, 1845–1910* (Cape Town, 1971)

Were, G.S., *A History of South Africa* (1974)

Williams, D., *An Account of a Journey into Transorangia and the Potchefstroom-Winburg Trekker Republic in 1843 by the Rev. John Bennie* (Cape Town, 1956)

Williams, M., *The Making of the South Australian Landscape* (1974)

Wilson, F., *Labour in the South African gold mines, 1911–1969* (Cambridge, 1972)

Wilson, M. & Thompson, L., *The Oxford History of South Africa* (Oxford, 1969–71)

Articles

Arrighi, G., 'Labour supplies in historical perspective: A study of the Proletarianization of African Peasantry in Rhodesia', *Journal of Development Studies* 6 (1970), 197–234

Best, A.C.G. & Young, B.S., 'Homeland Consolidation: The case of KwaZulu', *South African Geographer* 4 (1972), 63–74

Birkby, M.D., 'The Wattle Industry in Natal', *Geography* 36 (1951), 150–64

Botha, C.G., 'Early Cape Land Tenure', *South African Law Journal* 36 (1919), 149–60, 225–33

Botha, C.G., 'The dispersion of the stock farmer in Cape Colony in the eighteenth century', *South African Journal of Science* 20 (1923), 574–80

Browett, J.G. & Fair, T.J.D., 'South Africa, 1870–1970: A View of the Spatial System', *South African Geographical Journal (S.A.G.J.)* 56 (1974), 111–20

Christopher, A.J., 'The British settlement of Natal, 1848–1851: A geographical appraisal', *Journal for Geography* 3 (1969), 485–99

Christopher, A.J., 'The closer-settlement movement in Natal, 1875–1910', *Journal for Geography* 3 (1970), 569–78

Christopher, A.J., 'Colonial Land Policy in Natal', *Annals, Association of American Geographers* 61 (1971), 560–75

Christopher, A.J., 'Land Tenure in Rhodesia', *S.A.G.J.* 53 (1971), 39–52

Christopher, A.J., 'Air photo interpretation and urban sprawl', *Rhodesia Science News* 6 (1972), 207–12

Christopher, A.J., 'Environmental perception in southern Africa', *S.A.G.J.* 55 (1973), 14–22

Christopher, A.J., 'Land ownership in the rural-urban fringe of Salisbury', *South African Geographer* 4 (1973), 139–56

Christopher, A.J., 'Government Land Policies in southern Africa', in Ironside, R.G., et al, *Frontier Settlement* (Edmonton, 1974), 208–25

Cole, M.M., 'The Witwatersrand Conurbation: a watershed mining and industrial region', *Transactions, Institute of British Geographers* 23 (1957), 249–65

Cook, G.P., 'The Growth of Retail Activity on the East and West Rand', *S.A.G.J.* 54 (1972), 73–83

Daniel, J.B.McI., 'A Geographical Study of Pre-Shakan Zululand', *S.A.G.J.* 55 (1973), 23–31

Davies, R.J., 'The Growth of the Durban Metropolitan Area', *S.A.G.J.* 45 (1963), 15–44

Davies, R.J., 'The South African Urban Hierarchy', *S.A.G.J.* 49 (1967), 9–19

Davies, R.J. & Rajah, D.S., 'The Durban C.B.D.: Boundary Delimitation and Racial Dualism', *S.A.G.J.* 47 (1965), 45–58

Davies, R.J. & Young, B.S., 'Manufacturing in South African Cities', *Journal for Geography* 3 (1970), 595–605

Davies, R.J. & Young, B.S., 'Manufacturing and size of place in the South African urban system', *Journal for Geography* 3 (1970), 699–713

De Smit, A., 'A Brief History of the Surveys and Cartography of the Cape of Good Hope', *South African Survey Journal* 73 (1970), 5–14; 74 (1970), 3–11

Dicke, B.H., 'The Tsetse Fly's Influence on South African History', *South African Journal of Science* 29 (1932), 792–6

Dickson, K.B., 'Historical Geography in Africa', in Baker, A.R.H. (Ed.), *Progress in Historical Geography* (Newton Abbot, 1972), 187–206

Els,W.C., 'Die Besproeiingsakie in die Groot-Vis-Riviersbesproiings distrik tot 1925', *Journal for Geography* 3 (1968), 115–26

Fair, T.J.D. & Shaffer, N.M., 'Population patterns and policies in South Africa, 1951–1960', *Economic Geography* 40 (1964), 261–74

Gevers, T.W., 'Drying Rivers in the north-eastern Transvaal', *S.A.G.J.* 30 (1948), 17–44

Grasskopf, J.F.W., 'Vestiging en trek van die Suid-Afrikaanse Naturelle-bevolking onder nuwer ekonomiese voorwaardes', *South African Journal of Economics* 1 (1933), 261–80

Hart, G.H.T., 'The Bar problem of Durban Harbour', *S.A.G.J.* 49 (1967), 95–103

Hodder-Williams, R., 'The British South Africa Company in Marandellas', *Rhodesian History* 2 (1971), 39–63

Kirk, T., 'Progress and decline in the Kat River settlement, 1829–54', *Journal of African History* 14 (1974), 411–28

Kosmin, B.A., 'The Pioneer community of Salisbury, 1897', *Rhodesian History* 2 (1971), 25–37

Lewis, P.R.B., 'A "City within a City" — The creation of Soweto', *S.A.G.J.* 48 (1966), 45–85

Moolman, J.H., 'Growth and Settlement Pattern of the Pretoria-Witwatersrand-Vereeniging Region', *S.A.G.J.* 43 (1961), 34–40

Muller, E.K., 'Early Urbanization in the Ohio Valley. A Review Essay', *Historical Geography Newsletter* 3 no 2 (1973), 19–30

Nobbs, E.A. & Haselwood, B., 'Statistical Returns of Crops in Southern Rhodesia for the season 1914–15', *Rhodesia Agricultural Journal* 13 (1916), 28–44

Paish, G., 'Great Britain's Capital Investments', *Journal of the Royal Statistical Society* 74 (1911), 167–200

Reyburn, H.A., 'Studies in Cape Frontier History', *The Critic, University of Cape Town Quarterly* 3 (1934), 40–56

Reynolds, R.D., 'The Struggle against the Introduction of Convict and Reformatory Labour in Natal', *Archives Yearbook for South African History* 30 no 2 (1967), 70–133

Robertson, H.M., '150 Years of Economic contact between Black and White', *South African Journal of Economics* 2 (1934), 403–25; 3 (1935), 3–25

Robertson, H.M., 'The Cape of Good Hope and "Systematic Colonization" ', *South African Jounral of Economics* 5 (1937), 367–411

Rossouw, P.J., 'Die Arbeidskolonie Kakamas', *Archives Yearbook for South African History* 14 no 1 (1951), 347–450

Scott, P., 'The Iron and Steel Industry of South Africa', *Geography* 36 (1951), 137–49

Scott, P., 'The Witwatersrand goldfield', *Geographical Review* 41 (1951), 561–89

Scott, P., 'The development of the Northern Natal Coalfields', *S.A.G.J.* 28 (1951), 53–68

Siddle, D.J., 'Do-it-yourself policy for rural Zambia', *Geographical Magazine* 43 (1971), 569–73

Stigger, P., 'Volunteers and the profit motive in the Anglo-Ndebele War, 1893', *Rhodesian History* 2 (1971), 11–23

Tyson, P.D., 'Spatial variation of rainfall spectra in South Africa', *Annals, Association of American Geographers* 60 (1971), 711–20

Van Reenen, R.J., 'A Resumé of the Drought Problem in the Union

285

of South Africa', *South African Journal of Science* 20 (1923), 178–92

Van Rensburg, J.I.J., 'Die Geskiedenis van die Wingerdkultuur in Suid-Afrika tydens die Eerste Eeu', *Archives Yearbook for South African History* 17 no 2 (1954), 1–96

Van Zyl, D.J., 'Die Geskiedenis van Graanbou 1795–1826', *Archives Yearbook for South African History* 31 no 1 (1968), 167–290

Visagie, J., 'Enkele Aspekte oor die landmeter en sy beroep 1806–45', *South African Survey Journal* 75 (1970), 17–31

Unpublished Research Reports

Baumann, G., *Titles to Farms, The History in the O.R.C.* (Bloemfontein, 190?)

Christopher, A.J., *Natal: A study in colonial land settlement* (Durban, 1969)

Guelke, L., *The Early European Settlement of South Africa* (Toronto, 1974)

Herring, G., *The Pilgrim Diggers of the 70's: A short history of the origin of Pilgrims Rest (1873–1881)* (Pilgrims Rest, 1948)

Marshall, M., *The Growth and development of Cape Town* (Cape Town, 1944)

Palmer, R.H., *The Making and Implementation of Land Policy in Rhodesia, 1890–1936* (London, 1968)

Palmer, R.H., *The agricultural History of Rhodesia* (Lusaka, 1973)

Steynsberg, F.J., *Carnarvon: Sy Onstaan en Groei, 1839–1952* (Carnarvon, 1952)

Tow, L., *The Manufacturing Economy of Southern Rhodesia: Problems and Prospects* (New York, 1960)

Index

Figures in *italics* refer to an illustration
on the specified page

DUE DATE

APR 0 1 1996

MAR 0 6 1996

Printed
in USA